Against Authenticity

Against Authenticity

Why You Shouldn't Be Yourself

Simon Feldman

LEXINGTON BOOKS
Lanham • Boulder • New York • London

Published by Lexington Books
An imprint of The Rowman & Littlefield Publishing Group, Inc.
4501 Forbes Boulevard, Suite 200, Lanham, Maryland 20706
www.rowman.com

Unit A, Whitacre Mews, 26-34 Stannary Street, London SE11 4AB, United Kingdom

British Library Cataloguing in Publication Information Available

Library of Congress Cataloging-in-Publication Data

Feldman, Simon, 1972-
Against authenticity : why you shouldn't be yourself / Simon Feldman.
pages cm.
Includes bibliographical references and index.
ISBN 978-0-7391-8200-0 (cloth) -- ISBN 978-0-7391-8201-7 (electronic)
1. Self (Philosophy) 2. Authenticity (Philosophy) I. Title.
BD450.F3885 2015
170--dc23
2014036684

ISBN 978-1-4985-0678-6 (pbk)

∞ ™ The paper used in this publication meets the minimum requirements of American National Standard for Information Sciences Permanence of Paper for Printed Library Materials, ANSI/NISO Z39.48-1992.

Printed in the United States of America

Contents

Acknowledgments

This book would not exist if it were not for the community that is Connecticut College. It has nurtured me materially, psychically, and intellectually. I am so lucky that my colleagues at the College are my friends and supporters. Thanks to Larry Vogel, my Continental doppelganger; to Andy Pessin, whose philosophical energy and engagement is contagious and daunting; to Kristin Pfefferkorn, for a worldview that keeps me doubting my own; and to Derek Turner, with whom I've been talking philosophy daily for the past seven years and without whom my mind would not be half as good as I hope it is.

Thank you to my parents for making me think in the first place; to my brother, Noah, "my first friend, my first interlocutor;" to my brother, Ezra, for his ever-sharp provocations in every domain.

Finally, thank you to Allan Hazlett for his inspiration and wit and for the ongoing conversation that this book is a piece of.

Introduction

The Ideal of Authenticity

This above all: to thine ownself be true,
And it must follow, as the night the day,
Thou canst not then be false to any man.

–*Hamlet*, Act I, Scene 3

And since you know you cannot see yourself
So well as by reflection, I, your glass,
Will modestly discover to yourself
That of yourself which you yet know not of.

–*Julius Caesar*, Act I, Scene 2

Caitlin, a nineteen-year-old student in my bioethics class, walked into my office in tears. (Names and details have been changed in the interest of confidentiality and philosophical clarity.) The readings I'd assigned for a unit on abortion, she said, were not helping her at all. Caitlin was sharp and conscientious and a regular at my office hours. She always seemed to be engaged with the course materials and trying hard to work out her own philosophical positions—in short, an ideal student. She was also captain of the swim team and was performing in a student production of *Les Misérables*. I tried to reassure her that the readings were hard and that she shouldn't feel bad about not yet having a settled view on the ethics of abortion. Needless to say, her concern was more than philosophical. Through sobs, she told me that she was pregnant and she didn't know what to do.

She'd told her parents a few days before and they'd reacted badly, yelling at her for being irresponsible and demanding that she have the baby ("We're Catholic," Caitlin said). The one close friend she'd confided in had said she'd be crazy to have it, it would ruin her life—"but of course it's your choice," she'd added. Pulling herself together in my office, Caitlin proceeded to talk and think. She definitely felt a strong aversion to abortion and she was afraid of what would happen to her relationship with her parents if she didn't do what they wanted. But she definitely wasn't ready to be a mother; she did not want to quit school or swimming. She also thought it would be too painful to give up the baby for adoption. She didn't want to involve Jack (the almost-boyfriend and prospective father) who would, officially, be understanding, but would surely pressure her not to have the baby. At the same time, she did think he had a right to know what was going on. She had turned these considerations into a rough list of pros and cons (a strategy she'd thought worked well when she was trying to figure out where to go to college) but after looking at the list she felt like it was no help at all. How was she supposed to weigh the different points against each other?

Feeling a bit unhinged the day before, she'd gone to psych services on campus where the doctor on call, after confirming that she was not a threat to herself or others, reassuringly advised her to "figure out what you really want and just be true to yourself." On the one hand, she thought this was the best advice she'd gotten. On the other hand, it was totally useless—what she "really" wanted was not to be in this situation; and if she knew what her "true self" thought, she wouldn't be so confused. But Caitlin still thought the doctor's advice was sound. If she could only figure out how to be true to herself, she felt sure she could live with her decision. Coming to the conclusion that there was no "rational" or "philosophical" way to figure out what was right, Caitlin thought her best bet was just to "go with her gut." Her first reaction, when she had found out she was pregnant, had been "I can't have it," and she was pretty sure she should trust that. All her subsequent tortured thinking was just pulling her away from her first instinct, which felt "authentic" to her. Did I agree she should go with that?

As a philosophy professor who teaches ethics, I've been approached, on many occasions, by friends and students who think I must have some special insight into life. I was asked by a friend recently diagnosed with bipolar disorder what I thought about her taking lithium. "Will I still be me?" she wondered. A student I know well, whom I'd pass daily on the college green having his between-class smoke, was perplexed by his own behavior: "Why am I smoking when I don't really want to?" he wondered. And now Caitlin was asking me a question I was frankly unprepared to answer: how to be true to yourself.

This book explicates and criticizes the pervasive idea that one should be true to oneself (henceforth, The Ideal of Authenticity). The intuitive appeal of The Ideal of Authenticity can be captured by a slew of interrelated but distinct commonsensical thoughts: that sometimes we "aren't really ourselves;" that it's bad to be a phony, a poser, or "pseudo;" that we shouldn't submit to peer pressure or internalize other people's opinions as our own; that self-love and self-acceptance are the necessary preconditions for being loved by others and for genuine happiness; that it's bad to be weak-willed or in bad faith; that not knowing ourselves dooms us to make choices we will regret; that denying one's biological or psychological or metaphysical nature is a recipe for misery; that the best way to approach or resolve thorny ethical dilemmas is simply to be true to oneself. As we shall see throughout this book, the idea that one should be true to oneself has intuitive pull in many kinds of situations—when people are trying to overcome addiction, make choices about love, careers, and domestic roles, and resolve inner conflicts about identity (gender, sexual orientation) and ethics, broadly construed.

I claim that, under the guise of indisputable wisdom, The Ideal of Authenticity obscures a set of intersecting social, political, moral, and philosophical ideas that we would do well to give more attention. And I claim that The Ideal of Authenticity, as invoked in everyday life, presupposes various confused notions of the self (for example, that there is a discernible "true self" to be true to). For these reasons I claim that The Ideal does not help us figure out how to make good choices nor does it help us to live better lives. These claims should be surprising and of special interest to those who in fact take the goal of being true to themselves as something like a core personal philosophy. I conclude that The Ideal is one that we would be better off abandoning, independent of our other antecedent moral or ethical commitments.

What follows comprises five chapters. Chapters 1, 2, and 3 consider three overarching accounts of what makes The Ideal of Authenticity so seductive; chapter 4 discusses the nature of action-guiding norms, as such, and presents a framework helpful for seeing why The Ideal of Authenticity is often distinctively bad advice; and chapter 5 offers a set of redirecting suggestions for what we ought to be thinking about once we abandon The Ideal of Authenticity and stop thinking about our lives through the lens of true selfhood.

The remainder of this introduction is devoted to laying out some preliminaries that will be helpful as we proceed through my arguments. To that end, I first introduce readers to a brief history of authenticity-related ideas; I propose my analysis of what it means for something to be an ideal and lay out the five conceptions of authenticity that this book explores in detail; I explain the general contours of the three accounts of the appeal of authenticity that are explicated in chapters 1, 2, and 3; and I outline the key ideas of chapters 4 and 5.

AUTHENTICITY: A POWERFUL IDEA WITH A LONG HISTORY

"Be true to yourself." It's a dictum so ubiquitous that it can seem like an empty truism. But it is also a piece of wisdom held by many to be something like the meaning of life. On the first day of my First Year Seminar ("The Meaning of Life"), I typically poll my students about what parental or "adult" advice (if any) they were given as they were being carted off to college just days before, and a significant subset of them commonly report being told, "Just be yourself." If Caitlin's experience is at all representative, apparently trained psychiatrists tell their patients to just be themselves. Popular self-help ideologies like Oprah's love-yourself-first self-esteem boosterism (open any issue of *O, The Oprah Magazine*) and Dr.

Phil's self-improvement-through-tough-love philosophy (for example, in *Self Matters*) are saturated with the idea that being true to yourself is the key to happiness (and, of course, weight-loss, success in love, and making lots of money).

In a more serious vein, much of the liberatory discourse of LGBTQ rights activism appeals to the idea that it can't be wrong to be the way nature made us (see, for example, the "It Gets Better" Project). Indeed, the idea that a fulfilling life requires an authentic expression of one's sexual self in a safe environment is a virtual platitude of liberal thinking. Of course, there is a parallel conservative rhetoric whose racial, gender and sexual essentialism is equally shot through with a true-self metaphysics, sometimes supplemented by the thought that those who fail to conform to various traditional norms are deviants, alienated from their true and natural selves by a corrupt society's increasingly relativistic (or even nihilistic) atheism. I argue in chapter 5, where I take up Charles Taylor's influential conception of authenticity, that we should be suspicious of The Ideal of Authenticity in part because it is so plastic that it can be deployed in support of liberal, as well as reactionary (subjectivist and objectivist) moral thinking.

The plasticity of The Ideal is evidence of its power, but also its complicated embeddings in the history of western thought. The ancient Delphic motto, "Know thyself," and the famous Socratic dictum that "The unexamined life is not worth living," are among the earliest and most influential articulations of the insight that self-knowledge and, by implication, being true to that knowledge, is necessary for the good life. Both the rationalist (e.g., Cartesian) and empiricist (e.g., Humean) traditions in modern philosophy take introspection as the key method for investigating not only some of the most basic epistemological and metaphysical questions (e.g., What, if anything, can we know? What is the nature of the mind?), but also the fundamental questions in ethics (e.g., How should we live? What is right and wrong?). From Rousseau through the Romantic period philosophy, in its reaction against mechanism and modernity, appealed to the natural self as the basis of artistic and creative inspiration; and the conceptions of self and self-reliance in Transcendentalist thinkers like Emerson and Thoreau can be placed within the continuum of this tradition.

Arguably, the most influential sources of philosophical liberalism also emerge from ethical frameworks that place selfhood at the center. In his *Groundwork for the Metaphysics of Morals*, Kant goes so far as to claim that the law one freely and rationally gives oneself is the thoroughgoing guide to right conduct.[1] (John Rawls draws on the Kantian picture of the self in devising his liberal arguments in *A Theory of Justice*). In the utilitarian tradition, John Stuart Mill (e.g., in *On Liberty*) focuses on our privileged access to knowledge of our own individual good as a primary justification for his Harm Principle and the limits of the liberal state.

While none of these philosophers uses the language of authenticity (and I am not claiming that we ought to interpret them as talking about authenticity, as such), my intent is simply to highlight a set of ideas that turn out to resonate closely with the conceptions of authenticity that this book explores.

From Nietzsche and Heidegger to Camus and Sartre and de Beauvoir, the existentialist tradition is, of course, the first philosophical tradition to take up the idea of authenticity in its most explicit and recognizably modern forms. On Sartre's conception (which I discuss in detail in chapters 1 and 2), for example, to avoid "bad faith" is to avoid a particular form of self-deception and thus to be true to the one "truth" about oneself, namely that one is at once an embodied being, or a "facticity," and also a radically free, unconstrained "transcendence." Simone de Beauvoir's antiessentialist critique of gender made the self a touchstone of feminist and "post-feminist" thinking. And of course, theorizing about race and racial identity has been permeated with a concern for the metaphysics of authenticity (e.g., Du Bois, Fanon).

But the project of this book is explicitly *not* historical or exegetical. Charles Taylor and others have written illuminatingly on the history of the idea of authenticity.[2] This book is also not primarily cultural or political analysis of The Ideal of Authenticity. Again, others have done important work from these directions.[3] Rather, this book is an investigation of various ways in which we invoke the ideas of authenticity and true selfhood in everyday life. This is why I began this introduction with a personal anecdote and why I try, throughout this project, to keep my analysis grounded in examples that I hope will resonate with the lived experiences of readers situated in a social reality somewhat similar to my own. My aim is thus to use familiar examples both to sharpen and to challenge a set of ideas that I think properly fall under the label, "authenticity," but that are not identical to any one philosophical definition of the term. Nevertheless, my critique of The Ideal of Authenticity inevitably draws on ideas from these important historical precursors, and I invoke them now to remind us of the roots of an idea that converges with a piece of contemporary common sense "wisdom": that people achieve a kind of *ideal* when they are genuine or real or true to themselves.

THE CONCEPT OF AN IDEAL

Because this book is a critique of a certain ideal, it will be helpful if we first consider *what* an ideal might be. Most generally, we can say that a person who holds an ideal aspires to live in accordance with some overarching value or principle. Some ideals might be taken to be *overriding*. We can say that an ideal is overriding if it is *always* better to conform with the ideal rather than not to. If authenticity were an ideal in this sense, it would mean that it would always, under all circumstances, be better to be more rather then less true to oneself; the relatively *in*authentic person would always live a better life were she to become *more* authentic. More exactly, keeping everything else about the world fixed, any change in a person in the direction of authenticity (even at the possible expense of other values) would always be better, all things considered. This is, of course, a very strong claim and, while some may hold it, I think it would be uncharitable to attribute this view quite generally to advocates of authenticity. The claim that The Ideal of Authenticity is an overriding ideal can be rejected if we can identify cases where, intuitively, it is *not* best, all things considered, to be more authentic. In chapters 1, 2, and 3, I present such cases. So, among my aims is to show that authenticity is not an overriding ideal. (Indeed, I will be suggesting a broader and perhaps more interesting claim that no single ideal is likely to be overriding in the sense just described). But even if authenticity is not an *overriding* ideal, it might still hold strong appeal as a more modest form of ideal.

Charles Taylor suggests that contemporary common sense conceives of the authentic life as a "better or higher mode of life," and of authenticity as "a standard of what we ought to desire."[4] An *in*authentic life, on this view, is one that would be, by contrast, relatively "wasted or unfulfilled."[5] Now, I think this language is ambiguous with respect to whether it implies that authenticity is overriding. But it nevertheless captures something important about what it is to be an ideal. If we take something to be an ideal, we think, minimally, that aspiring to that ideal makes our lives better in *some* fundamental dimension that we take to be worth aspiring to, as a rule.

In explaining her theory of the virtues, Rosalind Hursthouse employs some language that will be helpful in our effort to articulate an appealing conception of an ideal. According to Hursthouse, "the virtues, for the most part, benefit the possessor."[6] "[F]or the most part" is an important qualification indicating that the virtues need not *always*, in every case, benefit the possessor. This means that it's possible that in certain particular situations, it may not actually be best for us to be virtuous. But the virtues are nevertheless to be sought. Hursthouse explains that this is because they are "one's only reliable bet as far as a flourishing life is concerned."[7] This claim has two components worth focusing on: the first is that the virtues *are* a reliable bet as far as flourishing is concerned,[8] and the second is that the virtues are the *only reliable* bet as far as flourishing is concerned.[9] The first point captures a modest version of the Taylorian idea that ideals make our lives better. The second point clarifies that Hursthouse does not think that virtue is always, without exception, better for us. If we construe Hurstouse as saying that virtue is an ideal, then what she is saying at least is that there is no alternative way of living that *more* reliably promotes flourishing. Importantly, this is compatible with particular, idiosyncratic, or local evidence, say, of unvirtuous people flourishing. In other words, the claim that virtue *is* an ideal is not falsified by the mere existence of the happily vicious. What would be needed to show that virtue is not an ideal is a "clearly identifiable pattern" of cases where virtuous people fare badly.[10] Correlatively, the claim that virtue is the *only reliable* bet would be falsified only by a "clearly identifiable pattern" of cases where vice promotes flourishing.

Hursthouse's is roughly the conception of an ideal that I think a reasonable defender of The Ideal of Authenticity ought to adopt. And it is the view that I will be challenging throughout this book. When someone says or implies that authenticity is an ideal, what I take them to be saying is that *being true to oneself is, all things considered, one's best or most reliable bet, as far is living the best life one can live.*[11] This means that our ideals are more than just our tentative or generally guiding principles; it means that if something is an ideal, it is more than just a *pro tanto* good that can be outweighed or overruled by competing goods. If something is our ideal, it is something that we are committed to, that we pursue *seriously*, and that we take to be a necessary component of the good life. If something is an ideal, then its opposite or inverse is something that we have standing reason to avoid.

With this conception of an ideal in mind, we will be asking whether authenticity (on various conceptions) is in fact an ideal, and this means not just investigating whether there are isolated counterexamples to the claim that it's always better to be authentic, but inquiring into whether there are identifiable *patterns* of cases where it is not best, all things considered, to be authentic. I will be claiming that there are. And this means that there are values, other than authenticity, such that acting on them in principled and patterned ways, in particular kinds of situations, facilitates our living better lives than we would if we took authenticity as our ideal. My aim is thus to show that there are many contexts where authenticity is not our best bet for living the best lives we can and that inauthenticity (on various conceptions) is.

Before moving on, I have one further clarification relating to the nature of an ideal. The conception of an ideal that I've attributed to Hursthouse is explicitly eudaimonic. As a virtue theorist, she is interested in what makes a flourishing life, what promotes our well-being. I will be taking the idea of "what makes our lives go well" quite broadly. As noted in the italicized statement of what an ideal is (above), I take it that following an ideal (if there are any) enables us to live "the best" lives we can. But our lives can be good in many ways and I treat "flourishing" as only one of them. I take it to be an open question whether "the best" life, full stop, is the life with the most happiness or whether it might perhaps be the morally best life or the most rational life or perhaps, most plausibly, the life with some complex balance among these. This is to say that I want to leave open the conceptual possibilities that being *morally* good or being *rational*, for example, might come at the expense of our experienced well-being or our happiness. Of course, many may think that well-being, morality, and rationality do, or even must, necessarily coincide. And some may think that authenticity is the key to one or all of these modes of good life. But because these connections are complex and the claims about them contentious, I will be treating these three particular domains—well-being, rationality, and morality—as, in principle, conceptually distinct. Each may, on its own, causally contribute to, or (in part or in sum) simply constitute, "the best" lives we can live. As we shall see in the context of our discussion of The Ideal of Authenticity, well-being, rationality, and morality often function as kinds of "supervalues," thought to be so important to human life that we can, perhaps, understand the value of everything else (authenticity included) in terms of them. For this reason, the three "accounts" of THe Ideal of Authenticity I consider correspond to these values.

THREE ACCOUNTS OF THE IDEAL OF AUTHENTICITY

As just suggested, there are many ways to understand the claim that it is "better" or "best" to be authentic: it might be psychologically or biologically healthier; it might be prudent; it might be socially or politically advantageous; it might be rationally (epistemically or practically) best; it might be morally best. With this in mind, in the next three chapters of this book, I propose and considerer three general accounts of why The Ideal of Authenticity seems so appealing. More technically, these are three possible accounts of the normative grounding of The Ideal. If you were to ask, in response to the advice to be true to yourself, "But why should I do *that*?" satisfying answers might be "Because it's good for you," or "Because it would be rational," or "Because it's right." Accordingly, the first account (developed in chapter 1) construes The Ideal of Authenticity as an ideal in virtue of the benefits that authenticity provides to the well-being of the authentic person (henceforth, The well-being Account of The Ideal of Authenticity). On this view, to say that authenticity is our best bet for living a good life is to say that it most reliably makes our lives go best *for us*.[12] So if someone were wondering why she should be true to herself, the powerful answer would be that it is *good for her* to be. The second account (the focus of chapter 2) interprets The Ideal as a mandate of practical or epistemic rationality (henceforth, The Rationality Account of The Ideal of Authenticity). On this view, the reason to be authentic is that *reason itself* demands it. The answer to the question "Why should I be authentic?" would be that being authentic is the way to be rational. Given that we, as (responsible) persons, are essentially rational beings, The Rationality Account of The Ideal of Authenticity would seem to carry a kind of normative inescapability that makes it powerfully attractive. The third account (presented in chapter 3) makes sense of The Ideal of Authenticity by linking it with some moral norm(s) (henceforth, The Moral Account of The Ideal of Authenticity). On this view, the reasons to be authentic are essentially moral reasons. If a person asks why she should be true to herself, the answer will be that it is *morally* right or best. And seeing that many think morality is a candidate for being possibly even an overriding ideal, if morality grounded authenticity, then authenticity, too, might even turn out to be an overriding ideal.

Because of the overwhelming appeal of well-being, rationality, and morality, I think that all three of these "supervalues" are compelling as possible groundings for The Ideal of Authenticity. For this reason, I focus on them in the central chapters of this book and argue that The Ideal of Authenticity does not reliably conduce to well-being or rationality or to moral goodness. But some might worry that I have ignored a fourth crucial (and perhaps the most fully philosophically investigated) possible grounding account of The Ideal of Authenticity and that is an Aesthetic Account of The Ideal. Versions of The Aesthetic Account of The Ideal of Authenticity have, I think, been best explored through a Nietzschean lens[13] which offers a philosophically provocative and important perspective precisely because of the ways in which it runs *against* a Moral Account and perhaps even a Rationality Account of The Ideal of Authenticity. This is to say that Aesthetic Accounts of the authentic life may take it to have certain formal qualities that make it worth idealizing even if—or possible even *because*—they come at the expense of other values, are "beyond good and evil," or perhaps are even beyond the norms of rationality itself. Defenders of an Aesthetic Account of The Ideal of Authenticity may thus be inclined to defend authenticity even when it is injurious to others (or to the authentic person herself) and even when it seems irrational in various ways. It is partly for this reason that I do not devote a chapter of the book to the Aesthetic Account. Because I am interested in the ways in which people invoke The Ideal in everyday life, I focus on conceptions of authenticity that I think have been under-theorized and that are not primarily endorsed for complex metaethical reasons (say, relating to the death of God or the possibility of radically self-created value). Moreover, I am interested in conceptions of authenticity that at least purport to be supported by commonsense intuitions about what is good for us and what is right, intuitions that are distinctively non-nihilistic, at least in their explicit forms. The Aesthetic Account of authenticity is, I think, a uniquely philosophical and important one, often adopted and endorsed by those invested, possibly for good reason, in rejecting a swath of other conventional values. This book is *not* a response to those who take this position. This book is aimed at those who think that authenticity is an ideal because of the ways it resonates with intuitive and commonsensical ethical thinking in its broadest form.

Now that we have a working definition of an ideal and three compelling accounts of what might ground an ideal of authenticity, I'll turn to the five substantive conceptions of authenticity which I will be developing and criticizing. After that, I'll offer short summaries of each chapter of the book.

FIVE KINDS OF AUTHENTICITY

In what follows, I consider five different kinds of authenticity. I will be thinking of these versions of authenticity as different conceptions of a single overarching concept and I do not take these conceptions to be exhaustive. Moreover, my aim is to be neutral on the question of how these different conceptions might coincide or compete with one another. I present them because I think each is compelling in its own right and each, I hope, captures something intuitive and deep about what we think it means to be true to ourselves in a variety of everyday situations. What the conceptions all, crucially, have in common is that they make being authentic a matter of how we relate *to ourselves* in a certain way. And I take this to be a conceptual constraint on any reasonable conception of authenticity (thus capturing the "aut-" of authenticity). In chapters 1, 2, and 3, I present a set of scenarios intended to clarify each conception of authenticity and to elicit intuitions supporting the prima facie plausibility of each conception. To get our thinking started, I'll now just suggest how each conception might apply to Caitlin, the student described above.

According to the first conception of authenticity (call it Authenticity as Strong Will), what it means to be true to yourself is to exercise the self-control necessary for acting in accordance with your best judgments. Imagine, for a moment, that Caitlin knew exactly what she thought she should do about her pregnancy but, feeling how hard that would be, was tempted to take some "easier" way out. If Caitlin sticks to her resolve and does what she judges best, even though it is difficult, we can say that she has been true to herself by exercising strong will. In general, sticking to resolutions will be paradigm cases of Authenticity as Strong Will.

A second kind of authenticity involves being robustly psychologically independent (henceforth Authenticity as Psychological Independence). In Caitlin's case, we would say that she is true to herself in this way if she resists simply submitting to the judgments of her parents or her friends or some other authority. When we are authentically psychologically independent, we think *for ourselves* and, in so doing, we may resist a variety of pervasive and oppressive social standards (for example, those telling us to be thinner, or richer, or to conform to racial, sexual, domestic, or professional expectations). If Authenticity as Psychological Independence is an ideal, then, by succeeding in living (or at least trying to live) the kinds of independent-minded lives *we ourselves* want and deserve to lead (rather than the kinds of lives *others* may want for us) we live as well as we can.

A third way of being true to ourselves is by resolving inner conflicts among our desires and values and identifying clearly and unambivalently with a coherent vision of ourselves and our chosen paths (call this Authenticity as Wholeheartedness). If Caitlin is irreconcilably conflicted about what she should do or if there is no determinate fact about what she thinks is best, then there is a sense in which she cannot be true to herself because there is no determinate self to be true to. According to The Ideal of Authenticity as Wholeheartedness, then, what Caitlin needs to do to be true to herself is *settle* what she thinks or how she feels and become a whole, integrated person. Resolving or settling ourselves in these ways (sometimes described as "finding ourselves"[14]) seems essential to making narrative sense of our lives and achieving the kinds of subjective meaning that makes our lives fulfilling.

A fourth way of being authentic is by avoiding various kinds of self-deception or bad faith. On this conception, we are true to ourselves by facing up to the sometimes painful and often obscure truths about ourselves (henceforth Authenticity as Self-Knowledge). By gaining self-knowledge, we also enable ourselves to live in accordance with that knowledge, which seems essential for making choices of the kinds that are ultimately best for us. If we imagine that Caitlin knows "deep down" what she really values, but for some reason is repressing or suppressing this knowledge, The Ideal of Authenticity as Self-Knowledge recommends to her that she be true to herself by acknowledging her true values.

Fifth and finally, there is a kind of authenticity that involves living up to our own best moral judgments. (We'll call this Authenticity as Moral Conscientiousness.) On this conception of authenticity, the moral self is the true self, so, in acting on conscience, we live authentically. For Caitlin to be authentic in this way, what she somehow needs to do is figure out what she thinks is *morally* right; by acting in accordance with that judgment, she would embody authenticity as moral conscientiousness.

THE WELL-BEING ACCOUNT OF THE IDEAL OF AUTHENTICITY

Why think that being true to ourselves is reliably best for our well-being? There are many reasons to think this. In being true to ourselves, we may avoid various harms associated with weak will (e.g., by kicking an addiction or overcoming an inclination to procrastinate). By overcoming the internalization of oppressive social norms and living (or at least trying to live) the kinds of lives we ourselves want to lead, we stand to benefit in profound psychological ways. By figuring out who we "really are," we enable ourselves to live wholeheartedly, without the depression and confusion that sometimes come from being conflicted about who we are or what we really want. In being true to ourselves, we may also avoid the guilt or shame that often comes from failing to do what we think is right.

I argue in chapter 1 that none of these claims about the benefits of authenticity ultimately supports the idea that being authentic is the reliably best way to promote our own well-being. Using a series of intuitive counterexamples, I argue that the apparent benefits to well-being from being authentic are contingent and unreliable. Moreover, in a variety of "normal" situations, it is reliably better *for* us to be *in*authentic. For example, when one's "best judgment" about what to do is unreasonably perfectionist or demanding, it can be better not to do what we ourselves think is best. Being deeply influenced by others is often best for our well-being (this is obviously true in the case of young children). Thinking too much about who we really are and what we really want, even entirely conscientiously, can lead to paralysis and narcissistic self-involvement. If well-being is what we ultimately care about, I claim that we should not take authenticity as our guiding value.

But even if authenticity did reliably conduce to well-being, this would not, I argue, vindicate The Ideal of Authenticity. After all, there surely seem to be some things that are more important than our own well-being—if we care about being good parents, children, friends, and citizens, then sometimes we will inevitably have to sacrifice our own well-being and perhaps even do things that threaten to alienate us from our deepest selves (for example, if those selves are conflicted or morally deficient in various ways). Those who think authenticity is justified as an ideal by its benefits to individual well-being can also be vulnerable to thinking that authenticity might be a standing defense against moral criticism. (Consider how we sometimes give "artists" or "geniuses" extra leeway to pursue their passions because of their apparently extra-special psychic need for authentic self-expression.) I argue that this should not be tolerated; the well-being benefits of being true to oneself, such as they are, are not a trump against otherwise standing moral constraints. The best life (full stop) cannot reliably be expected to be the best life *for us*.

THE RATIONALITY ACCOUNT OF THE IDEAL OF AUTHENTICITY

Suppose, for a moment, that when Caitlin's doctor told her to be true to herself, she thought that Caitlin knew, at some level, what she really wanted to do, and her aim was to help motivate her to have the courage of her convictions. On this understanding of the advice, the doctor would be encouraging Caitlin to gain self-knowledge, to avoid the undue influence of others, to act in accordance with her own best judgment, and to do what she thinks is right. We might say, more technically, that the advice would be aimed at promoting Caitlin's rational autonomy. The Rationality Account of The Ideal of Authenticity holds that authenticity and (practical and/or epistemic) rationality go hand in hand. If this is right, it might turn out that being true to oneself is always, *necessarily*, the rational thing to do. Now, if we add the very intuitive claim that being subject to the norms of rationality is, at least in part, *constitutive of being a person*, then The Ideal of Authenticity will be no less essential to our very personhood. Rationally speaking, there would be no getting off the hook of The Ideal of Authenticity; The Ideal might acquire the inescapable force of a Kantian categorical imperative.[15]

In chapter 2, I argue against the Rationality Account of The Ideal of Authenticity. I lay out two sets of patterned cases that conflict with the account. The first set consists of cases where, intuitively, being authentic does not seem rational, overall. (Consider that our true selves, if we have them, might not be rational). The second set consists of cases where inauthenticity, perhaps (or hopefully) surprisingly, is perfectly rational or even more rational than authenticity. I argue, in turn, that it can be rational to be weak-willed; that it is often rational to be deeply psychologically dependent; that ambivalence, as opposed to wholeheartedness, is often rational; that it is often rational to forego self-knowledge; and that it can certainly be rational to act against conscience.

The chapter thus aims to undermine the intuition that apparently paradigmatic instances of inauthenticity (being weak-willed, or submissive to the judgments of others, or self-deceived) are necessarily irrational. So, to return to Caitlin, if Caitlin goes *against* her gut, or her conscience, or if she does what her parents want her to do, or if she fails to achieve self-knowledge, none of these things necessitate that Caitlin has not been rational.[16]

This chapter also defends a contention that many philosophers will find discomfiting. Even if the value of authenticity could be derived from the normativity of practical and/or epistemic rationality, I claim there are sometimes, perhaps even often, more important things than being rational. The best lives we can live may in fact be ones that are deficient with respect to a variety of rational norms (for example, being perfectly means-ends rational, and believing the truth). To begin to see why this is so, we need only imagine the miserably impoverished life of a person who obsessively fetishizes rationality (something that some philosophers may be especially prone to doing). So, in this chapter, I consider some of the apparent dangers of valuing rationality too highly. I suggest that even if being subject to the norms of rationality is in part constitutive of being a person, this does not suffice to show that that the norms of rationality are normatively overriding or even that they should be adopted as a practical ideal; in short, there are clearly identifiable patterns of cases where it is not best to be rational. The Rationality Account of The Ideal of Authenticity thus fails to vindicate authenticity as an ideal because rationality turns out not to be as important to the good life as many philosophers would have us believe.

THE MORAL ACCOUNT OF THE IDEAL OF AUTHENTICITY

If the value of well-being or rationality cannot vindicate our attraction to The Ideal of Authenticity, perhaps a Moral Account can do better. The Moral Account of The Ideal of Authenticity aims to show that being authentic makes us morally better or more virtuous people or, perhaps even that authenticity, as such, is really the only legitimate moral ideal there can be. If being authentic paradigmatically involves having a strong will or resisting temptation, then authenticity would seem to be a virtue, along the lines of temperance. We often say, by way of praise and admiration, that the strong-willed person has "integrity" or is "conscientious," words almost synonymous with moral character. Relatedly, the idea that authenticity is about thinking for oneself seems to have significant moral import. Thinking for oneself is thought by many to be an essential, if not the essential, component of an ethical life. It is an assumption among many liberal arts faculty, for example, that teaching students to think critically and independently is the basic way to foster a community of socially engaged, progressive, and upstanding citizens. (I have regularly heard my college's honor code explained in terms of the ethical requirement to be true to oneself, to live up to *one's own* values rather than conforming to social pressures.)

In this chapter, I offer two strategies of objection to The Moral Account of The Ideal of Authenticity. The first strategy is, again, to lay out a patterned set of cases that conflict with the claim that being authentic is reliably the best bet if our aim is to be morally good. So, I suggest a variety of contexts in which people are intuitively authentic, but also predictably bad. It seems clear, for example, that we can be conscientiously true to ourselves in the pursuit of what are in fact morally despicable ends. The perpetrators of the September 11 attacks are aptly characterized as strong-willed in the face of danger. People who commit crimes despite widespread social disapproval may be highly psychologically independent and so, in that sense, authentic. But thinking "for oneself" has no special connection with morality, especially if one's iconoclasm involves flouting pro-social norms dictating cooperation and respect. Further, as noted above, artists or "geniuses" who may, so to speak, rank highly on the authenticity-as-psychological-independence scale, often do so at the expense of moral virtue.[17] Similarly, I argue (as we shall see, contra Aquinas, Martin Luther King, Jr., and Kant) that thinking rigorously, consistently, and self-critically is no guarantee of thinking (morally) *rightly*. Despite liberal platitudes about the value of a liberal-arts college education, the skill of critically thinking for oneself is, as such (notwithstanding the value of epistemic rationality itself), value neutral, so orthogonal to moral virtue.

The second strategy of objection to The Moral Account suggests, correlatively, that it is often morally better to be inauthentic. It can be morally good to be weak-willed and to violate conscience (as when our best judgments are morally flawed). It can be good to be psychologically dependent (as when one's character is being formed under the influence of those who are themselves virtuous, or conditions which themselves attune us to the good). It can be morally good to be ambivalent (when ambivalence is a kind of modesty or when it is a proper response to the complexity of a situation). And it can be morally best to lack self-knowledge—or even to live in bad faith—when the alternatives would lead us to harm others, in accordance with our "true" and perhaps vicious or simply amoral selves.

Methodological Note

So, to recap, the primary strategy I will use to challenge The Ideal of Authenticity will be to propose patterned *counterexamples* to the claim that being authentic is an ideal. By appeal to a series of everyday situations, I argue for the (at least initially) counterintuitive conclusion that in fact *inauthenticity* often reliably conduces to the best lives we can live. For example, when one's "best judgment" about what to do is unreasonably demanding or just plain wrong, being strong-willed in the furtherance of that judgment is not ideal. It can, indeed, be best for us—and also both rational and right—not to do what we, ourselves, honestly think is best for us; in this sense it can be better for us not to be true to ourselves. Being deeply influenced by others, thought by many to be incompatible with being "truly ourselves," *is* often best for our well-being, our rationality, and our virtue (this is obviously true in the case of young children, but I will suggest this is much more generally correct). More controversially, I argue that the aim of avoiding inner conflict and ambivalence about our lives may not be compatible with having the range of passions and the diversity of values and commitments that are present in most good lives. It should also be clear that thinking too much about who we really are, even in the conscientious effort to avoid self-deception or bad faith, can be a form of narcissistic self-involvement that leads to paralysis and depression (which can come at significant rational and moral cost). We can easily overvalue self-knowledge. And, finally, I argue that being conscientiously true to our best moral judgments is not reliably good for us, or rational, or even, ironically, morally best. The implication is that there is not a sufficiently tight connection between authenticity and well-being, rationality or morality to establish The Ideal of Authenticity.

That said, the appeal of The Ideal of Authenticity does, I think, hinge on the appeal of rationality, well-being and morality. Each of these, individually, has been thought by theorists of the Good Life to be a comprehensive guide to human conduct. In the course of criticizing The Ideal of Authenticity, therefore, I will also be contributing arguments for why none of these (rationality, well-being, or morality) should be accepted as practical ideals.

As we will be construing The Ideal of Authenticity, those committed to it are committed to three important claims. The first is that being authentic is essentially a matter of how one relates to *oneself* rather than to others (it is to be, in some relevant sense, true to oneself); this is meant to capture a conceptual truth about what authenticity *is*. The second is that authenticity is one's most reliable bet, all things considered, for living a good life. This captures our notion of what it is for something to be an *ideal*. The third claim that I think many defenders of The Ideal of Authenticity will want to endorse is that The Ideal applies to all who are capable of complying with it. You don't get off the hook of a charge of inauthenticity just by saying that you don't feel like being authentic (consider the apparent absurdity of someone resisting The Ideal by saying, "But why should I be true to myself?"). This third claim is important because, without it, the charge of inauthenticity would seem to lack the kind of normative force it is typically taken to have. The normative force of authenticity advice, and the plausibility of this third claim, is the topic of chapter 4.

BAD ADVICE: THE NATURE OF NORMATIVE FAILURE

Those who think that authenticity is an ideal typically take "being true to yourself" to be a central and *practical* guiding value. Because of this, they are also disposed to give authenticity *advice* in contexts where others are struggling with important life decisions (we've already seen this in Caitlin's case, where her doctor explicitly offers true self advice as practical guidance for Caitlin). But what are the conditions in which a piece of advice or a practical ideal is actually helpful in guiding action? By identifying what makes advice good (here taking "advice" broadly enough to allow that we can give ourselves advice by invoking our ideals), we will be in a better position to see why The Ideal of Authenticity so often fails as good advice.

In exploring this issue I assume that good action-guiding rules are in the business of providing *reasons* for pursuing certain courses of action. So I take up a set of fundamental metaethical questions: How and when do the norms we invoke in the form of ideals or advice provide us with reasons for action? What, if anything, gives reasons their normative force? Are there "objectively prescriptive" normative facts that ought to guide people, independent of their actual concerns or interests? Or must all practical reasons somehow derive from, or "tap into," the psychologies or personal interests of the people to whom they apply? The purpose of taking up these questions in the context of The Ideal of Authenticity is to show that purportedly action-guiding authenticity advice is prone to fail in two main ways—by being so indifferent to the actual concerns and interests of advisees that they fall on deaf ears (what I will call the problem of normative alienation) or by being so sensitive to those concerns that they turn out to be trivial or contentless. (Very plausibly, Caitlin perceived her psychiatrist's advice to be true to herself as supportive and validating precisely because it had no action-guiding content that she could conceivably disagree with).

I claim that good advice, as such, must minimally, (a) have action-guiding *content*, (b) be in some way *informative* to the subject (tell her something that was not already obvious to her), and (c) be capable of *rationally motivating* the subject in the direction of a decision. I proceed to develop seven criteria for good action-guiding rules and show how, in different contexts, The Ideal of Authenticity fails to meet one or more of these criteria. By turns, The Ideal reduces to something tautological or trivial (like "You got to do what you got to do"), uninformative (as in "I should do what I think is best"), self-defeating (when given as advice of the form "Don't take anyone's advice but your own") or just plain wrong (for example, when what a person authentically thinks is best is downright terrible). This chapter thus provides a larger framework for thinking about advice within which the book's local arguments against The Ideal of Authenticity can be situated.

ETHICS WITHOUT AUTHENTICITY: LOOKING OUTWARD NOT IN

Having rejected what I take to be the three most powerful accounts of the appeal of The Ideal of Authenticity in chapters 1, 2, and 3, and having given general reason to be suspicious of The Ideal as good advice in chapter 4, in chapter 5, I offer an articulation of the ethical benefits of abandoning The Ideal of Authenticity. The chapter is devoted to two projects: the first is diagnosing what values *other* than authenticity are often implicitly or indirectly endorsed by our talk of authenticity. To put it differently, this is a matter of *rediagnosing* the appeal of The Ideal of Authenticity. I show in this chapter how being true to oneself is invoked as a clever way to motivate people to live in accordance with very particular and often contentious conceptions of health, romance, sexuality, professional productivity, and even elitist intellectualism. I suggest that The Ideal of Authenticity functions as a kind of rhetorical cover for a set of moralisms that themselves deserve our critical attention. The second project of the chapter is to show how we might make *better* ethical arguments—I claim ones we are often tacitly and badly making via our authenticity talk—without invoking authenticity at all. I explain why I think there is *something* right about our intuitive attraction to The Ideal of Authenticity and why I think we can better retain what is of philosophical value there without committing ourselves to The Ideal or to any of its metaphysically confused and, I argue, ethically problematic elements.

Finally, I want to clarify that I think we can and should get on board with a version of the antiessentialism that resonates with certain conceptions of authenticity and that has played an especially important role in shaping feminist and antiracist thinking. So, my critique of authenticity is not a rejection of the fundamental values of individual freedom, or rights, or choice, liberally construed. There *are* ways of thinking of ourselves and others as free and responsible that can and should be separated from the robust and problematic authenticity fetishism that saturates discourses on both sides of the "culture wars."[18] To demonstrate this, in my concluding chapter I suggest the distinctive turn the ethical discourse of the left might take if, for example, gay rights arguments were purged of the ideology of authenticity. To this end, I take up Charles Taylor's discussion of homosexuality in *The Ethics of Authenticity* and compare it with Leslie Green's discussion that is explicitly critical of Taylor. I show that while Taylor's "dialogical" conception of authenticity avoids some of the pitfalls of both essentializing and subjectivizing versions of authenticity-based gay rights arguments, his approach does not succeed in vindicating authenticity, as such, as a *moral* ideal of the kind he thinks it is.

The lesson I draw in the end is that The Ideal of Authenticity sets up false dichotomies between self and other, and between what "really" is and is not us, which divert us from the more substantive overarching questions about how we should live our lives. I suggest that by abandoning The Ideal, we can (re)focus our attention *outward* on the personal and social questions that matter in a way that escapes the objectionable narcissism, relativism, and essentialism that our collective obsession with authenticity often perpetuates. I suggest that charges of inauthenticity obscure various unexamined philosophical assumptions that we would do better to bring to light: for example, the dubious assumption that one's "gut" or conscience is a reliably good guide to one's "true" values; or the assumption that we should be suspicious of "external" influences on ourselves; or the assumption that self-knowledge is the key to psychological health. By bringing to light and then challenging the plausibility of The Ideal of Authenticity, I claim, we will be better able to recognize the complexity of personhood and the diversity of values that are properly brought to bear in difficult situations of practical decision-making. We are prone to change over time and to experience inner conflict and alienation and self-deception. Our subjectivity may be utterly fraught and fragmented. But, for both metaphysical and ethical reasons, we should not be led to think that these are conditions that must be overcome through the aspiration to The Ideal of Authenticity.

NOTES

1. The relationship between autonomy and authenticity is an interesting one that I do not explore here. See Oshana (2007).
2. See Taylor (1991, p. 25) on "The Sources of Authenticity."
3. See Guignon (2004) and Varga (2011).
4. See Taylor (1991, p. 16).
5. Ibid., p, 17.
6. Hursthouse (1999, p. 173).
7. Ibid., p. 174.
8. To be more precise, what Hursthouse says is that there is no "regimen," other than virtue, that "will serve one better" (p. 174). This may technically leave open the possibility that the "regimen" of virtue is not an especially reliable bet, just the most reliable of the options.
9. Thanks to Allan Hazlett for this observation.
10. Hirsthorst (1999, pp. 173–174).
11. The idea of a "reliable bet" is not a straightforwardly quantitative one. If it turned out that, in the statistical majority of cases (how we would enumerate "all" the cases is itself conceptually and metaphysically obscure), authenticity were better than inauthenticity, this would not confirm The Ideal of Authenticity. Consider that on the statistical majority of roads, the more reliable bet when it comes to avoiding a crash is to drive on the right. But we wouldn't want say that, for all roads, driving on the right is the most (or even more) reliable bet. The right thing to say is that *sometimes* driving on the right is the more reliable bet, and *sometimes* driving on the left is the more reliable bet. Driving in the UK is not an abnormal, exceptional circumstance. It is a clearly identifiable pattern of cases in which driving on the left is the more reliable bet, when it comes to avoiding a crash. (Thanks to Allan Hazlett for these clarifying observations).
12. I take this in the spirit of Derek Parfit's question: "What would be best for someone, or would be most in this person's interests, or would make this person's life go, for him, as well as possible?" (Parfit, 1984, p. 493).
13. See Nehamas (1985) and Berkowitz (1995).
14. The language of "finding oneself" might suggest an antecedent fact of the matter (about who we are) which, heretofore being unknown, is now discovered. But I think the idiom is broad enough to include the idea that we can "find out" who we are by becoming determinate selves or by making ourselves; before we "find ourselves," on this conception, we don't know who we are because we aren't yet ourselves.
15. See Dreier (2001). In chapter 4, I consider the normative authority of different kinds of imperatives.
16. Of course, philosophers of various stripes will be disposed to count her as inauthentic and irrational of she *does* go with her gut.
17. See Williams (1999).
18. On the one hand, defenders of The Ideal of Authenticity "on the left" sometimes seem committed to the radically relativistic assumption that *whatever* one does, so long as one does it authentically and conscientiously, must be okay. This captures the intuition that none of us are ultimately in a privileged position to judge each other, so the only standard that remains is the standard that each of us chooses for ourselves. I argue that this is an implausibly permissive ethical stance (and is, in fact, self-defeating if authenticity is itself given a privileged or objective moral/normative status). On the other hand, others who invoke The Ideal of Authenticity do so with the assumption that it has specific and nonrelativistic moral content. Some think that being authentic requires a very specific expression of one's racial identity or sexual orientation or gender identity (e.g., not "passing," or being out, or being a "real man," etc.). In contexts like this, I argue, The Ideal of Authenticity functions to disguise various contentious and problematic ethical views that would be better articulated without the distorting framework of true-self metaphysics.

ONE

The Well-being Account of The Ideal of Authenticity

Consider *Alison, the Smoker*:

> Alison, thirty-five, has struggled with smoking since she was sixteen. She thinks it's a disgusting habit and she's been feeling the effects lately; she wants to turn over a new leaf, get healthy, and quit for real. On New Year's Eve, she resolves that, starting tomorrow, she's not going to smoke anymore. It's two o'clock New Year's Day, and Alison is hungover. She and her friends meet up for a late brunch. She orders a coffee and then thinks she would probably also benefit from a bit of the hair of the dog and she orders a Bloody Mary. Alison's friend, Jen, gets up from their booth, says she's going outside for a smoke and, as she normally would, asks Alison to join her. Suddenly, Alison really wants a cigarette. But she remembers her resolution and tells herself, "That's just the nicotine talking. I'm not a smoker anymore. What kind of person am I if I can't even stick to my guns for a day?" She tells Jen she's quit, Jen looks at her (equal parts suspicious, beckoning, and judgmental), but Alison stays strong and feels good about her decision and herself.

It seems natural to say that in resisting both the temptation of her addiction and the social pressure Jen puts on her to smoke, Alison has succeeded in being true to herself. It also seems to be very good for her. She feels good about her self-control; she avoids the guilt that would have kicked in had she had the cigarette. If she sticks to her resolution, over time, she stands to reap the health—and financial—benefits of not smoking; and in habituating herself to the exercise of her strong will and her independent mind, she also likely improves her chances of making a variety of other good choices in the future. According to what we will call The Well-being Account of The Ideal of Authenticity, none of this should come as any surprise. According to this view, being true to ourselves is, fundamentally, about doing what is *good for us*.

If being true to ourselves reliably makes our lives go best, and if well-being is something that is entirely appropriate for us to take as an ideal (and we will question this in what follows), then authenticity would likewise be something we have reason to prize as an ideal. Corresponding to our five conceptions of authenticity, the initial case for the Well-being Account of The Ideal of Authenticity looks like this: by figuring out and being (or becoming) who we "really are," we (1) avoid the harmful effects that come from being weak-willed and (2) from internalizing others' oppressive standards. We gain the meaningful benefits of (3) being wholeheartedly committed to our life projects and (4) the rewards that come from knowing who we are. And (5) we also stand to reap the psychic, social, and material rewards of living in a morally conscientious way. In short, by being true to ourselves we live the lives that are the best lives for us. This is the heart of the Well-being Account of The Ideal of Authenticity. With this in mind, the driving question of this chapter is whether aiming for authenticity really is our best as far as promoting our individual well-being is concerned. But as we proceed we should also keep a second question in mind: whether lives that take well-being as an ideal are themselves the best lives we can live, all things considered. To vindicate an Ideal of Authenticity grounded in well-being, the answer to both these questions would have to be "yes." As we shall see, as we explore our five different conceptions of authenticity, these yeses are not forthcoming.

To challenge the Well-being Account of The Ideal of Authenticity, I propose a set of patterned *counterexamples* to the claim that being authentic is reliably conducive to our well-being. These counterexamples are meant to represent everyday situations where being authentic does not promote well-being and, indeed, where being *inauthentic* may be reliably better for us. For example, when one's "best judgment" about what to do is unreasonably demanding or self-injurious, being strong-willed in the furtherance of that judgment will not normally benefit us. It can, indeed, be best for us *not* to do what we, ourselves, honestly think is best for us; in this sense it can be better for us *not to be true to ourselves*. Being deeply influenced by others, thought by many to be incompatible with being "truly ourselves," is also often best for our well-being (this is obviously true in the case of young children, and I will suggest this is much more generally correct). I argue that avoiding alienation and ambivalence may not be compatible with having the range of passions and the diversity of values and commitments that are present in most good lives. And thinking too much about who we "really are," even in the conscientious effort to avoid self-deception or bad faith, can lead to paralysis and depression. We can easily overvalue self-knowledge. Finally, I argue that being morally conscientious is not plausibly our best bet for making our own lives go well. The implication is that there is not a sufficiently tight connection between authenticity and well-being to establish anything close to the Well-being Account of The Ideal of Authenticity. But even if this connection were clear and tight, I suggest that there are more important things in life than what is good for us. So even if being authentic *did* reliably or even *always* conduce to well-being, this would not vindicate Authenticity, as such, as an ideal.

Before proceeding, I should also clarify the conception of well-being employed here. For reasons that will become clear in the next two chapters on rationality and morality, I mean "well-being" to be comprised of *experienced* goods like joy and pleasure and happiness. The totality of a person's well-being, on this conception, would thus be a function of the balance of these goods along with all the experienced pains and suffering of life.[1]

WELL-BEING AND AUTHENTICITY AS STRONG WILL

The idea that the good life requires the exercise of strong will can be traced back to Plato's allegory of Reason as the charioteer and our passions the winged horses to be harnessed and controlled.[2] Kant's conception of autonomy, with its similar view of the passions, is another antecedent here.[3] The unifying and intuitive idea is that the properly functioning person is, in some basic sense, *in control* of herself.

For present purposes, we will say that to be strong-willed (as opposed to weak-willed or *akratic*) is to act in accordance with one's best judgment, to live up to one's own explicitly held values and expectations.[4] It is in this sense to be true to oneself. It should be clear from Alison's case that her being strong-willed is closely connected to her well-being. When we are strong-willed, we avoid the guilt and shame that often come from failing to do what we think is right. We can also expect to avoid various harms associated with succumbing to our weaknesses. If we manage to kick an addiction or overcome an inclination to procrastinate, we stand to reap the rewards like improved health and productivity. We also may stand to benefit in a deep "meaning-of-life" kind of way by succeeding in living the kinds of lives we really want to lead. One piece of evidence to support this is the appeal of being able to look back on our lives and say, honestly, "I may have made mistakes but at least I did what I thought was best."[5] This seems to confirm that we take strong will, or resolve in the face of obstacles and temptations to be an essential component of the well-lived life. By the lights of common sense, it should come as a surprise if sticking to our own best judgments were not a worthy ideal.

But how reliably does strong will in fact conduce to well-being? To help us begin to see the problems with the Well-being Account of The Ideal of Authenticity, it is worth noting, first, that the psychological benefits of strong will are contingent upon variable facts about our psychological makeups (e.g., our dispositions to feel guilt and pride under different conditions, etc.). Quite clearly, our individual psychologies vary widely. Some of us may know people who do not seem to suffer the typical negative psychological effects of weak will. We've all probably met people so easy on themselves that they don't give it a second thought when they fail to uphold their best judgments. Some people simply have a gift for rationalizing. One can easily imagine Alison joining Jen for the cigarette and telling herself "It's just one and I'm hungover and it's still New Year's, so I haven't really broken my resolution. I can still quit today just like I said I would." The familiarity of this kind of thinking suggests that the psychological costs of weak will may not generally be as high as we might have initially thought.[6]

While some people are great rationalizers, others simply might not take themselves too seriously. They may put in modest efforts to follow through on their resolutions, but they have an easygoing nature and don't feel too bad if something interferes with their best-laid plans. To their credit, such people might also not be disposed to strong feelings of pride or satisfaction when they succeed in sticking to their resolve. Perhaps some of these people see things with a modicum of "philosophical" perspective that comes from appreciating the absurdity of life and the pervasive effects of good and bad luck on our ability to exercise self-control.[7]

It also might be possible to derive a variety of the benefits of strong will without in fact *being* strong-willed. Just as rationalization can help us avoid guilty feelings, a bit of everyday self-delusion about our achievements might suffice to generate many of the psychic benefits of actual strong will. (I just graded a measly three papers but wow, I feel good about myself!) Put differently, the point is just that if feeling good about our choices is normally good for us, we may be able to generate these feelings without actually doing what we, when we are most honest with ourselves, think is best. Studies have shown, for example, that non-depressed people, as contrasted with depressed people, disproportionately believe they have control over their lives.[8] If this is right, then perhaps our disposition to the self-enhancement bias—to think better of ourselves than we actually are—is our good luck.

Now, I grant that it is hard to imagine someone not deriving *any* satisfaction from the exercise of strong will, and not feeling any guilt or regret at the failure to exercise it. This shows something that is fundamentally correct about the vision of the person that The Ideal of Authenticity as Strong Will assumes: it's not clear that we would fully recognize *as a person* someone who evinced a consistent lack of concern to devote herself to her own ends or who was genuinely indifferent to the outcomes of her own efforts. I presume we normally take it as evidence that something is seriously wrong with a person if she lacks all affective response to the successful or unsuccessful implementation of her own will. But is this enough to show that, all things considered, it is best for us to be strong-willed? Is it enough to show that being strong-willed is an *ideal*?

Perhaps the best reason to think *not* is that we can be strong-willed in the pursuit of things that are bad for us. People can "bravely" do stupid, self-injurious things. (Indeed, there seems to be an epidemic of just such behavior among kids performing crazy stunts, modeling themselves on the self-injurious "jackasses" on shows like MTV's *Jackass*). One can be inappropriately strong-willed in the face of danger or obstacles. Sometimes it might be better for us if we allow what we ourselves (rightly or wrongly) judge to be cowardice to govern our actions. So, while Alison, in her particular circumstances, gets healthier and saves money by exercising her strong will, these benefits are entirely dependent on the particular activity to which her strong will directs her and are not simply a product of strong will itself.[9] Those whose resolute self-control is manifested, say, in anorexic behavior, do not achieve comparable benefits to well-being. Even if the resolutely self-harming person always felt good about her self-control (say, the anorexic takes some pleasure in her self-denial), this would not make strong will good for us, all things considered. As we shall see in a moment, given the kinds of flawed beings we are, it may quite often be good for us to be *weak*-willed.

THE WELL-BEING BENEFITS OF WEAK WILL

We've just pointed out that, though strong will may be reliably good for us in some respects, in others it may not. So it is not *always* good for us, all things considered. I now turn to the more surprising claim that there are in fact patterns of everyday cases where it is best for us to be *weak-willed*. Consider a case inspired by Nomy Arpaly, *Hailey, the Hyper-Perfectionist Student*:[10]

> Hailey is a perfectionist when it comes to academic achievement. She reflectively judges that she should spend pretty much all her waking hours studying and making the most of her academic opportunities. She thinks that many of her friends are wasting their college years partying. She does sometimes go out and have fun, but when she does she feels guilty and wishes that she had stayed in the library and studied.

Let's make the following three further assumptions about Hailey. First, let's assume that, in fact, her academic perfectionism motivates her to work much harder and perform at a higher level than she would if she were not a perfectionist; second, assume that her academic success is going to benefit her in the long run in several important ways (say, she's going to get a better job and she's going to live a richer inner life because of the way she has cultivated her mind); and, third, and most importantly, let's assume that her life would not have been better had she followed her own best judgment and never gone out (because in fact having fun keeps her sane and at least somewhat balanced). The hypothetical possibility we are considering, then, is that Hailey's having extremely high expectations for herself *and* failing to live up to those expectations—even allowing for the inevitable guilt she feels as a result—generates the best outcome *for Hailey*. While the guilt she feels is not, as such, good for her, her life, as stipulated, is actually better, all things considered, *in virtue of* her pattern of weak will.

Consider another, perhaps more familiar example: Priscilla, who loves ice cream, adopts (say, for health reasons) an absolute rule against eating it. Every so often, though, she succumbs to temptation and has a delicious bowl of mint chip. Priscilla feels regret after eating the ice cream and, by hypothesis, she would have been strong-willed had she not eaten it. But she'd also have missed out on what is, for her, one of life's real pleasures. Imagine that Priscilla is psychologically constituted such that if she abandoned her abstemious rule, she'd eat *much* more ice cream and be substantially less healthy (which is among her highest priorities). If this seems like a reasonable possibility, it looks like her failing to be strong-willed, and correspondingly true to herself, is reliably best for Priscilla, given her (I claim typical, albeit flawed) psychological makeup.

The general point is this: setting very high standards for ourselves, which we then consistently fail to live fully up to, may be reliably best for us in a variety of everyday situations. In these kinds of cases, it wouldn't be better for us to *either* lower our expectations for ourselves so that we could more easily succeed in meeting them *or* be so strong-willed that we never enjoy the very activities that our (unreasonably) high standards preclude.

Now, the defender of strong will might object here that what would be best for Hailey and Priscilla would be for them to adopt more reasonable or balanced practical judgments. If their resolutions were more modest they might enjoy their lives with less guilt, and also be sufficiently motivated to achieve the goals that correspond to what they really value (education and health). I think this is right, in a sense. Hailey and Priscilla might be better off *if* they could adjust their standards and their behavior in this way. The problem is that there is no guarantee that this is compatible with their actual psychological makeups. It might turn out, for example, that if Hailey were less of a perfectionist or more forgiving with herself she would be led to slack in her work substantially more. If she decides that her work, while important, is not *that* important, she might start to rationalize more and more time away from her work and this, in the end, might not be best for her. She might even know this about herself and for this very reason, rationally and prudently, commit herself to her perfectionist ideals. If this is possible (and I think it may in fact be a quite common psychological profile familiar to anyone who has tried to stick to a diet), then it's not clear what is gained in this context by saying that nevertheless, it would be better *for Hailey* not to be weak-willed. If Hailey were very different, then all sorts of different things might be good for her. But, given her nature and her actual dispositions in the real world, it seems clear that there could be many circumstances in which it will not be best for her to live up to her own best judgments. And if we are like Hailey or Priscilla in our imperfect patterns of desire and self-control, we can conclude that actually being strong-willed may not be reliably best for our well-being.

There are two more objections that might be raised here against my argument that weak will is best for us in a variety of normal circumstances. The first is that this argument seems to presuppose an objectivist view of well-being. That is, the argument seems to rely on the contentious assumption that what is best for a person is not simply determined by each person's individual best judgment, and this is at odds with an appealing liberal conception of the good life. (If Hailey really thinks that studying all the time is best for her, who are we to disagree?) The second objection is that "best judgments" like the anorexic's or even Hailey's, which seem to be pathological, are not well understood as reflecting the person's true self and thus acting from strong will, *in accordance with those unhealthy judgments*, is not plausibly understood as acting authentically. I return to these objections in detail in chapter 5, where my aim is to show how intuitions about what constitutes the true self are suspiciously *ad hoc*. In that chapter, I show how conceptions of authenticity are easily manipulated to accommodate objectivist or subjectivist accounts of well-being—and, indeed, of morality as well—and I argue that what judgments and desires are attributed to another person's "true self" often track the authenticity advocate's own value commitments rather than any principled metaphysics of the self. These points will also be crucial to my critical assessment of Charles Taylor's explicitly moralized defense of The Ideal of Authenticity. For now, I turn to our next conception of authenticity and consider whether being authentically psychologically independent is reliably best for us.

WELL-BEING AND AUTHENTICITY AS PSYCHOLOGICAL INDEPENDENCE

Many share the intuition that being unduly influenced by other people is a way of failing to be true to oneself. Consider *Jamie, the Sorority Sister*:

> Jamie is captain of her school's rowing team, state champion in shot-put, and has the muscles to prove it. She's got an athletic build, and her sorority sisters tease her mercilessly for being "thick" and call her "The Russkie" (by which, apparently, they mean that she looks like a ste-

roided-up, gender-ambiguous, Soviet Olympian). Her sisters tell her that her chosen sports are not good for the "feminine physique" and that she'll never get a boyfriend (something she wants), unless she loses weight, stops wearing workout gear all the time, and grows her hair. These comments really get to her. She quits track and field (which she loves), makes an effort to dress more "like a girl" (which she hates), and starts trying to lose weight (even though she's got basically no fat on her). Whatever she does, she feels terrible about herself. She hates her body, but she also resents having to conform to the social expectations of her sorority sisters.

A passage (with the heading "To Thine Own Self Be True") from a popular addiction-recovery website touts the benefits of psychological independence this way:

> Trying to live out somebody else's life script is like putting a size ten foot into a size seven shoe. The size simply does not fit. No matter how hard you force yourself to adjust to your situation, the discomfort continues . . . Why not start off with the right fit? Acknowledge your unique gifts and talents, as well as your wants and needs. Then seek out situations and circumstances that will allow them their full expression. This route may take time, but the results are worth it: a life of peace and fulfillment that comes from being true to yourself.[11]

The clear idea here is that much unhappiness is the product of our having internalized a variety of "external" standards (e.g., that we should be thinner, richer, conform with various sexual or domestic norms, etc.) that are not "our own" and that are incompatible with our true selves' true natures. Unhappiness comes from living in accordance with a "false self" that masks who we "really are" and that must be removed by processes of self-recognition, self-acceptance, and self-love. At least superficially, this is the kind of self-help ideology that Oprah Winfrey propagates. As Kathryn Lofton puts it in an interview on The Immanent Frame, Oprah crystallizes her guiding philosophy when she tells her audience, "Girls, I'll guide you to your total originality."[12] Interestingly, this formulation resonates closely with Johann Herder's eighteenth century idea that each of us has an *original* way of being. (Charles Taylor argues that this Herderian idea is among the most important sources of our contemporary "culture of authenticity."[13]). According to The Well-being Account of The Ideal of Authenticity as Psychological Independence, the key to living a good and happy life is to know who you really are deep down, beneath the layers of social influence, and embrace that "originality." This, of course, can be difficult in a world where our families and friends, our religious leaders, our own celebrity obsession, and, of course, the history of sexism, racism, and homophobia (and other forms of institutionalized oppression) exert competing and distorting influences upon us.

THE COSTS OF PSYCHOLOGICAL OPPRESSION AND THE BENEFITS OF INDEPENDENCE

The kind of well-being that comes from Authenticity as Psychological Independence can be incredibly difficult to achieve because of the structure of what Sandra Bartky and others call "psychological oppression."[14] As Bartky puts it,

> "[T]o be psychologically oppressed is to be weighed down in your mind; it is to have a harsh dominion exercised over your self-esteem. The psychologically-oppressed become their own oppressors; they come to exercise harsh dominion over their own self-esteem. Differently put, psychological oppression can be regarded as the 'internalization of intimations of inferiority.'"[15]

What Bartky is noting here is that what is bad about oppressive social norms is not simply that they produce social stigmatization; nor is it just that the stigmatizing norms are themselves ethically problematic or unreasonably difficult to live up to; it is the fact that these norms are internalized and imposed by the "victims" themselves. This creates a distinctive problem within the self, comparable in some ways to the popular understanding of "Stockholm Syndrome," in which prisoners or abductees may come to identify with their captors, "willingly" comply with their dictates, and even express gratitude for the most minimal care they are given. To make things even worse (from a first-person phenomenological perspective), another dimension of psychological oppression is that the internalization is incomplete—the demeaning internalized judgments are at once (consciously or unconsciously) endorsed by the person who has internalized them but also at the same time (consciously or unconsciously) *resisted*, resulting in a confusion about one's own self and self-worth famously characterized by W. E. B. Du Bois as "double consciousness."[16] As Iris Marion Young puts it, double consciousness is double "because the oppressed subject refuses to coincide with these devalued, objectified, stereotyped visions of herself or himself."[17] The fragmentation of the self that results from internalizing oppression is thus experienced as an acute form of alienation. Jamie, the sorority sister, comes to want to conform to the social conventions determining what is feminine and fashionable. Unfortunately, those conventions run up against her desires to be athletic and comfortable. If both sets of desires remain, she is doomed to frustration, whichever desires she chooses to accommodate.[18]

Beyond the pain of having unsatisfied desires (when those desires are non-cosatisfiable), there is another kind of pain (a meta-pain perhaps better characterized as *suffering*) associated with double consciousness that arises from the *awareness* of one's own inner conflicts. The *self*-conscious doubly conscious person endures an additional anxiety in virtue of not knowing how to resolve the conflict or knowing that whatever one does will not be fully satisfying. Those experiencing double consciousness may also experience the pain of feeling like they don't know what they "really" want or who they "really" are. Yet another kind of suffering can arise from seeing oneself as irrational. We normally aim to develop roughly coherent narratives about ourselves as persons with more or less consistent beliefs, desires, and values. The lengths to which we will go to avoid cognitive dissonance is some evidence of what we might call "the pain of irrationality"[19] that can be overcome by overcoming double consciousness. The feeling that we are not in full control of our desires and values can also be distressing. While feelings of inferiority relative to the dominant social norms are the paradigmatic symptom of psychological oppression, we shouldn't neglect the significance of the guilty feelings that may come from the realization that one has not measured up to one's own standards. And, again, the self-conscious person suffering from psychological oppression may even feel bad *about feeling bad* about not living up to her own standards. Imagine, for example, an anorexic person who feels guilty when she eats *and also when she doesn't*, say, because she's conceptualized her condition as an illness that requires her utmost effort to overcome. But now imagine that she also feels guilty *about feeling guilty* when she eats because she blames herself for failing to fully internalize the therapeutic paradigm that her doctor is trying to instill in her.[20] We are sometimes able to disavow desires that we come to see as the products of cultural hegemony or illness; but this is rarely enough to make those desires go away completely, and it is natural to blame ourselves for a failure to resist the oppressive social norms in question.[21]

Framing all this in terms of Jamie's situation, if Jamie can just get herself to reject the gender norms of her sorority sisters and see them as entirely external, she stands to overcome her predicament. In fully embracing *her own* values, she can avoid the conflict and internalized shame that comes from her affinity for "unfeminine" sports and clothes. More generally, in successfully purging ourselves of oppressive internalized norms, multiple layers of painful self-loathing can be removed. By disavowing externally imposed and oppressive values and becoming whole, integrated, psychologically independent people, we free ourselves from the self- and world-imposed psychological pain that comes from judging ourselves through the eyes of others. When psychological independence is achieved, the result is a clear and stable sense of self, accompanied by new and positive feelings of self-respect and self-esteem. In achieving Authenticity as Psychological Independence, the thinking goes, we put ourselves in a position to pursue our own conceptions of the good life, undistorted by the internalized expectations of others.

This is a strong case for the pervasive benefits to well-being of The Ideal of Authenticity as Psychological Independence. But is the aim of achieving psychological independence reliably best for us, all things considered? As we shall see, if the arguments in Tina Rosenberg's recent book, *Join The Club*, are right, the way to help people emerge from self-damaging cultures of oppression is not to glorify some version of authentic, free originality. It is, rather, to make them *followers* in progressive movements that promote individual and collective well-being.[22]

THE WELL-BEING BENEFITS OF PSYCHOLOGICAL DEPENDENCE

In *Join the Club*, Rosenberg presents a powerful case for the benefits of complex forms of unconscious social influence on our choices and values. She shows, for example, how campaigns for AIDS awareness in South Africa, and against smoking in the United States, succeeded by means of carefully crafted media messages and the recruitment of "cool" kids to spread ideas in often indirect and non-transparent ways. The gist of her argument is that people can be leveraged into self-benefitting behaviors (engaging in protected sex, not smoking) by being attracted to communities of people whose explicit job it is to instill and spread pro-social values. The ways in which these values are transmitted and the behavioral norms instilled are explicitly incompatible with the kind of authentic, "original" thinking that is supposed to be characteristic of the truly independent-minded person. These are powerful examples of an unsurprising observation: it is mostly a contingent social question whether being "independent minded" is good or bad for us. Beyond Rosenberg's great and serious examples of the well-being benefits of widespread conformity, I want to consider an interesting sort of case where the kind of fragmentation of the self characteristic of psychological oppression and double consciousness seems to be good for us: the case of guilty pleasures. If I am right, the phenomenon of the guilty pleasure reveals something that should be quite surprising to advocates of psychological independence: internalized norms, even when experienced as "external" and constraining, can be good for us. And even when such internalized norms are not obviously good for us in themselves, it may still often be best, all things considered, if we do not free ourselves from them because such norms, even the oppressive ones, can be the very condition of everyday pleasures.

THE WELL-BEING BENEFITS OF GUILTY PLEASURES

To start with a light example, consider *Shlomo, the Lobster Eater*:

> Shlomo grew up eating a strictly kosher diet but abandoned his religious beliefs and his observance of the *kashrut* laws in his college years. He soon discovers that he loves lobster (a non-kosher food) and realizes that his enjoyment is enhanced by a feeling of transgressive

> pleasure. His youthful internalization of the norm against eating lobster has a continuing residual effect on his experience of eating it that is distinctly positive. In hindsight, Shlomo is glad that he was raised to think that eating lobster was sinful because of the (possibly perverse) pleasure it allows him now. Even as time passes, and the salience of the internalized prohibition fades, Shlomo's enjoyment of the lobster continues to be enhanced by his nostalgia for a time when eating it felt transgressive.[23]

Versions of this kind of case should be psychologically familiar to many. Such cases suggest that there are certain kinds of pleasures, the very possibility of which depends on transgressing internalized norms from which one is alienated. It seems that Shlomo is demonstrably *better off* in virtue of his incomplete psychological liberation from a norm that he reflectively rejects.[24]

In this spirit, Jean Grimshaw suggests that certain kinds of common fantasies essentially involve a similar kind of inner tension. She asks, "Why is there a 'split' between sexual fantasy and that which one might find pleasurable in real life?"[25] Her explanation is that, having been socialized to have certain desires, those desires often persist, even after we come to see them as objectionable (say, because they are sexist or because they normalize violence or some other kind of inequity). In these cases, the only way to enjoy a version of the pleasures that would be attainable by acting on the objectionable desires is to fantasize about their satisfaction. This kind of fantasy might come along with feelings of guilt or disgust or self-loathing and we might even prefer, on ethical grounds, that the problematic desires and fantasies did not persist. But it's also possible that the pleasure of such fantasies is enhanced by the sense that they are "naughty" or "dirty" or just plain wrong. Moreover, one might prefer not to be purged of those admittedly less than noble or emancipated desires precisely because they are the condition of a certain kind of pleasure. I claim that it is at least not obvious that we would be better off overcoming the feelings of alienation that are the necessary precondition for these kinds of pleasurable fantasies. In other words, the fact that certain pleasures depend, for their existence, on internalized oppression or on feelings of transgression does not preclude those pleasures from contributing in meaningful ways to our well-being.

The implication is that a fully psychologically *independent* person, devoid of the internalized desires that enable such transgressive fantasies, would seem to be *denied* a range of normal pleasures. Now I certainly grant that there may be many cases where the pleasure of a transgressive fantasy or behavior might be bad for the person, all things considered. If the guilt is too severe, or if the person is in the grip of a psychological complex that makes her think she deserves sustained ill treatment, or if the *only* pleasure a person could derive was from engaging in activities that are experienced as fundamentally degrading, then such a person's overall well-being may well be in jeopardy. The negative affects of the fantasy or the behavior might well outweigh the benefits. We also might just think that some kinds of fantasy are so morally fraught that it would be better not to have them at all, no matter the pleasure involved. For example, fantasies which essentially consist in imagining the suffering of the innocent might seem beyond the pale to most of us. But if the desires in question are not especially morally problematic or morally problematic, as such (let's assume this about the desire for lobster, or the phenomenologically transgressive desire to be sexually submissive), and cause no serious damage to the person who has them (Shlomo is not tormented by the guilt of his lobster-eating), it seems that we can, indeed, benefit from the alienation that comes from internalizing—and resisting—constraining social norms. Grimshaw observes that it is

> "Signally obvious in the experience of many women, myself of course included . . . that it is perfectly possible to agree 'in one's head' that certain images of women might be reactionary or damaging or oppressive, while remaining committed to them in emotion and desire. I suspect that this 'split' happens at times in all women, and perhaps particularly in those who have some commitment to feminism."[26]

While Grimshaw's is simply an empirical observation, I think it is hard not to see the appeal of a modest normative corollary: given our socialization in this terribly imperfect world, and given the kinds of radical shifts in society that would be necessary for our socially conditioned desires to change to ones that are not problematic, say, from a feminist perspective it is reasonable and even good for us, to continue to enjoy many of the admittedly problematic pleasures that are available to us.[27] Recall that Hailey's admittedly flawed psychology meant that it could be best for her to fail to live up to her perfectionist resolution. The corresponding point here is that those of us for whom everyday pleasures depend not just upon our socialization by others, but even upon psychological oppression as Grimshaw defines it, may well be better off, all things considered, indulging in those pleasures and even sometimes reveling in the accompanying feelings of transgression.

WELL-BEING AND AUTHENTICITY AS WHOLEHEARTEDNESS

Consider *Sergio and his Love Life*:

> Sergio has been going out with David for the last few months. They've got great chemistry and they enjoy the same activities: they go dancing and hiking, they cook together. David even likes the same stupid TV shows from the 1980s that Sergio likes (*Magnum, P.I.; Simon & Simon*). But Sergio can't help thinking about the fact that David doesn't appreciate his more serious side. They don't talk much about books or ideas, and David gets really annoyed when Sergio starts to "overanalyze"

> things. For example, when Sergio went on a ten-minute rant about whether Magnum's campiness redeems its objectionable sexual politics, David groaned and said, "Why can't you just enjoy things without thinking about what they *mean* all the time?" Overall, Sergio likes David a lot but isn't sure how deep his feelings for him go and thinks maybe his attraction to him is objectionably superficial. Then again, Sergio is worried that maybe he's just being an elitist snob. Not everyone has to want to *theorize* all the time. Sergio asks his best friend, Bethany (herself a romantic), for advice and she says, "Just be true to yourself and you'll know what to do." But Sergio is despondent.

This situation certainly does not seem ideal for Sergio. Because he's conflicted about how he feels, *he's unsure what to do.* Says Harry Frankfurt, "[C]onflict within the will precludes behavioral effectiveness, by moving us to act in contrary directions at the same time."[28] Sergio's interest in David, let's presume, brings him to profess his affection for him and spend time with him. But his doubts, sparked by David's apparent anti-intellectualism, generate different and contrary motives. Sergio is incapable either of breaking up with David or decisively "going for" the relationship.

To generalize, when we are ambivalent about things, we characteristically feel that we don't know what we really want or who we really are, and as a consequence, it may feel impossible to be true to ourselves. *Whatever* we do, when we are ambivalent, won't feel quite right and the result may be a kind of paralysis, the product of indeterminate or self-defeating and contradictory motives. Frankfurt's advice to Sergio would be to *get wholehearted,* to somehow resolve how he feels one way or the other so as to facilitate his practical decision-making. Being enabled to make decisions thus seems like a standing benefit of overcoming ambivalence.[29] As we shall see, Frankfurt also thinks that becoming wholehearted is necessary for self-love. Translating into the terms of authenticity, we might say that Sergio's problem is that he cannot be true to *himself* because his ambivalence renders the content of his true self indeterminate. In the absence of any fact of the matter about what he "really" wants or how he "really" feels, there is a sense in which there is no self for him to be true to. The unfortunate consequence of this is that he is stymied in his pursuit of his own vision of the good romantic life. As we shall see, Frankfurt actually goes so far as to argue that the ambivalent person is precluded from living a *meaningful* life.[30]

So, Frankfurt's analysis of ambivalence suggests that being wholehearted is good for us in at least three main ways. First, the wholehearted person's ends are in harmony, yielding a coherent motivational set that facilitates the kind of "behavioral effectiveness" that Sergio seems to want and need. When our passions are conflicted, we are pulled in multiple directions at once and this may block us from achieving our own goals.[31] Second, according to Frankfurt, wholeheartedness—wholehearted love in particular—is a necessary condition of self-love. On Frankfurt's view, what it is to love someone is to be wholeheartedly committed to the promotion of the concerns of the beloved.[32] The ambivalent person is not so committed and for this reason does not express love. (To evince only half-hearted concern for someone's well-being is, intuitively, not to love them.) Accordingly, to love one*self* is to be wholeheartedly committed to the promotion of one's *own* concerns. But if one is ambivalent about what one cares about, then one cannot resolutely promote one's *own* concerns and thus one cannot properly love oneself.

Third, and most importantly, Frankfurt suggests that wholeheartedness is a necessary condition of living a *meaningful* life. Living a meaningful life seems to require that we pursue our projects with "zest,"[33] or in Susan Wolf's terms, with "active engagement."[34] In light of this, the importance of self-love becomes clear. If we cannot be true to ourselves in wholehearted pursuit of our own passions, then we are cut off from the kind of subjective fulfillment that a full life seems to require. Frankfurt concludes that the ambivalent person's life lacks *purpose* and for this reason lack meaning.

To sum up, in achieving authenticity as wholeheartedness, we overcome ambivalence and in doing so we render our practical lives coherent, thus enabling ourselves to pursue projects of worth, to love ourselves, and to live meaningful lives. Simply put, subjective well-being of the deepest kind seems to require wholeheartedness. To see if these claims about the well-being benefits of authenticity as wholeheartedness support an *Ideal* of Authenticity as Wholeheartedness, it will be useful to consider Sergio's situation in some detail, keeping in mind three questions: Does Sergio's ambivalence "preclude[s] behavioral effectiveness" in a way that is clearly bad for him? Does Sergio fail to *love* himself in a way that is bad for him? Does Sergio's life lack purpose or *meaning* in a way that would be (best) remedied by his becoming wholehearted?

What's So Bad About Ambivalence?

Frankfurt describes an experience of ambivalence this way:

> It may happen that a person truly loves something but that, at the same time, it is also true that he does not. . . . Part of him does love it, as we might say, and part of him does not. There is a part of him that is opposed to his loving it, and wishes that he did not love it at all. In a word, the person is ambivalent.[35]

How might this apply to Sergio's case? Well, let's suppose that Sergio loves David, but, at the same time, as Frankfurt puts it, there is also "a part of him that is opposed to" loving him. Let's also assume, for the moment, that Sergio is not "unequivocally clear" about which "part" of himself, or which side of his own feelings about David, he identifies with.[36] But since there are many ways to be conflicted about love, let's consider five different scenarios of romantic ambivalence. In the first scenario, let's imagine that Sergio oscillates between loving and not loving David. We might say that earlier and later "parts," or "time-slices" of the temporally extended person, Sergio, feel differently about David. A second possibility is that Sergio loves David in some respect but does not love him in some other respect. Here we might say (metaphorically and somewhat reductively) that the *part* of Sergio that attends to the attractive and fun things about David loves him, but the *part* of Sergio that attends to David's anti-intellectualism does not love him.[37] A third possibility is that there is simply no fact of the matter about whether Sergio loves David or not. In this scenario, we are imagining that it is just indeterminate whether Sergio loves David.[38] Sergio neither loves nor does not love him.[39] Of such a situation, Frankfurt says, "His will remains obstinately undefined and therefore lacks effective guiding authority."[40]

Let's consider two more interpretations of what it might intuitively mean to fail to love wholeheartedly, neither evidently compatible with Frankfurt's own characterization of ambivalence as a matter of being divided or lacking determinacy of will.[41] The fourth scenario is that Sergio loves David, just not very passionately. We might say that this love is "half-assed" and not wholehearted. The remaining possibility is that Sergio unambivalently loves David but he also unambivalently loves someone else, say, Geoffrey. Given Sergio's limited resources (e.g., his time and energy), these two loves conflict. So his behavior toward each of his loves is constrained by his love for the other and, in this sense, is not fully wholehearted.

What all five scenarios seem to have in common is that Sergio is, in some sense, not fully committed to loving David. And, in light of this fact, we might be inclined to think that all of these scenarios generate a problem of "behavioral ineffectiveness" for Sergio. At least *qua* the norms of romance, Sergio cannot *act* as he should toward David if he (Sergio) is (1) constantly switching between different attitudes toward him or (2) focusing intermittently on his attractive or less-than-attractive qualities or (3) if his feelings are indeterminate or (4) half-hearted or (5) if he loves Geoffrey, too. In all of these cases, Sergio's behavior toward David may appear to be, as we standardly describe it in the romantic context, "fickle." But is it bad *for him*?

Recall that in our original description of Sergio, we said that he was "despondent." By hypothesis, then, his ambivalence would be somewhat bad for him. In blocking him from living out his romantic dreams, say, his ambivalence fills him with stress and anxiety. But what if Sergio were not bothered by his ambivalence? What if Sergio were happily fickle? What if he were the kind of lover who was content with his own erratic emotions, his own inconstancy, or his own polyamorous inclination? (Romantic literature is filled with examples of such people, usually characterized, moralistically, as cads). Or maybe Sergio is the kind of romantic who believes that love cannot be controlled and he submits himself to its vagaries with the absolute certainty that it is the best life he can live.

These possibilities suggest three things. The first is that the assessment of Sergio's behavior as "ineffective" presupposes a specific and not uncontroversial set of romantic conventions (I return to this in chapter 5). The second is that whether Sergio's ambivalence is bad for *him* depends significantly on what romantic conventions *he* endorses. The third is that it is not evidently *Sergio* whose well-being is most clearly threatened by his ambivalence. It is, rather, *David* whose well-being seems most vulnerable in virtue of Sergio's ambivalence (again assuming that we attribute certain conventional romantic expectations to David). So, in answer to our first guiding question, even if we do think that Sergio's ambivalence results in "romantic ineffectiveness" (or perhaps especially if we think this and even *because* we think this), we cannot conclude that it is necessarily bad for him, as such.

What should we say about our second and third questions? Does Sergio's ambivalence mean that he fails to love himself? Does Sergio's life lack purpose or meaning? Recall that Frankfurt thinks that in failing to love *others* wholeheartedly, we fail to love *ourselves* because self-love requires wholehearted devotion to the things (and people) we love. In the absence of clarity about what (and whom) we love, there is no way to express our self-love. Now, Sergio's life does fail to have a *certain* purpose: he is not fully committed to David and he is not successfully pursuing a certain romantic ideal. But self-love only seems precluded if Sergio fails to pursue *anything* he cares about deeply. And we have already established that he may well (unambivalently) value the kind of love he is pursuing. Correspondingly, his life does lack a *certain* kind of meaning—the kind of meaning achievable only by those committed to a very specific set of romantic ideals. But there is no clear reason to think that it's bad for Sergio, or bad in general, not to embrace these particular ideals.

So, the strongest anti-ambivalence conclusions we can draw are these: contingently, *if* (and to the degree that) Sergio is unhappy with his lack of idealized romantic "effectiveness," *then* it is bad for him (and to just that degree); *if* Sergio has the goal of experiencing or pursuing wholehearted love, *then* his behavior seems "ineffective" and perhaps even an obstacle to his life having subjective meaning. But none of these "ifs" need be the case. If we are content to be fickle or indecisive, if we are fully happy to be less than fully passionate, or to love multiple people, it seems *ad hoc* to insist that nevertheless our lives are going badly *for us*.[42] The insistence that loving less than wholeheartedly must be bad for us seems to reveal a commitment to a certain kind of romantic ideal, not a general truth about the well-being benefits of wholeheartedness, as such. Many may think that a certain kind of idealized love *is* vital to our well-being. We may, for example, be comforted by the fate Don Quixote suffers for his romantic vices, but if we remain subjectivists about well-being and nonmoralistic about love (as I argue we should in chapter 5), there is no reason to assume that "cads" must lose in the end, or that even egregious violations of the conventional norms of romantic love must be bad for those who commit them.

The Well-being Benefits of Ambivalence

I've suggested that if we can imagine a happily ambivalent anti-romantic, then we've got a powerful counterexample to the claim that authenticity, construed as wholeheartedness, must be reliably best for us, as such. Let's consider another possible counterexample. Imagine Jordan, a person whose occasional serious doubts about everything and his curiosity about the world are an important part of his sense of self. Suppose that Jordan has restlessly cycled through a series of jobs, never content to "settle down" and stick with what he's doing for too long. At the age of fifty-five, he has already been, in succession, a lawyer, a high-school teacher, a doctor, and a nature guide. Imagine that he will hold many other jobs in the course of his (from my perspective) incredibly interesting and varied life. His family and many of his friends think that there is something seriously wrong with him, that he is, quite frankly, stunted, like a permanent student or a confused teenager trying to "find himself." Jordan's critics think (perhaps correctly) that if he had stuck with just one of his pursuits, he might have become great at it, done something important with his life, and found a modicum of meaning in his life. My own reaction to this kind of criticism is that it may say more about the conventionality of the values of Jordan's critics than it does about their concern for his well-being. Yes, he is restless, and yes, he was never fully committed to what he was doing (which is not to say that he could not do his jobs exceedingly well). But it's far from clear that, given his apparent disposition, simply "settling down," or, in Frankfurt's terms "resolving" his will and becoming "unequivocally clear" about his life would be better (or psychologically possible) for him. Given the kind of person he is, it seems unreasonable to insist nevertheless that, *for his own good,* he ought to become wholehearted in the relevant sense and adopt a stable professional life-plan.[43]

As for wholehearted love, it can be monomaniacal. And while I have no strong objection to those who endorse romantic risk-taking, or who make romantic love a central component of their lives, it also seems clear that, in the context of love, a degree of ambivalence about things might conduce to a kind of temperance and prudence. Recall that in our second interpretation of Sergio's case, it was his *accurate* perception of David's various qualities that led to his ambivalence. A steady awareness of others' flaws may keep us from falling head-over-heels with the wrong person. Ambivalence in this context may thus be a manifestation of *sensitiv-*

ity to how other people really are. Such sensitivity may keep us wary and less than wholehearted, but such clear vision (rather than blind love) is also thought by many to be necessary for the stability of enduring relationships.[44]

So, if the ambivalence that comes from being aware of others' flaws can be good for us, what about the kind of ambivalence that involves oscillating between different attitudes toward people (or things) or the kind of ambivalence that involves being torn by competing or incompatible or incommensurable loves? Could it be good for Sergio to oscillate between loving and not loving David or for Sergio to love both David and Geoffrey? Though people are admittedly not quite like ice cream, the analogy may be helpful: consider that on Monday, I like coffee ice cream best. On Tuesday, I prefer mint chip and am completely indifferent to coffee. On Wednesday, I may either go back to preferring coffee or I might discover rum raisin and be torn amongst them all, each competing for the rank of favorite. Not only does this not seem bad for me at all, it involves the kind of varied experience that exposes me to a range of worthwhile pleasures. By contrast, a fully wholehearted commitment to coffee ice cream would seem to preclude change and the discovery of other good things. The clear difference between people and ice cream is that obvious *moral* considerations are implicated when we think about inconstant love or friendship. But, importantly, as far as the question of *well-being* goes, the analogy holds. Shifting, serially, between feeling one way and then another about David could be good for Sergio. When he is down on David, he may get into someone or something else. Suppose that, in loving David *and* Geoffrey, Sergio gets to experience a range of good things that he would not otherwise experience. Loving David in either of these ways (i.e., while also not loving him or while also loving someone else) may well be the best Sergio can do and certainly better than not loving him at all. So, against Frankfurt, we have shown, again, that being ambivalent, being moved "in contrary directions," might sometimes be the reliably optimal course, given the options available to us.[45]

To conclude our discussion of Authenticity as Wholeheartedness, it is worth pointing out that Frankfurt himself acknowledges that there are some things of value that can preclude wholeheartedness. Says Frankfurt, "Other things being equal, being wholehearted is better than being ambivalent."[46] The "other things being equal" clause seems to amount to a concession that wholeheartedness is *not* an ideal if we acknowledge that other things are rarely equal in the real world. If ambivalence is a "necessary evil,"[47] as Frankfurt suggests, then it is in fact necessary in a predictable way. If we are charitable to Frankfurt, we might take his view to be that it would be better if we lived in a world where being wholehearted about everything never interfered with anything else we cared about. But this world would be quite unlike our own. It would be a world in which there could be no conflict between the various things worth caring about for their own sake. After all, being wholeheartedly committed, for example, both to one's work and one's family would seem incompatible with sacrificing either for the other. But we have to make such choices. Everyday experience suggests that such sacrifices are inevitably necessary and, when they are, it is entirely normal to feel ambivalent about them, whatever they may be. A world in which we never had to sacrifice in this way would, by necessity, be a world in which we were committed to just one thing, unconcerned about devoting time to other worthy activities. Most of us will think this would be a seriously impoverished world.[48] In the actual world, being ambivalent, filled with inner conflict, lacking determinate convictions about the relative value of things is often the best we can *and should* hope for.

WELL-BEING AND AUTHENTICITY AS SELF-KNOWLEDGE

The ancient Delphic motto "Know thyself," and the famous Socratic dictum that "The unexamined life is not worth living" are among the earliest and most influential articulations of the insight that self-knowledge, and by implication, being true to that knowledge, is necessary for the good life. It is also a dogma of many forms of psychotherapy that uncovering and accepting certain deep truths about ourselves is necessary for moving in the direction of psychological health and promoting our overall well-being. Bringing our unconscious beliefs and desires to the surface, discovering the ways in which we rationalize our choices (often against the available evidence) and overcoming bad faith are evidently enormously instrumentally valuable to our well-being. According to the Well-being Account of The Ideal of Authenticity as Self-knowledge, it is reliably best for us to know the truth about ourselves.

Consider *Jack the Starving Artist*:

> Jack has been trying to make it as a painter for fifteen years but has been feeling especially dispirited and unsure of himself of late. He is thinking of giving up his dream and applying to law school. Jack's friend, Andrew, a successful artist himself and a good judge of Jack's talents, gets up the courage to tell Jack, with the best of intentions, that he should be honest with himself and face up to the fact that he's better at analytical thinking than creative expression; he's probably never going to make it as a painter, but he'd be a fantastic lawyer and he might just love it.

To make the case for self-knowledge even more powerful, let's imagine that Jack has a ten-year-old son to support, is pretty deep in debt, and for years has been relying on his friends and family for financial assistance. And if we add that Jack really would be a great lawyer (and that, after a bit of adjustment of his sense of self, he would love his work), it seems pretty straightforward that Jack ought to accept the truth about himself and go to law school. If he does so, he stands to overcome a set of long-standing practical worries (e.g., about his finances and his future), as well as the existential ones that derive from his justified doubts about his artistic talents. In coming to a more accurate picture of himself, he enables himself to choose a path that makes the most of his actual abilities. Self-knowledge, for Jack and the rest of us, thus seems essential to being true to our talents, which itself seems a necessary condition for making the most of our lives. Of course, given that our self-conceptions can be out of touch with reality, and given that our hopes and desires are thus themselves sometimes quite unrealistic, acceptance of the truth about ourselves can be quite painful. So it takes a certain strength to live up to The Ideal of Authenticity as Self-knowledge. Says Charles Taylor, "The Ideally strong character . . . would be able to face unflinchingly the truth about himself or herself."[49]

Jean-Paul Sartre's critique of bad faith in *Being and Nothingness* is explicitly focused on the importance of self-knowledge and the avoidance of self-deception.[50] As David Jopling notes, Sartre endorses self-knowledge about "the whole of our way of life, individual life history, or basic moral framework."[51] The imperative of authenticity is the imperative to bring to light "the always presupposed background or horizon of our life experience," and to become aware of "what we are really up to, and who we are."[52] While figuring out exactly why Sartre is so critical of bad faith is beyond our current scope, in "Existentialism is a Humanism," Sartre suggests that bad faith can be criticized simply in virtue of the value of truth:

> [W]e may judge (and this may be a logical rather than a value judgment) that certain choices are based on error and others on truth. We may also judge a man when we assert that he is acting in bad faith. [I] do not pass moral judgment against him, but I call his bad faith an error. Here, we cannot avoid making a judgment of truth.[53]

But it is natural also to see an ethical idea in play in the existentialist critique of bad faith. Bad faith essentially involves a failure to recognize that we are both "facticity" and "transcendence," and this failure is closely connected with a failure to appreciate the normative import of the existentialist mantra, "Existence precedes essence." In other words, the condition of bad faith (i.e., absence of certain self-knowledge) precludes us from taking *responsibility* for our lives and living as we ought. So, for example, if Jack thinks he *is* or *must be* an artist, then he is in the grip of an essentialist delusion that psychologically blocks him from making certain choices that are in fact radically open to him. If, for example, he is subconsciously trying to fulfill his college art teacher's bohemian-romantic aspirations for him, then he fails to appreciate his own freedom which is a condition of his agency. Very plausibly, what is bad, generally, about being self-deceived is that it harms us by undermining our agency. Marcia Baron argues that self-deception is dangerous for precisely this reason. Since "self-deception can become a habit, a strategy one falls back on too often," and since "self-deception often requires, for its efficacy, further self-deception," it is particularly dangerous.[54] If self-deception undermines agency and agency of this kind is a condition of making properly informed decisions, then the Well-being Account of Authenticity as Self-Knowledge looks quite compelling.

Sartre's own paradigm case of bad faith involves a salient prospective cost to well-being. In Sartre's narrative, a woman on a date is paralyzed when the man she is with takes her hand in his. Not wanting "to realize the urgency" of the situation, "she concerns herself only with what is respectful and discreet in the attitude of her companion."[55] Sartre continues, "We know what happens next; the young woman leaves her hand there, but she does not notice that she is leaving it."[56] It is not hard to see a powerful prudential lesson in this example. Though this is not obviously Sartre's point, the case highlights the importance to our own well-being of not deluding ourselves about others' intentions or about our own freedom and thus of making responsible choices in light of the total evidence available to us about our options. Sartre's case is a powerful prefiguring of the ethical issues surrounding responsibility and consent in date rape scenarios. It is clear that not taking responsibility for ourselves, in light of an understanding of our own agency, can be quite dangerous for us. By contrast, maintaining an awareness of ourselves as free and responsible, and properly reactive to what others are doing, is *empowering* and may put us in a position to make better choices. Avoiding dissociation of the kind Sartre's woman on the date engages in amounts to a kind of vigilance that can make us safer. The alternative to this kind of epistemic vigilance, would seem to be a kind of blind passivity or acquiescence. Taylor's observation that "[t]he Ideally strong character . . . would be able to face unflinchingly the truth about himself or herself" resonates nicely with this idea. The Well-being Account of The Ideal of Authenticity as Self-knowledge thus holds that while it might often be hard to face certain painful truths about ourselves and our circumstances, in the end, it is best for us to do so.

To sum up, according to the Well-being Account of The Ideal of Authenticity as Self-Knowledge, in order to be fully autonomous and to live lives that are good for us, we need to know the truth about ourselves. If our life plans are not in harmony with who we are (our interests and desires as well as our nature as free agents) or with the reality of our circumstances, we will be destined to make bad or dangerous choices, to live unfulfilled lives, to waste our talents. In the absence of self-knowledge, there is a good chance we will not end up living in accordance with our values. If we don't know who we are, we may, by sheer luck, live well, but not in a way that is ultimately good for us: deliberately, responsibly, autonomously. If we think living in these ways is essential to our well-being, then, in this sense, the unexamined life really may not be worth living.

The Limited Value of Self-Knowledge

Now, on the face of it, there are counterexamples to the claim that self-knowledge is reliably best for us. There is some self-knowledge that causes us pain and yields no apparent benefits. Consider a grim example to make a grim point: If your ninety-five-year-old grandfather, suffering from end-stage heart disease, has been given a prognosis of a week to a month to live, there seems to be no point in telling him that his most recent MRI shows a small inoperable brain tumor that would probably kill him in a year were he not going to die from heart disease first. Is there any well-being-based reason to think that it would be better for this poor man to know this truth about himself?

According to an appealing account of well-being, it would not be better for him to know. Derek Parfit characterizes "preference hedonism" as the view that what is good for a person are her "introspectively discernible" experiences of having her desires satisfied.[57] Correlatively, what is bad for a person are the introspectively discernible experiences of unsatisfied desires. There are two important implications of this view. The first is that if an event has *no* subjectively discernible experiential effects on a person, then that event can be neither good nor bad for that person. The second is that whatever a person does not know about, and will not find out about, cannot in itself be bad for that person (though its subjectively experienced consequences could be). This means that it is an open question whether being in the grip of false beliefs about things we care about is bad for us, because it's an open question whether what we don't know about will have any introspectively discernible effect on us. If preference hedonism is correct, then the Well-being Account of The Ideal of Authenticity as Self-Knowledge is subject to significant doubt.

But how plausible is preference hedonism? Consider another scenario: suppose you want very badly not to be cheated on by your partner. As a matter of fact, you are being cheated on, though you don't know it, and you never will. Moreover, out of guilt, your partner has never treated you better, and you are feeling happy and loved. According to preference hedonism, this situation is not bad for you. Indeed, given your introspectively discernible experience, it is *good* for you. For those who think that being deceived in this way cannot be good for us, a natural response here (and the response most often articulated by my students in Introduction to Ethics) is simply to refuse to accept the stipulations that you will never find out about the cheating and that it will not produce any negative introspectively discernible effects on you. This line of thought insists that it is always better to know you are being cheated on, no matter the short-term pain, because that knowledge can always be usable to prevent present or future pain and/or enable the possibility of better experiences (in this case perhaps a better relationship with the cheater or with a different, more suitable partner). Applying this logic to the grandfather case, the defender of the well-being benefits of self-knowledge might suggest that we don't *know* that the heart disease will kill him and, in light of being informed of the brain tumor, he might make some different choices about how to use his remaining time. For example, he might have decided to write a brilliant, darkly comic short story about death, irony, and the metaphysics of overdetermination. The consequence of denying him knowledge about himself is that he might not achieve something he's always wanted (say, to write something good) and something that would be good for him. (Instead of just lying in bed depressed and waiting for death he spends his last days engaged in a rewarding and ultimately successful intellectual and artistic project.) The difficulty we may have in imagining that ignorance could, ultimately, be bliss is evidence of how strongly we associate self-knowledge and well-being.[58]

It might also be further evidence of how strongly we associate knowledge with the capacity for rational autonomy.[59] Self-knowledge, in particular, seems necessary for full agency, which is itself, presumably, both a constituent of, and a means to, individual well-being. Decisions made in light of full information about ourselves and our options would seem, as a rule, to be those most likely to be good for us. Again, though, as we saw in the cancer case, it turns out to be a contingent matter whether more information leads to better decision-making or overall improved well-being. Jean Grimshaw has argued convincingly, from a feminist perspective, that bringing it about that people are in a better position to evaluate their circumstances and their options can be socially disruptive and sometimes even dangerous.[60] If someone living under less than ideal social conditions comes to see, for the first time, that there are alternatives, this can sow the seeds of resistance and conflict. Such knowledge can often be used to improve one's conditions and make the world a better place. But it can also result in violence directed at those who resist. Knowing that you are oppressed and that others have it better than you will be good for you if you can do something about it. If you can't, it may simply compound your suffering.

J. David Velleman has argued, in the context of the debate about physician-assisted suicide, that knowing your options can sometimes make your life go worse.[61] He suggests that people in vulnerable positions (e.g., the old or the sick), who would otherwise want to extend their lives, might feel an undue pressure to end their lives if informed that assisted suicide is an "option." Even granting that the range of autonomous possibilities is expanded by knowing our options, it seems clear that sometimes, simply knowing what those options are, can make things more difficult for us. This will be especially true when those options involve significant self-sacrifice and when they appeal to our altruistic impulses (for example, in the assisted-suicide context, the impulse not to be a burden to our families).[62]

So it would be a mistake to assume too close a connection between self-knowledge and the kinds of practical freedom that we really want. More self-knowledge, even when it conduces to an expanded understanding of our life options, does not necessarily make our lives go better. As we saw above, a defender of the well-being benefits of self-knowledge may always be able to imagine how the knowledge of even the most tragic and painful truths *might* benefit us. But this falls short of what must be established in order to vindicate the Well-being Account of The Ideal of Authenticity as Self-Knowledge. If we can equally well imagine everyday situations where such knowledge *does not* benefit us, then The Ideal has been undermined. Trivially, there is information about ourselves that is of no particular value to us. Knowing the number of cells in your liver is a fact about yourself that, except in some crazily gerrymandered thought experiment, cannot be presumed to be good for you. The more general point is that there are infinitely many such obscure facts about ourselves, knowledge of which seems entirely irrelevant to our well-being. If self-knowledge, as such, were an ideal, it would entail an imperative to pursue all such truths. The Ideal of Authenticity as Self-Knowledge is patently not an ideal in this sense.

What this shows is that what we value is not self-knowledge, *per se*. What we want, for our own well-being, is to know some subset of important facts about ourselves. Might there be a way to specify what these facts are in order to preserve the appeal of The Ideal of Authenticity as Self-Knowledge? Perhaps there is a set of truths about ourselves that is the proper target of an ideal of self-knowledge? Perhaps, for example, the *important* self-knowledge is of the kind that psychotherapy is meant to elicit (whatever that may be). Or perhaps the important self-knowledge is knowledge of our basic talents or our core values. Or perhaps the relevant self-knowledge is of the Sartrean metaphysical kind. Each of these kinds of self-knowledge seems valuable because each enables the kind of accurate (re)framings of our lives that seem necessary for making good choices. Unfortunately, each of these proposals seems problematic. This is because, for any proposed subset of purportedly valuable self-knowledge, we will be able to identify patterns of cases where the absence of such knowledge will be reliably better for us. We will take each of these three proposals in turn, starting with psychotherapeutic knowledge.

While some psychotherapeutic models take it as an orthodoxy that there are true and false selves, and that facilitating an awareness of the true self is the *telos* of therapy, others explicitly forgo or reject the idea of a true self and focus on the project of devising functional narratives of the self independent of their "truth."[63] Moreover, evidence that different versions of talk therapy are about equally efficacious, independent of their particular conception of self-knowledge, suggests that no *particular* form of self-knowledge is necessary for mental health. Equally important for our purposes, though, is evidence that medication seems to be about as, if not more, effective in producing various well-being benefits than therapies aimed at eliciting self-knowledge. On the plausible assumption that the primary causal mechanism by which psychiatric drugs improve well-being is not by promoting self-knowledge (though it shouldn't be ruled out that there could be an indirect correlation between medication and self-knowledge), the obvious lesson is that some forms of well-being causally produced by inquiry into the self may be, as a rule, achievable by other means (for example, by brute alteration of a person's neurochemistry). We thus cannot assume that the kinds of self-knowledge that various psychotherapeutic approaches take to have value are more reliably conducive to well-being than are treatments that have nothing directly to do with the pursuit of self-knowledge.[64]

The Well-being Benefits of Self-Ignorance

Suppose we say, alternatively, that the Well-being Account of The Ideal of Authenticity as Self-Knowledge requires just that we have an understanding of our basic abilities and our core values. Such understanding would seem both necessary and sufficient for putting a good life plan into action. But is it always reliably best for us to have even this limited self-knowledge? Again, there is evidence that it is not. There is plenty of anecdotal evidence that having false beliefs about our abilities can be *good* for us. It is a platitude among competitive athletes, for example, that believing in one's competitive superiority, even against the evidence, often yields better performance. As for more rigorous evidence, studies have shown that those of us who are non-depressed are consistently in the grip of an "enhancement bias" about even some of the most important things about us. As it turns out, overestimating our talents, our popularity, and our control over the world around us are all consistently good for us. By contrast, having a more realistic self-conception tends to correlate with a greater disposition to depression.[65]

What about knowing our core values? Can it be reliably better for us *not* to know what they are? There are two reasons to think it can be. The first is that there seem to be situations where knowing what we really care about might change our behavior in harmful ways. Imagine that, upon reflection, a person came to the honest conclusion that he is an egoist, that at bottom, he really only cares about himself. Suppose that realizing this affects his behavior; unless he is a very good actor, his friends will start to picking up on his newly discovered egoism. They might begin to see that he doesn't care about them as ends in themselves, but only as means to his own ends. His relationships might crumble, and he may become miserable. More generally, whenever self-reflection reveals to a person that her deep values are in conflict with the prevailing social norms, this can be potentially personally costly. This is because acting against such norms can lead to social ostracization and even violence against the antisocial person. The sad lesson is that it can be good for a person to conform, even in bad faith, to various social norms.[66] In places where the prevailing social norms are extremely oppressive to a minority, taking a stand against them can be dangerous. In such conditions, even "good" people may be disposed to rationalize their acceptance of injustice. This seems to be part of Dr. King's critique, in his "Letter from Birmingham Jail," of certain liberals who refused to join the civil disobedience movement. Fearing the reprisals that more activist civil rights leaders in fact suffered, these people argued, plausibly in bad faith, that slower change would ultimately be best. Surely it could be better for such people to tell themselves they are doing what's right and avoid the sacrifices that would be necessary if they acted on their deep values.

A second reason to think that knowledge of our core values can be bad for us is that the introspective and philosophical project of *figuring out* what we value can be harmful to ourselves. The pursuit of ethical knowledge is difficult and can lead to paralysis and depression. It can also result in the undermining of the very values we were trying to discover. A person living a happy unreflective life in pursuit of worthwhile ends might suddenly find himself doubting whether his choices are really of any value. This kind of doubt, if compartmentalized and taken with a grain of salt, might be good for us—indeed we have noted that Charles Taylor and Thomas Nagel take the capacity for this kind of doubt to be in part constitutive of a good human life. But if it becomes pervasive, it can undermine our capacity to think our lives have meaning. If The Ideal of Authenticity as Self-Knowledge is really an *ideal*, and if we take it seriously, then by hypothesis, it is something we would have to be deeply committed to, increasing the likelihood of potentially pervasive and troubling doubts. (Of course, if we are able to adopt a Nagelian comfort with the comic absurdity of life, we might be able to stave off some of the troubling implications of the doubt.)

What about Sartrean self-knowledge? Can we expect it to be reliably good for us? Recall that, on our well-being interpretation of the badness of bad faith, the idea was that it is good for us to appreciate fully that we are both "facticity" and "transcendence," embodied beings who are nonetheless radically free. Being in denial about this fundamental condition, it was suggested, leads to failure to take responsibility for ourselves. At least construed as a requirement that we hold a certain obscure philosophical doctrine about human nature (or lack thereof), the Sartrean requirement is absurd on its face. Perhaps, though, *some* basic recognition of our condition as both free and responsible for making ourselves who we are might reliably make our lives go better? Again, the possibility of imagining situations where this philosophical wisdom *would* clearly benefit us (which we've granted above) is not enough to vindicate self-knowledge as a well-being ideal. The question is whether it is reliably best for us to avoid bad faith. Perhaps unsurprisingly, there are many cases where it is entirely psychologically beneficial to deny we are free, to chalk up some bad circumstance in which we are stuck to forces beyond our control. Imagine, for example, a teenager averse to conflict and "forced" by his parents to practice the violin; he might tell himself, by way of rationalization, that he *has* to practice, that he has no choice in the matter. This lie might help him get through many unpleasant hours. Rather more seriously, the forms of dissociation that people sometimes experience while suffering various kinds of violence or abuse can be functional coping mechanisms. Thinking, "This is my body, but this isn't happening to *me*" can be a way of dealing with the worst of treatment. It is presumably also a paradigmatic case of Sartrean bad faith. In dissociating from her body, the person is denying her facticity and *taking refuge* in the delusion of pure transcendence. There may certainly be cases where the effect of keeping the existentialist doctrine in mind will be extremely beneficial, producing an empowering sense of agency and the capacity to resist unwanted treatment. But sometimes such resistance is dangerous or impossible. To deny that dissociation of this kind can be psychologically necessary for well-being seems both odd and cruel.[67]

Put simply, the problem with the Well-being Account of The Ideal of Authenticity as Self-Knowledge is that it overestimates the value of self-knowledge to the good life. This is a mistake unsurprisingly endemic to a certain kind of *philosophical* worldview. Though we don't often take the Socratic dictum literally, the arguments in *The Apology* really are aimed at showing that the unexamined life isn't *worth living*, that in fact we ought to prefer death to a life that is not devoted to the pursuit of virtue or wisdom or truth. If we return to a more commonsense worldview, it seems nearly impossible to imagine a person living a life so devoid of self-knowledge that it would not seem worth living. No degree of bad faith, for example, seems so detrimental to well-being that, on its own, it renders the life valueless, from the perspective of well-being. Of course, The Ideal of Authenticity as Self-Knowledge is not committed to the radical idea that death is preferable to any deficit in self-knowledge. The point here is just that the appeal of an ideal of radical self-knowledge, which The Ideal of Authenticity as Self-Knowledge does endorse, should only seem appealing if we are already in the grip of an austere and demanding philosophy (e.g., of the Socratic or Sartrean kind). For those already disposed to think that inquiry or truth is of utmost importance, it is only natural to think that there can't be too much knowledge, that it is absolutely essential to the Good Life, that everyone should be pursuing it as a (or even *the*) basic life project. But it is also telling that those of us professionally devoted to the pursuit of such knowledge do not seem to be especially well-adjusted or possessed of any preternatural aura of well-being. (The same is often observed about professional psychologists and other kinds psychotherapists who engage in their own relentless pursuit of "therapeutic" self-knowledge.)

Returning to our example from the beginning of this section, I am inclined to think it really is bad for *Jack, The Starving Artist* not to know the truth about himself.[68] Given his current unhappiness and the prospect of his future success as a lawyer, it seems that his friend's advice is sound, purely from the perspective of Jack's well-being. But I think there is reason to be suspicious that our judgment is really (only) about the well-being benefits to Jack of self-knowledge. This is because many of us also endorse the following claim about the good life: that one's central life choices ought, when possible, to make use of one's best talents.[69] Now, using one's talents often does require self-knowledge—after all, to make use of one's talents, one normally needs to know what they are. Likewise, it seems that matching one's choices to one's talents is a way of being true to oneself. So there is evidently a close connection between the good-life claim we have just introduced and The Ideal of Authenticity as Self-Knowledge. I return to this claim once again in chapter 5, in order to suggest that our intuitions about the likes of Jack are not best understood as stemming from a commitment to authenticity, but rather as manifesting a commitment to other values, values orthogonal to (and sometimes at odds with) our purported concern for Jack's knowledge of his true self.

WELL-BEING AND AUTHENTICITY AS MORAL CONSCIENTIOUSNESS

It is axiomatic for many that we do well by doing good—that being good must be good for us. Now, if it turns out that being authentic is essentially connected with being good, there will be a strong case for a Well-being Account of The Ideal of Authenticity as Moral Conscientiousness.

Consider *Annie and the Honor Code*:

> Annie is in the grip of what feels like a moral dilemma. She's thinking about smoking some marijuana with her friends (she's never done this before, she thinks it might be fun, and she doesn't think it's wrong in itself). But she's a diligent student, attending a college with an honor code she's sworn to uphold. Annie has a great relationship with her mother and, knowing that she did some drugs in her day, decides to call her up and ask her what she thinks. Her mother, sympathetic, gives her the advice she almost always gives her: just be true to yourself. After some hard thinking, Annie sheepishly tells her friends that she's not joining them, she has too much homework (she doesn't want to sound self-righteous). The next morning, she finds out that Campus Security, having been called about noise in an adjacent room, smelled the pot and busted her friends, who are now facing a disciplinary hearing and the possibility of serious penalties.

It seems natural to say about this case that in being true to herself, Annie has been *conscientious*. She's been guided by her deep values and has acted in accordance with what she thinks is right. In being conscientious, she also benefits in a variety of specific ways. First, her choice has clear prudential value. Breaking her school's honor code carries significant risks, prospectively affecting her education, her future employment options, and her economic opportunities. It also stands to affect her relationship with her parents (who, we can assume, would be none too pleased by her cheating, or suspension or expulsion). In keeping her word and doing what she knows is right, Annie also keeps herself in good social standing with her community—a strong standing benefit of being morally conscientious. In general, following conscience is good for us, in no small part because of the reciprocal benefits to be gained by treating others in accordance with moral rules. There is a straightforwardly pragmatic, "If I scratch your back you'll scratch mine," support for pro-social moral behavior. Only if we are conscientious about keeping our word, for example, will people be disposed to engage in mutually rewarding projects with us. When we break our word, others are warned that we are not to be trusted. We can also expect people who follow conscience to avoid moral guilt and alienation, to derive positive feelings of moral pride or satisfaction, and even to achieve a kind of moral peace of mind.[70] In following conscience, Annie enables herself to continue to think of herself as a person of integrity who takes her moral commitments seriously and is worthy of trust.

Now, before turning to what I take to be decisive objections to the Well-being Account of The Ideal of Authenticity as Moral Conscientiousness, I want to consider two interesting challenges that I think have some weight but are not decisive. The first is that a person primarily concerned with promoting her own well-being might be able to accrue the benefits of moral conscientiousness by *appearing* to be conscientious, rather than *being* conscientious. What is reliably good for us, according to this thinking, is others *believing* that we have moral integrity. If people believe this about us and for this reason *trust* us, we will be in a position to maximize our own well-being by violating moral rules and exploiting others whenever we can do so without getting caught. Being conscientious thus functions as a constraint on our own well-being that can be overcome so long as others still take us to be conscientious people. Could it be reliably best for us to fake conscientiousness and exploit others when we can do so for our own benefit? My guess is that it would be better for most of us simply to *be* good rather than to engage in the case-by-case calculations necessary to decide whether, in any given situation, we might benefit by breaking moral rules. It also seems likely that, in cultivating genuinely moral motives—in becoming the kinds of people who sincerely care about others for their own sake—we will be more stably and reliably disposed to treat others well and to receive the corresponding reciprocal benefits.[71]

Those who are not motivated primarily by the promotion of their own well-being will also be in a unique position to feel love and to have real friendships, two things many of us take to be absolutely essential to a good life. The genuinely morally conscientious person, unlike the self-interested pretender, will also be in a position to experience the moral satisfaction that comes from being conscientious. But, perhaps most significantly, those of us with reasonably powerful and deep moral motives would pay a significant psychological cost for acting against conscience. To pursue one's own self-interest at the expense of conscience can be expected to involve living with substantial moral guilt about our own wrongdoing. So, even if there might be well-being to be gained by acting against conscience, the costs for those of us who have been successfully morally socialized will be unappealingly high. So I believe this first challenge to the well-being benefits of conscientiousness is not too compelling.

A second, related challenge to the well-being benefits of moral conscientiousness comes from observing that bad things happen to good people and that at least some obviously bad people do quite well in life, never paying the price for, and even benefitting from, their wrongdoing. For those of a theistic bent, the question "Why do bad things happen to good people?" is often an especially troubling one. After all, if God is both omnipotent and benevolent, and good people do not deserve to suffer, then why does God allow (or even cause) bad things to happen? The evidence that being morally good does not reliably conduce to well-being can seem overwhelming. Theists, of course, typically approach the problem by positing some guarantee that being good is rewarded by God in this world or the next. But, even independent of theological commitments, many share the intuition that it would somehow be absurd if being good were not good for us. George Mavrodes goes so far as to say that it would be a "crazy world" if the fulfillment of moral duties could "result in the net loss of good to the one who fulfills them."[72] There would seem to be something cosmically *unjust* about a world like this.

Perhaps for this reason, some non-theists think that something like karma brings good returns to those who do good. Others hold the view that being good must be good for the psyche or the soul, even when we are not immediately experientially aware of these benefits. Those of a somewhat less metaphysical bent might be compelled by this line of thought to adopt ethical egoism, the view that what is in fact morally right is the pursuit of self-interest. If ethical egoism were correct, this would guarantee that what we ought to do necessarily coincides with what is good for us. The crucial point here is that, despite the evidence of bad things happening to good people, one the idea that being good must be good for us is nonetheless a very powerful one, which finds expression in philosophies from Plato to Christianity to new age spiritualism and ethical egoism. The shared intuition is that it would not make sense for us to be good if being good were not in some important (spiritual, cosmic, or material) way good *for us*. Simply given the power of this intuition for so many, the Well-being Account of Authenticity as Moral Conscientiousness is one that we must take seriously.

The Costs of Conscience

To recap, I've suggested three main ways that being morally conscientious seems to be reliably good for us. It normally yields practical social advantages; it is a source and condition of moral (self-)satisfaction; and it is thought by many to yield benefits to the soul or psyche. For those not yet convinced that authenticity is plausibly a matter of acting on conscience at all, I direct you to the beginning of chapter 3 on the Moral Account of The Ideal of Authenticity, where I consider five powerful accounts of the connection between morality and the true self. The idea that the moral self is the true self is an idea deeply embedded in western moral thought. As should become clear, I do not ultimately think this identification is right; but in the remainder of this chapter I accept the idea that to be true to oneself is, in some fundamental sense, to be morally conscientious. I argue that there are a set of predictable costs to the well-being of the conscientious person that undercut the plausibility of the Well-being Account of The Ideal of Authenticity. Specifically, I consider counterexamples to the three purported benefits of conscientiousness that show that it is not reliably best for us; I argue that there are distinctive benefits that those of us with pretty typical moral motivations can achieve by acting against conscience.

It seems to be true, in general, that following conscience leads us to treat others well and that this normally results in others treating us well. But there are clear patterns of cases where no such benefits seem to accrue, for example, when doing what is right involves the radical self-sacrifice of a martyr. In sacrificing one's life, the possibility of reciprocal benefit is immediately precluded. Now, it might be pointed out that the person who sacrifices in this way may still benefit from the sacrifice. If we imagine that the person could not live with herself if she had not made the sacrifice, then we might think that in making it, she is promoting her well-being; the sacrifice might well be the best thing for her. I think we should grant that such benefits of self-sacrifice are *possible* (these will be tragic situations where the alternatives to moral self-sacrifice are worse for the person). But this possibility is far from sufficient to vindicate the claim that following conscience is reliably best for us. We need only imagine that the person would not feel overwhelming guilt if she didn't make the sacrifice or that with time and therapy she'd end up living a wonderful and rewarding life. These possibilities show that when following conscience has immediate and predictable costs to the conscientious person, there is no reason to think that following conscience is the best way to promote our own well-being.

Still, it is worth noting that the martyr may accrue the benefit of moral satisfaction in *doing* the right thing while doing it. Is there any principled reason to think that *this* moral satisfaction must reliably outweigh the loss of all future benefits the martyr might otherwise have experienced had she lived? Even granting the possibility that it can be good *for the martyr* to be thought well of after death, it seems not.[73] There is no reason to assume that the benefit to the martyr of posthumous good moral standing (or the avoidance of guilt) must be so great as to automatically outweigh the loss of all the future *experienced* well-being she might have had had she lived. This assumption would be plausible only if one thought that being good were best for us *no matter* the phenomenal content of our lived experience in this world, or in other words, only if one thought that loss of experienced well-being were always compensated for in some other way. Some may (perhaps for theistic reasons) think this, but in the absence of supernatural or other independent moral commitments, the idea does not seem very compelling.[74]

The Benefits of Violating Conscience

The case of the martyr suggests that acting on the very demanding requirements of conscience might often not be best for us (especially if we can learn to live with our unconscientiousness). Susan Wolf's idea that some things are more important than morality—even for a morally committed person—provides what I think is the strongest evidence that following conscientiousness is not reliably best for us.[75] Wolf's analysis points out that the demands of morality can conflict with the goods of friendship and humor and even musical or athletic achievement. If it can be best for us, all things considered, to "indulge" in these goods at the expense of what impartial morality asks us to do, then this might require *not* acting on conscience. Consider, for example, what I take to be a compelling moral claim in the spirit of Peter Singer: if we can prevent something very bad from happening, without thereby sacrificing anything of even approximately equal moral significance, we are morally required to do it.[76] If conscience required acting on this principle, it is quite clear that this would mean drastic sacrifices to our well-being. After all, many of us are in a position to use our time and resources to prevent many quite horrible things from happening without sacrificing anything of even vaguely equivalent importance. Instead of going to the movies or having a nice dinner with a friend, we are imagining that conscience could require us to send that money to Oxfam, where it could be used to save lives. While I might derive some moral satisfaction from doing this, it seems implausible to insist that it must be reliably better *for me* to send my money to help strangers in need than to enjoy dinner and a movie.

The lesson is just that if the dictates of moral conscience are very (materially or psychologically) demanding, then promoting our own well-being might well almost certainly require *not* acting on conscience. Perhaps more surprisingly, we can conclude that unless one's moral commitments are pretty minimal, always acting on conscience will be extremely materially and psychologically costly. In the absence of evidence that we are guaranteed to be compensated for these costs in some way, we ought to reject the idea that being good is best for us.

There is one further piece of evidence supporting the idea that it may often be best for us to violate conscience, and this is the fact that conscience is not *always* a very deep or powerful voice. Sometimes we may experience conscience as simply offering us a bit of moral advice that we take to be relevant to our overall practical deliberations but far from decisive. Conscience might tell us that we really should invite that somewhat annoying but evidently lonely coworker to our dinner party; but knowing that this person's presence will come at the cost of a fun time, we may simply ignore the moral consideration that conscience presents to us and act on our overwhelming nonmoral motives. Even granting that there is some psychological cost to ignoring conscience in cases like this, the generalizable point is that the costs of violating conscience can often be minimal (especially when the moral stakes seem low to us) and the corresponding benefits to well-being in cases like this can easily outweigh them. (In chapter 3 I suggest that cases like should also lead us to be skeptical of the idea that the voice of conscience has any special connection with the true self.)

If the preceding was right, then it may sometimes be reliably best for us not to heed conscience. Interestingly, a similar line of reasoning suggests that it might sometimes actually be best for us to abandon conscience altogether. Intuitively, conscience is a psychological constraint that deters us, with the threat of guilt, from doing things we would otherwise do, and enjoy, with impunity. If we could somehow purge ourselves of conscience, we would stand to benefit in three ways: we would be freed to act as we please, and thus enjoy the benefits of the activities that we would pursue were it not for conscience; we would be freed from the psychological weight of the looming *prospect* of guilt; and we would also be freed from the actual guilt that inevitably comes when we violate conscience.

Of course these benefits of overcoming conscience would only accrue to those with strong nonmoral or immoral desires and for whom the prospect of guilt is psychologically taxing. Presumably, though, there are many for whom conscience does not function in this psychologically oppressive way. These would be people we properly think of as *virtuous* people, basically inclined in an unconflicted way to do what is in fact right and good. Interestingly, though, even these people might benefit from overcoming conscience, for example, if their moral sensibilities lead them to be especially self-sacrificing or altruistic. This is a central point made by some feminist critics of "the ethics of care," who note that a disposition to care for others is in fact heavily gendered in societies like ours.[77] Given the asymmetric distribution of gender roles in our patriarchal society, women are more likely to think it is their duty to care for friends and family members and are thus more likely to take their own interests as secondary to the interests of those to whom they provide care. In a context where men's and women's moral frameworks are structured this way, conscience actually functions as a form of institutionalized sexism, keeping women disproportionately in positions where they serve others. Those disposed by conscience to sacrifice their well-being for others as a matter of course would benefit from purging themselves of the other-serving demands of conscience. In doing so, they might even come to see their own interests as mattering as much as anyone's—surely a liberating and beneficial attitude.

THE LIMITED APPEAL OF WELL-BEING AS AN IDEAL

In this chapter, I have suggested that, in many, everyday kinds of situations, our individual well-being is not reliably promoted by our being true to ourselves. And, indeed, being *inauthentic* in many situations seems reliably best for us. If this is right, then the Well-being Account of The Ideal of Authenticity should seem quite implausible. But what of the connections between authenticity and rationality and authenticity and morality? For those who think that the reason to be rational or to be moral has something essentially to do with our own well-being, the appeal of the Rationality Account and the Moral Account of The Ideal of Authenticity will already be significantly diminished. But the idea that the value of rationality and morality is merely instrumental to well-being is itself contentious and, I think, implausible. Intuitively, the reason to be rational is not that it is good for us; it is that we are rational beings for whom the very activities of thought and responsible action presuppose the binding norms of reason. Moreover, contrary to George Mavrodes' idea that it would be absurd to be good if being good were not good for us, I hope that many of us will think that the reason to be good is simply that it is good. This is just to say that rationality and morality are appealing ideals in their own right and, if this is so, we should be drawn away from the idea that the best lives, full stop, are simply the lives with the most subjectively experienced well-being. As we shall see, there is also compelling reason to think that being true to ourselves is fundamentally conducive to practical and theoretical rationality and to moral goodness. So, in the next two chapters I turn to these ideas. And I argue that though being authentic in the five ways we are considering bears on our rationality and our moral goodness, ultimately being authentic in these ways does not reliably conduce to rationality or to being good. I argue, furthermore, that even if it did, this would still not suffice to establish that authenticity is an ideal or to establish that being true to oneself is something appropriately adopted as a central action-guiding principle for living.

NOTES

1. One of the reasons I restrict well-being to the domain of experienced goods is to allow a conceptual distinction between well-being and the goods of rationality and morality, which are the subjects of chapters 2 and 3. Rationality and morality are thought by many to be important constituents of the good life (broadly construed) independent of their direct contributions to subjective experience. For this reason, I treat them separately in this book.
2. See Plato (1997, p. 524).
3. See Kant (2002).
4. See chapter 2 for a discussion of the metaphysics of weak will and the conceptual connections between the will and the self.
5. Interesting to note here, as a strike against the Rationality Account discussed in the next chapter, how much more appealing "I did it my way" sounds than "At least I was rational."
6. While "successful" rationalizers may avoid the bad feelings that typically arise when we are weak-willed, we might still wonder about other costs to well-being that come from habitual rationalizing.
7. See Nagel (2000, pp. 22–23) for a discussion of some of the virtues of such an attitude.
8. See Hazlett (2013) for a full philosophical discussion of this phenomenon.
9. There is also a curious tension between the view that overcoming addiction is a paradigm case of strong will and a very pervasive ideology of recovery. Recovery, for many, is thought to require recognition of one's relative powerlessness over one's life, and a willingness to depend on an intimate community of support. These are, of course, dogmas of Alcoholics Anonymous and they conflict with a version of The Ideal of Authenticity that connects being true to yourself with strong-willed self-sufficiency. Simply committing to being strong-willed and radically self-sufficient is widely thought to be a very bad strategy for reaping the rewards of recovery. Rather, dependency on others and the acknowledgment that one's essential, alcoholic self needs a lot of support seem to be very good for many people.
10. See Arpaly (2003).
11. See Soberrecovery.com (2002).
12. See Lofton (2010).
13. Taylor (1991) sees Herder as an essential precursor to the contemporary Ideal of Authenticity (pp. 28–29, 61)
14. See Bartky (2005, p. 105).
15. Ibid.
16. See Du Bois (1994).
17. Young (2005). Sandra Bartky captures the characteristic confusion this way: "It is hard enough for me to determine what sort of person I am or ought to try to become without being shadowed by an alternate self, a truncated and inferior self that I have, in some sense, been doomed to be all the time" (Bartky 2005, p. 106).
18. In other cases, such conflicts might result in a paralysis that precludes the satisfaction of either set of conflicting desires.
19. Thanks to Allan Hazlett for this coinage.
20. See Freedman (unpublished) for a discussion of how different therapeutic paradigms conceptualize the relationship between self and illness.

21. Among other things, this shows how the desire to see ourselves as rational, and the desire to see ourselves as in control of our own desires, converge.
22. Rosenberg (2011).
23. Assume here that Shlomo unequivocally disavows the view that eating lobster is sinful. His alienation consists in the conflict between this (let's assume rational) disavowal and a nonrational feeling that eating lobster is somehow wrong. The reverse is also possible. Anthony Bourdain, host of TV food show *No Reservations*, appears to take pleasure in a kind of self-professedly vicious gluttony. As B. R. Myers reports in *The Atlantic* (2011), Bourdain enjoys eating illegally obtained "ortolan, endangered songbirds fattened up, as he [Bourdain] unself-consciously tells us, in pitch-dark cages." The point here is just that Bourdain seems to have internalized the moral norms against gluttony and against eating tortured and endangered animals just sufficiently to enjoy violating them.
24. Assume also that, on balance, Shlomo's religious upbringing has promoted his well-being.
25. Grimshaw also draws a helpful distinction between two kinds of psychological tension: the first is "between one's fantasies and what one would actually do or enjoy doing in real life." This kind of tension needn't involve any alienation, as it might simply be a manifestation of prudence. The second kind of tension is "between one's understanding of the oppressive nature of some discourse or practice and one's continuing investment of desire and finding pleasure in it." This is the kind of tension characteristic of psychological oppression and, I argue, of the same structure as that which can generate guilty pleasures. (2005, pp. 334–335)
26. Ibid.
27. This is, of course, a contested position. For example, radical feminists in the tradition that sees all heterosexual sex on the continuum of rape have gone so far as to disavow all heterosexual desire and, presumably, all of the associated pleasures, tainted as they are by the ongoing conditions of patriarchal oppression. For discussions of these issues, see Frye (2005), Hoagland (1992).
28. Frankfurt (2004, p. 96).
29. "Resolution requires that the person become finally and unequivocally clear as to which side of the conflict *he is* on." (Frankfurt, p. 81).
30. It is worth noting an important common feature of psychological oppression and ambivalence: they both involve a kind of inner tension and the prospect of alienation. What is distinctive of psychological oppression, though, as considered through the lenses of Du Bois and Grimshaw, is that it is presumed to have an "external" and morally oppressive cause or origin. By contrast, Frankfurt's critique of ambivalence is distinctively nonmoral (see Frankfurt, p. 98).
31. In our next chapter, we will question whether the kind of ambivalence that Frankfurt is criticizing is a (problematic) form of irrationality.
32. Ibid., p. 79.
33. According to Philip Quinn (2008, p. 35), "[A] human life has positive teleological meaning if and only if (i) it contains some purposes the person who lives it takes to be non-trivial and achievable, (ii) these purposes have positive intrinsic value, and (iii) it also contains actions that are directed toward achieving these purposes and are performed with zest." Items (i) and (iii) are the key ones for our purposes, as they seem to be incompatible with ambivalence.
34. See Wolf (2008, p. 232). If Frankfurt is right, then Susan Wolf's *activity* requirement on a meaningful life ("Meaningful lives are lives of active engagement in projects of worth") also seems incompatible with ambivalence.
35. Frankfurt, p. 91.
36. We need to assume this because, if in fact Sergio is alienated from his love of David in the sense that his *considered judgment* is clearly opposed to the love, then, by Frankfurt's own definition, Sergio is not in fact ambivalent. According to Frankfurt, "[R]esolution [of ambivalence] requires only that the person become finally and unequivocally clear as to which side of the conflict *he is* on" (Frankfurt, p. 81). So there is

an important kind of well-being that wholeheartedness, defined this way at least, does not guarantee—the kind that comes from purging feelings which one has reflectively disavowed. This might pose a challenge for Frankfurt if we think that the pain associated with being alienated in this way might be even worse for our subjective well-being than the experience of straightforward Frankfurtian ambivalence.

37. I argue in our next chapter that neither scenario even involves any clear irrationality or incoherence on Sergio's part. Consider, for example, that there is nothing irrational, as such, about having non-cosatisfiable desires. I may have only a dollar in my pocket and desire both a drink and a small fries. I can't *have* both, but there is no contradiction in wanting them.

38. We are putting aside here any metaphysical problems with this kind of indeterminacy (e.g., whether it violates a requirement of bivalence). Also note that such indeterminacy differs from cases of being "torn" or of having a "divided will" (Frankfurt, p. 92); there is nothing obviously incoherent or irrational about being in a state that is in some way indeterminate.

39. My guess is that this is an entirely commonplace romantic occurrence. The normalcy of such situations would be especially explicable if "love" turns out to be a vague concept; it wouldn't then have to be an indeterminacy about the self that was responsible for the feeling of ambivalence; it might simply be an indeterminacy about what love is—compatible with the psychological state in question being completely determinate.

40. Frankfurt, p. 92.

41. Ibid., pp. 92–93.

42. It is noteworthy that advocates of wholehearted love often presuppose some kind of voluntarism about love. Those of us who have experienced ambivalence of the kinds we are attributing to Sergio might have serious doubts about whether the kind of "resolution" that wholeheartedness requires is something that can be achieved through any act of will. Sergio might be able to be decisive about how to *treat* David, and perhaps as a moral matter we might think he should be (say, if David is being hurt), but if "ought implies can" (see chapter 4), it is less than clear that wholeheartedness can be a practical norm. Of course, it is also possible that it is part of our human condition that we aspire to forms of coherence and wholeheartedness that are painfully elusive. I return to this question in a discussion of Nagel and Taylor in our next chapter.

43. See "Interlude on Objectivism, Subjectivism and the Dangerous Plasticity of The Ideal of Authenticity" in chapter 5.

44. Wholehearted love may, despite all this, still be desirable in itself. But we should at least be clear that its appeal is not obviously reducible to the appeal of the prospective well-being benefits it has to offer. The idea that it is better to have loved and lost than never to have loved at all highlights this point. Interestingly, there is both a consequentialistic/well-being-based interpretation of this claim as well as a deontological one. The consequentialistic view would be that it's better for us, all things considered, to take the risk of love; the deontological view would be that that value of love trumps the risks to well-being, as such. For our purposes, we need only acknowledge the possibility that for some people, loving and losing may be worse than never having loved at all. If this is a real possibility, then avoiding wholehearted love might well sometimes be best.

45. Speaking not of love, but of all things, what he defines as "sexual perversion," Nagel writes:

> Finally, even if perverted sex is to that extent not so good as it might be, bad sex is generally better than no sex at all. This should not be controversial: it seems to hold for other important matters, like food, music, literature, and society. In the end one must choose from among the available alternatives, whether their availability depends on environment or on one's own constitution. And the alternatives have to be fairly grim before it becomes rational to opt for nothing. (Nagel, 1969, p. 17)

Replacing "ambivalent love" for bad or perverted sex in this context yields the quite reasonable conclusion that ambivalent love may often be better for us than no love at all. The evidence of our romantic choices suggests that most of us think this is probably true.

46. Frankfurt (2002, p. 250).

47. Ibid., p. 251.

48. I take this to be close to the heart of Bernard Williams' critique of utilitarianism in *Utilitarianism: For and Against* (Smart and Williams, 1973). The utilitarian requirement that we be permanently ready to do whatever is necessary to maximize utility amounts to a requirement to be *wholehearted* utilitarians. But to be wholehearted in this way means we must be willing to abandon our other projects when they conflict with the utilitarian calculus. (See chapter 2 for a fuller discussion of Williams.)

49. Taylor (1989, p. 33).

50. For a fuller discussion of bad faith and possibility of self-deception see Feldman and Hazlett (2010).

51. Jopling (1992, p. 121).

52. Ibid.

53. Sartre (2007, p. 47).

54. Baron (1988, p. 437).

55. Sartre (1956, pp. 96–97).

56. Ibid.

57. Parfit (2011, p. 128).

58. A critic of preference hedonism might also respond here by broadening the relevant conception of well-being. Ignorance might simply be bad for us as such, independent of its introspectively discernable effects. The idea here is just that a person's life is going better if she knows certain important facts about her life, no matter the material or psychological consequences. Alternatively, even if it turns out that the cheating is never discovered or that the cancer gets the old man first, we might think they both are worse off simply because they've been denied the opportunity to exercise full autonomy, which seems, in itself, bad for them.

59. See Baron (1988).

60. Grimshaw (2005).

61. Velleman (1992).

62. More mundanely, anyone who has perused the toothpaste or breakfast cereal aisles may have experienced how overwhelming it can be to choose among so many options. More toothpaste to choose from is not always better; neither, it seems, is more self-knowledge.

63. This will be true of psychotherapeutic paradigms with constructivist or anti-realist theories of the self, for example, pretty much all post-modern theories.

64. I have been focusing on forms of well-being that are causally produced by self-knowledge. A defender of the well-being benefits of self-knowledge might hold, however, that certain forms of self-knowledge are essential *constituents* of a person's well-being. It might simply be good for us, full stop, to become aware of some of our unconscious motives or desires and *not* because knowing this might help alleviate some pain or conduce to better future choices. My reply here is that it seems like any such self-knowledge *could* be painful and thus fail to conduce to well-being. To insist that it is nevertheless best for us is to abandon one of our basic working assumptions, that well-being is something that we experience.

65. See Hazlett (2013).

66. Keep in mind that this is not to say that it is *morally good* to be deluded or to conform in this way. The present claim is only about the possible well-being benefits of lacking self-knowledge.

67. See Brison (2005).

68. Those who agree with this judgment would do well to note how paternalistic it is. For all we know, Jack might take his friend's advice, abandon his artistic aspira-

tions, devote himself to the law, all the while regretting his choice and feeling like he abandoned his dreams.

69. Our judgments in Jack's case may also be affected by various cultural assumptions we make about authenticity and the arts. We often conceive of artists as specially engaged in the project of authentic self-expression in ways that others are not. For example, we don't presume that corporate lawyers or waiters are following their muses or their soul's call. This may explain the intuition of some that the failure of an artist to know the truth about his talents is especially pernicious.

70. Keep in mind here that even the unseemly self-satisfaction that a "self-righteous" person might derive from following conscience will count here as promoting the well-being of the self-righteous person.

71. See Gauthier (2011).

72. Mavrodes (2007, p. 587).

73. See Parfit (2011) on "success theory."

74. Can things be good or bad for us even if we do not experience these good or bad things, as such? I think there is sense in saying that posthumous events or states of affairs can make it so that our lives have gone better or worse. There is a fine sense in which a life devoted to certain ends (like the success of one's children or world peace) has gone better if the efforts exerted toward those ends actually contribute to those outcomes, even after one is gone. Likewise, there may even be a sense in which it is good *for* us to be thought well of after we are gone (and here I do not mean to be invoking the thought that our souls are looking down in appreciation). But even granting the somewhat odd-sounding thought that it is good *for* the martyr to be in good moral standing in death, this is not sufficient to establish the well-being claim in question because there is no guarantee that the life she might have lived might not have been so good as to outweigh the costs of her moral infraction.

75. Wolf (2011).

76. Singer (1972, p. 231).

77. Kittay (2005).

TWO

The Rationality Account of The Ideal of Authenticity

In chapter 1, we explored the first of our three accounts of why authenticity might seem like an ideal—The Well-being Account of The Ideal of Authenticity. On that account, authenticity was proposed as an ideal because well-being looked like an ideal and authenticity and well-being seemed to go hand in hand. The approach to the Rationality Account of The Ideal will be structurally parallel, so it will be helpful to remind ourselves up front of the three claims that I think defenders of an Ideal of Authenticity should want to defend. The first claim is a conceptual one about the nature of authenticity and it is simply that authenticity is, essentially, a matter of how one relates to oneself. This will be especially plausible on The Rationality Account because being rational on various construals essentially involves internal consistency. When we are not true to ourselves we often contradict or delude ourselves in some way (say, by being weak-willed or in bad faith). The second claim is that being authentic is our all-things-considered most reliable bet for living the best lives we can. And the third claim is that The Ideal of Authenticity is normatively inescapable. These latter two claims also gain intuitive support if we think that authenticity and rationality are tightly linked. If to *be* a person is, perhaps by definition, to be the kind of being who is properly held to standards of rationality, and if being authentic is a matter of being ideally rational in certain ways, then The Ideal of Authenticity would seem to reflect our aspiration to be full persons and might in fact constitute something like an inescapable categorical imperative (see chapter 4). I will be arguing, however, that purportedly paradigm cases of inauthenticity are not best understood as cases of irrationality; and I will also argue, perhaps more counterintuitively to many philosophers, that rationality itself is not an ideal because it may often be reliably best, all things considered, to be *irrational* in various ways. But before turning to these criticisms, I want to be sure that the case for the Rationality Account of The Ideal of Authenticity is made as compellingly as it can be.

Recall Caitlin, from our introduction. Caitlin was struggling with her decision about whether to have an abortion. She went to the doctor for advice and her doctor told her to just be true to herself. In one version of this scenario, we can imagine that Caitlin has a clear sense of what she ought to do but is having trouble committing to that course because it looks to be so psychologically or practically difficult. If this is her situation, the doctor's advice might be construed as encouragement to Caitlin to be strong-willed, to stick to her resolve—whatever it may be—and not let herself take what might look for a moment like an easy way out, but would really mean going against her best judgment (a pretty clear case of practical irrationality). In a second interpretation of the scenario, Caitlin's doctor might be advising her to avoid being unduly influenced by the people in her life who are putting various pressures on her. This kind of authenticity advice seems aimed at promoting Caitlin's rational autonomy. If she decides for *herself* what to do, rather than submitting to various social pressures, she is self-governing and taking responsibility for her own thinking and decision-making. In a third construal of the situation, the doctor's advice might be taken as a kind of tacit moral advice. Caitlin is trying to figure out the "right" thing to do, and the thought here is that if Caitlin is true to herself by being true to her *conscience,* then she will do what is right. Now, if it turns out that following moral conscience is a way to be rational (see chapter 4 for a discussion of moral rationalism), then again The Ideal of Authenticity would be aligned with a form of practical rationality. In a fourth interpretation of Caitlin's case, we might see the doctor's advice as advice to introspect and gain some clarity or self-knowledge about what she really wants. In this interpretation, the advice is aimed, straightforwardly, at promoting Caitlin's epistemic rationality. If she can *discover* what she really wants by looking inward, she achieves self-knowledge (and avoids self-deception). This self-knowledge can also then be translated into action, which further facilitates Caitlin's practical rationality. Finally, in a fifth version of the case, there may as yet be no fact of the matter about what Caitlin really thinks she should do and we might take the doctor's advice as acknowledging this fact and recommending that Caitlin *settle,* rather than discover the answer to the question of what she really thinks she should do. In settling or deciding what she wants, she determines who she is and thereby brings into being a determinate self to be true to. Put differently, this last proposal is that Caitlin may not have available any distinctively rational course of action precisely because her inchoate or conflicted psychological state blocks her from making any decision at all. So overcoming her ambivalence or uncertainty and forming an internally coherent judgment about what she should do may be necessary to facilitate the possibility of rational choice itself.[1]

The overarching thought that is meant to emerge from all these interpretations of what it could mean for Caitlin to be true to herself is that being true to ourselves in each of the five ways this book explores may facilitate practical and epistemic rationality. The idea at the center of the Rationality Account of The Ideal of Authenticity is just this: that being rational is at the core of what it is to be a person and, because being authentic reliably promotes rationality in various concrete ways, in aspiring to authenticity we are simply aspiring to be what makes us most fully ourselves. We can thus sum up the initial case for the Rationality Account of The Ideal of Authenticity this way: by figuring out and being or becoming who we "really are," we avoid weak will and resist internalizing others' oppressive standards; we live morally conscientiously; we achieve self-knowledge and avoid self-deception; and we become wholeheartedly capable of making and committing to our choices. In short, by being our authentic selves we embrace our rational nature and in so doing we exemplify what is most distinctive of us as persons.

As we proceed to consider whether The Ideal of Authenticity is in fact supported by an ideal of rationality, we will be appealing to a set of four (sometimes overlapping yet distinct) intuitive claims about rationality. A first claim about rationality is that practical rationality normally involves matching our actions to our best judgments about what we should do. Being rational in this way is a matter of consistency between judgment and action. In sticking to her resolution and not smoking, for example, Alison would be rational in this way, and this suggests why Authenticity as Strong Will seems to have a powerful rational grounding.[2] (One thing to keep in mind here, and that we will return to, is that being consistent in this way is no guarantee of *overall* practical rationality. For example, if one's "best judgments" are seriously flawed, it won't necessarily be rational *tout court* to act on those judgments.) A second claim is that epistemic rationality requires that we avoid self-deception and seek self-knowledge. While a person who has false beliefs may not always be culpable for being in this state (and may not always be properly charged with being irrational), having false beliefs is presumptively not fully epistemically rational.[3] The Ideal of Authenticity as Self-Knowledge seems well supported by this epistemic claim. A third claim is that it is rational to be morally conscientious; to do (or at least try to do) what we (upon proper moral deliberation)[4] think is morally right. We will also consider a fourth claim that is connected with the first two, and this is the claim that it is rational to have somehow "consistent" values and practical commitments. What this consistency might amount to will be developed below.[5]

With these claims in mind, the questions that drive this chapter are these: Is there reason to think that being true to ourselves is our most reliable bet if our aim is to live rationally? Is rationality itself an ideal?

To vindicate the Rationality Account of The Ideal of Authenticity the answer to each of these questions must be "yes." If being authentic is not fundamentally connected with being rational, or if being rational is not reliably best for us, this will leave The Ideal of Authenticity as yet ungrounded.

As in our last chapter, I offer three main strategies of argument against the Rationality Account of The Ideal of Authenticity. I argue, first, that some paradigm cases of inauthenticity don't seem like cases of irrationality at all. If this is right, then, as just noted, the value of authenticity can't consistently or generally be grounded in the norms of rationality. Second, I argue that it is sometimes reliably more rational to be inauthentic. And, finally, I offer a contention that philosophers will find discomfiting: that there are sometimes, perhaps even often, more important things than being rational. The morally and ethically best lives we can live may in fact be ones that are deficient with respect to a variety of rational standards. There is a danger of valuing rationality too highly. I suggest that, even if being subject to the norms of rationality were in part (or even in whole) constitutive of being a person, this would not suffice to show that the norms of rationality are themselves normatively overriding or even appropriately taken as ideals: in a variety of situations and in a variety of ways, it is better not to be rational.

We now turn to considering how our five conceptions of authenticity fair with respect to practical and epistemic rationality (starting from what I take to be the weaker cases and moving to the stronger).

RATIONALITY AND THE IDEAL OF AUTHENTICITY AS STRONG WILL

Recall *Alison, the Smoker*: Alison is thirty-five and has been trying to quit smoking off and on since she was sixteen. It's New Year's Eve and she resolves, once and for all, to quit—starting the next day. The next day comes, she's hungover, and she desperately wants a cigarette. But she remembers her resolution and tells herself to stick to her guns. She doesn't light up. It seems natural to say that, in sticking to her resolve, Alison exercises strong will and in so doing is true to herself. Moreover, in resisting temptation and thus acting in accordance with her best, all-things-considered judgment, Alison seems to be a paragon of practical rationality. When our behavior corresponds to the beliefs and desires we reflectively endorse—when our choices match our values—we thus manifest a salient kind of rational integrity. According to The Rationality Account of The Ideal of Authenticity as Strong Will, the fundamental reason to be strong-willed is that in doing so we reliably manifest this kind of rationality. This claim looks quite compelling because it does seem that being strong-willed *just is* a way of being means-ends rational and means-ends rationality is a basic principle of practical rationality. Could it ever fail to be rational to act on our best, all-things-considered judgments? Are there patterned cases where doing so could manifest *ir*rationality?

The Irrationality of Strong Will and the Rationality of Weak Will

To see why it might sometimes be irrational to be strong-willed, it will be helpful to recall a case of weak will that we discussed in the last chapter: *Hailey, the Hyper-Perfectionist Student*. Hailey's "best judgment" is that she should be spending pretty much all of her time on her studies, rather than socializing with her friends or "having fun." While Hailey generally stays late at the library reading and working, she doesn't consistently live up to her own very demanding best judgment and she "weakly" hangs out with her friends every now and then. Earlier, we invoked this case to suggest that being weak-willed might, in a commonplace and predictable kind of scenario, be good for us. Here the point is closer to the one Nomy Arpaly makes when she introduces this kind of case.[6] We can easily imagine that Hailey's weak will is more consistent with her overall motivational psychology than is her "best judgment." That is, if we knew Hailey well, we might see that she in fact cares a lot about her friends, that her past behavior, though indicating a strong concern for academic achievement, reflects a more balanced rather than hyper-perfectionist view of the good life and that her pattern of weak will itself suggests that she cares quite a lot about being social and having fun. There are two important implications of this possibility: the first is that her "best judgment" may in fact be mistaken. The idea here is not just that she is wrong about what she ought to do in some objective sense, but that she may be wrong about herself. She intends her best judgment to reflect her fundamental values but in fact, in this case her "best" judgment reflects a distortion of those values induced, perhaps, by the salience to her of her anxiety about her grades. So, the correlative second implication is that in cases like this, weak will as we have defined is actually more rational, overall, than strong-willed adherence to one's "best" judgment. This suggests, further, that when our apparent best judgments are not accurate reflections of the beliefs and desires we would endorse under better conditions of rational reflection, acting on them with strong will is not obviously rational.[7] This intuition is well-captured by the thought that Hailey would seem, overall, more rational if she were to change her "best judgment" to match her behavior, rather than if she were to conform her behavior to match her judgment. As noted in our earlier discussion, cases like this might be quite common for those with perfectionist bents or for those generally disposed to make overly demanding resolutions in response to a sense of our own less-than-perfect dispositions. My guess is that making unnecessarily abstemious resolutions is a common occurrence for those of us who are especially self-conscious about our weaknesses—be they for procrastination, junk food, or bad television. It seems that many of us would be reliably irrational if we were strong-willed in pursuit of such overly abstemious resolutions.[8] One interesting thing to note here is that the preceding analysis does not allow us to derive any action-giving rule *against* being strong-willed. This is because there is something fundamentally paradoxical about advising someone to act *contrary* to her best judgment. (I return to this puzzle in chapter 4, where I suggest that the advice to be strong-willed is problematic precisely because it appears to reduce to the merely trivial advice to be subjectively rational.)

A lesson here is that if practical rationality is something we care a lot about, as such, we ought not focus our efforts exclusively on being strong-willed; we would do well to focus more attention on the ways in which we form our "best judgments" in the first place and in particular on the ways in which these judgments can come to misrepresent the content and balance of our beliefs, desires, and values. That said, I don't think I've established conclusively that it is not a *fairly* reliable bet, as far as practical rationality is concerned, to make it a rule to try to be strong-willed. What I take myself to have shown so far, is that we should be skeptical of a very tight connection between strong will and practical rationality; if this is right, we've got some good initial reason to be skeptical of the Rationality Account of The Ideal of Authenticity as Strong Will.

Because our "best judgments" are often identified with (and as) the judgments of conscience, The Ideal of Authenticity as Moral Conscientiousness has much, structurally, in common with The Ideal of Authenticity as Strong Will, so to this we turn next.

RATIONALITY AND AUTHENTICITY AS MORAL CONSCIENTIOUSNESS

The Ideal of Authenticity as Moral Conscientiousness holds that a person is true to herself when she is (or tries to be) morally good. We are authentic, this view holds, when we live up to our own best judgments about what is morally right or morally good because, on this view, our true selves are essentially our moral selves (or are at least selves properly constrained by morality). The idea at the center of the Rationality Account of The Ideal of Authenticity is that, if it turns out that it's rational to be moral and being authentic is essentially about being moral, than authenticity would be rationally grounded. In chapter 3 (on the Moral Account of The Ideal of Authenticity), I develop five accounts of the relationship between morality and true selfhood that I introduce here. (They are, roughly, Augustinian/Thomistic, sociobiological, Kantian, relativistic, and culpability-based.) In this section, I simply assume the plausibility of the idea that being true to oneself is a distinctively moral enterprise. This is, of course, a huge topic in metaethics and this book will not survey this literature but will rather sketch, in turn, several compelling lines of argument and objection that seem especially relevant to our project. The present aim is to demonstrate the appeal of the idea that it is rational to be authentically morally conscientious. Ultimately, of course, I will be arguing that the link between being conscientious and being rational is not strong enough to support a compelling case for the Rationality Account of The Ideal of Authenticity as Moral Conscientiousness.

Consider, first, the Thomistic ideal that there is something like a divine imprint of the moral law on our minds or our souls and that we access this moral law by employing our faculty of "natural reason." If morality were in fact imprinted on us in this way, then rational reflection—or perhaps, better, a form of *intro*spection—would yield moral knowledge. And in acting morally, we would be acting in harmony with our true moral selves. On a parallel non-theistic, sociobiological account, our social or intellectual or affective natures may have evolved in such ways as to provide us with something like a moral center or compass. On such views, our evolved nature would provide us with the sources of standing reasons to be morally good.[9] The Kantian model, though perhaps least easily integrated into the paradigm of authenticity, is nevertheless the most clearly rationalistic. If something like the Categorical Imperative can be derived from principles of reason alone, then being moral would simply be equivalent to following the rules we are rationally bound to give to ourselves. On this conception, to be moral is just to be rationally autonomous. On the relativistic model, the key idea is that, ultimately, each of us is our own and only moral measure; if there is no objective standard determining what is right and wrong, then all that could be involved in being good would be being true to ourselves. Finally, on the culpability-based model, the idea is that all any of us can fairly or justly be held accountable or culpable for doing is what *we* ourselves think is right or best.

If any of these lines of thought is correct, then there will be substantial support for the claim that being morally conscientious conduces to or simply constitutes our being rational: on the Augustinian/Thomistic and sociobiological models, being moral would be practically rational because we'd be acting *consistently* with the dictates of our deepest selves; on the Kantian view, our rational nature, in virtue of which we count as persons and moral agents altogether, dictates that we are bound by morality; and on the relativistic and culpability-based views, it seems that the only grounds for holding people morally accountable would be a charge of moral hypocrisy grounded in an observation that a particular action failed to match a person's own moral judgment. If being true to ourselves amounts to, or consists in, or is essentially constrained by, a rational requirement to be moral—and the above philosophical traditions can be construed as suggesting this—this would make the Rationality Account of The Ideal of Authenticity as Moral Conscientiousness quite appealing. Of course, there are also strong theoretical and empirical reasons to wonder about the purportedly strong connections between morality and rationality.

Irrational Conscientiousness and Rational Immorality

Consider another case, inspired by Arpaly: imagine a self-identified Nazi with Jewish friends during World War II. Despite his personal sympathies, he "conscientiously" turns his Jewish friends in for deportation, acting in accordance with his apparent "best" moral judgment. Even ignoring the pretty evident non-universalizability of his judgment, it's at least possible to see this person's judgment as mistaken and, like Hailey's misjudgment of her own deep concern for friendship, not indicative of his "true" values (suppose he is plagued by genuine guilt over his actions for the rest of his life). In light of this, it seems reasonable to say that he's acted in a way that was conscientious (he was, subjectively, doing his best to act on conscience) but nonetheless irrational. Of course the Augustinian/Thomistic reply will be that though the Nazi may have acted in a way that felt or maybe even was *subjectively* conscientious, he has nonetheless failed to act on conscience itself. The Nazi's "conscience" seems so obviously perverted that it is more compelling for us to say that some corrupting passions (surely the result of powerful social and ideological influence) must have had improper influence on his moral reasoning; he has thus failed in his employment of Natural Reason and thus failed to act truly conscientiously. If this Thomistic analysis looks right, we still want to challenge the claim that conscience and rationality go together, we must see if there are cases where a person evidently does what conscience dictates, where we think the person has in fact done what was is right, but where it is also compelling to say that the person has acted irrationally.

To investigate this possibility, it will be helpful to consider a case where the moral considerations in play seem clear but somewhat weak and the nonmoral ones more powerful. Imagine Paula, a successful stand-up comedian whose wry humor typically comes at the expense of other people (she's some kind of insult comic).[10] She makes fun of the way certain people think and talk and act and she does so in a way, let's say, that hurts people's feelings. Let's add that she has honed her act over the years, that her identity is deeply bound to her distinctive comedic sensibility, and that she is also very popular among a certain subpopulation of disaffected people. Let's stipulate also that what she's doing is morally wrong, and that she herself doesn't think it's right—she doesn't think her jokes are somehow *morally* justified on utilitarian or deontological grounds. (She may in fact think the jokes wrong and even enjoy making then for this reason.[11]) Is it irrational for Paula to perform her routine? It seems *ad hoc* to insist that if Paula were thinking "properly" or "correctly," she wouldn't make these jokes. This is so in part because Paula is acting perfectly consistently with her own beliefs, desires and values. Unlike the Nazi, she is not in the grip of any obviously distorting influences; her values are utterly transparent to her. We might say that the balance of her "internal reasons," the rationally motivating considerations stemming from her distinctive motivational psychology, supports her comic choices.[12] The point is that, even if we grant that there are standing "external" or objective moral reasons for Paula not to make her jokes, it seems like they could potentially be outweighed by other nonmoral reasons—either internal ones stemming from Paula's own psychology or external ones deriving from various nonmoral considerations like the value of humor or entertainment or art. The idea is that all things considered, the nonmoral reasons that bear in favor of telling the modestly immoral jokes could simply outweigh the moral reasons not to. If this seems plausible, then we would have a compelling case of rational immorality.

But what if Paula were suddenly to tell us that she was abandoning her act, at the expense of her whole career, on moral grounds, because of the offense that her jokes cause? Should we think that Paula's newfound moralism is rationally necessary? Could we think this? Surely we could imagine her fans thinking that she's somehow come under the spell of religion or that her transformation is some kind of practical joke. Her acting on this moral judgment makes no sense in light of her explicit comic and artistic values and identity. She's an insult comic, after all. If she were suddenly to insist that she must follow conscience, we would surely conclude that Paula had radically changed and that conscience was now playing a role in her practical identity that it had not done thus far. *Given such change*, Paula's moral decision could be rational. But in its absence, the mere fact of her acting on conscience, as such, seems to have little power to rationalize her choice in our eyes. The implication is that in all sorts of normal circumstances, whether we think a person's acting on conscience is rational or irrational will depend on the functional role that conscience plays in that person's practical life. The mere fact that moral considerations, on their own, dictate some course of action is no evidence that rationality, as such, dictates it.

Returning to Caitlin and her abortion decision for a moment, the relevant question to ask here would be whether we can imagine it being appropriate for her to make her decision on the basis of something *other* than morality. Suppose that her education or her athletic endeavors or her personal freedom were her primary concerns and that, though concerned with the moral status of her fetus and even sympathetic to the idea that it has a significant moral interest in living, she nevertheless makes her decision on other grounds. Could this be rational? To insist that it could not be leaves us in the paternalistic position of having to say that Caitlin, who's thinking hard and thoroughly about her situation, is not thinking *well*, simply because of the way she is weighing moral and nonmoral considerations against each other. More importantly, for our discussion of authenticity, we'd be in the position of having to say that Caitlin is not being true to herself because, by *our lights*, her true self essentially is (or is to be constrained by) her moral self. This is paternalistic in yet another way because it entails not just that she isn't thinking well (despite her thinking that she is), but also entails an attribution of self-deception to Caitlin because The Ideal of Authenticity as Moral Conscientiousness presupposes that our true selves are (or are constrained by) our moral selves in any transparent way and this seems not to be the case for Caitlin, on this reading.

So, even if we were to grant that there were always good reason to be good,[13] it wouldn't follow that it was always rational, all things considered, to act on conscience. In fact, it seems like it could at least sometimes be *irrational* to be conscientious and *rational* to do what one believes or knows to be wrong. The argument that it is always rational to act morally presupposes that morality is rationally overriding; that moral reasons are always weightier than other kinds of reasons. There are two important reasons to doubt this presupposition: the first is that it seems that by our own lights, nonmoral internal reasons (grounded in our own motivational psychologies) can sometimes outweigh external moral ones and when they do it is at least subjectively rational to act on them; the second is that it seems like there are some weighty nonmoral reasons that can outweigh less important moral reasons.[14] The general point is that it seems like it is at least in part a contingent matter—depending on the relative weights of moral and nonmoral reasons and on how important morality is to particular people—whether failing to be morally conscientious is a form or irrationality or not. Now, given that there are competing conceptions of rationality, even if we grant that it is rationally overriding on *some* conception of rationality to be morally conscientious, it may also be more rational, on some *other* conception, to not be (e.g., if being rational is a matter of prudence or of acting on one's all-things-considered best judgment, both of which may plausibly come apart from conscience). If this is right, it would at least be hasty simply to say that The Ideal of Authenticity as Moral Conscientiousness is supported by an ideal of rationality.

RATIONALITY AND AUTHENTICITY AS PSYCHOLOGICAL INDEPENDENCE

Consider *Critical Cal*:

> Cal, a white, straight, thirty-five-year-old man, has always identified as a fiscally and socially conservative Republican. Cal's social, political, and moral values were formed by his growing up Christian and fairly wealthy in The South. But in recent years, Cal has come to doubt some of his social and political convictions. He found Obama's run for the presidency inspiring in 2008 and he started reading some "liberal" political magazines. Over time, he begins to feel that he's never really seen more than one side of the important social and political issues of the day. He becomes an ever more voracious reader and begins to think about the ways in which religious and class ideologies have shaped his thinking. He registers as an Independent and begins to think of himself as a political iconoclast. He is intellectually energized and feels like he's really *thinking* for the first time in his life.

Forming one's beliefs under the powerful influence of others is, intuitively, a form of epistemic irrationality; and being unduly influenced by others in one's decision-making is, intuitively, a form of practical irrationality. As a phenomenological matter, when we experience ourselves as submitting to various kinds of social pressure, we may feel weak-willed or psychologically alienated. By contrast, when we are psychologically independent, we avoid a distinctive form of heteronomy. By living (or at least trying to live) the kinds of independent-minded lives *we ourselves* judge best, we seem to manifest a variety of epistemic and practical virtues. Independent thinking seems characteristically critical, rather than dogmatic or ideological. For example, only when Cal begins to think for himself does he see his own privilege as something that isn't the product of his own efforts; he begins to see that some of his beliefs about himself and the world were self-privileging and in bad faith. He is newly able to recognize some painful truths about himself and the community in which he was raised. By distancing himself from ways of thinking that he'd internalized over a lifetime, Cal seems to be figuring things out for himself and in so doing, embodying epistemic virtues like curiosity, open-mindedness, intellectual modesty, and even a new kind of objectivity. As a result of this new clarity of thought, he is able to make his worldview more coherent. As a practical matter, he is also able to make clearer practical and policy judgments about what would be best for himself and even for American society as a whole. According to the Rationality Account of The Ideal of Authenticity as Psychological Independence, being true to ourselves is fundamentally a way of facilitating the proper function of our rational faculties.[15]

But is thinking for ourselves always or even reliably a way of thinking more rationally? What is the relationship between our *quality* of thought and its psychologically *independence*? If being psychological independent just means being disposed against dogmatism or ideology, it would seem to be essentially rational, by definition. But if there are characteristic modes of rational thinking that do not seem especially independent (or that seem especially dependent on others), or if we think that independence, as such, is no safeguard against dogmatism, then we might do better than to equate independent thinking with good thinking, or authentic thinking with epistemically rational thinking.

The Irrationality of Psychological Independence

Imagine that little Jimmy is being told to eat his broccoli and his response is a willful "no." A first-year art student is being taught to draw realistically but she refuses, insisting that that's not how she sees the world. A romantic cad is told he should be concerned with the emotional pain he's causing his "conquests" and he declares himself above such bourgeois rules of love. A self-styled "Zarathustran" declares that conventional morality is bunk and fashions herself a moral iconoclast, setting her own moral standards guided only by her "natural" passions.

In each of these cases, the person in question is asserting a meaningful kind of psychological independence. In saying "no," children begin to form identities separate from their parents. In refusing to paint "within the lines," an artist may free herself to produce something creative and original. Rejecting the conventions of romantic love may be liberating and fulfilling. And overthrowing Judeo-Christian morality may be a first step toward moral revolution. But, as we shall see, none of these things demonstrate the essential rationality of psychological independence. Young people who resist authority as a kind of developmental stage often end up refusing the council of those with greater knowledge than themselves and simply conforming to some other cliquish subculture; rebellious teenagers sometimes do dangerous things simply to assert their independence. Refusing to learn how to draw realistically is likely to be contrary to the aims and interests of aspiring artists. And the rejection of romantic or moral conventions—for the purpose of being independent or iconoclastic—may prevent the iconoclast from taking seriously or being guided by the aspects of those conventions that, by no accident, conduce to our individual (and collective) well-being. The point of these examples is just to show that, in many situations, asserting one's psychological independence can itself manifest a set of epistemic and practical vices: the child is stubborn, the budding artist is close-minded, the cad is imprudent, and the pseudo-Nietzschean may be morally blind.

When other people and the conventions they propagate are reliable sources of information and guidance, the rational thing to do is to be influenced and guided by them. Of course, the defender of the rationality of psychological independence has an important reply here: in order to know when it's appropriate to be guided by others, one must make one's own best assessment either of the content of the others' guidance or the reliability of their expertise. And this means thinking *for ourselves* about the quality of the sources and information available to us. Some philosophical anarchists take this point to be so powerful as to imply the impossibility of any legitimate authority of one person (or government) over another. If a piece of advice is correct or good, the anarchistic argument goes, the reason to "follow" it is never that it is issued by an authority. The reason to follow it is that it is correct or good, and this is something that must be independently assessed by each person.[16] This seems right, in part. Each of our examples of nonconformity, above, *could* be the product of antecedent critical reflection on the merits of the directives or conventions being proposed. If they are, and the resistance to those directives is based on the conclusions of that reflection, then the resistance may seem reasonable. So my claim is not necessarily that submitting to advice that is substantively good is rational (though it is always at least rational in the sense that it is consistent with the relevant good reasons). Rather, my claim is that psychological independence, commercially understood, can lead us away from substantively correct judgments and those influences that might induce or facilitate our thinking well and that it is, in itself, formally orthogonal to rational thought. More specifically, the idea is that resisting social influence may require forgoing kinds of collective and intersubjective thinking that are often thought to be distinctively rational, including scientific thinking and philosophical thinking.

The Rationality of Psychological Dependence

Involuntarists about belief hold that what we believe is not normally under our voluntary control.[17] Perceptual beliefs are typically the simple causal consequence of our senses being open. Deductive beliefs are typically formed on the basis of exposure to compelling arguments.[18] When a simple deductive argument convinces us of a conclusion, we normally cannot resist accepting that conclusion. We are under its sway. And we don't think it would be better were we immune to this kind of cognitive influence.[19] One thing this shows is that if we value psychological independence, this cannot be understood as valuing immunity to the influence of what is outside of us. My guess is that if we had to choose either being reliably, even deterministically, influenced to believe what was correct (even in the absence of a full understanding of what makes those beliefs correct) or suspending judgment about what to believe (in virtue of our limited capacities for independent assessment), many of us would happily select the first option. This is just to say that it's good—and perhaps even a defining mark of rationality—to be *responsive* to the truth, to have our minds shaped by it and its evidence and by those in possession of it.[20]

Interestingly, psychological dependence—or perhaps, better interdependence—actually seems especially virtuous and important in domains of inquiry where our epistemic standards seem the highest: in science and in philosophy. These are domains of inquiry where self-criticism, collaboration, dialogical and dialectical thought and a concern for widespread replicability of observation and intuition seem completely central. Ideas are sparked in response to the ideas of others; they are developed in communities of thinkers interacting in such dynamic ways that it is often impossible to say where a particular idea came from or who was its originator. Indeed, contemporary historians of science have largely abandoned—on both conceptual and empirical grounds—the idea of the lone genius and his "eureka" moment of discovery.[21] And, *pace* certain hyper-rationalistic conceptions of philosophy, it is a platitude among philosophers since Socrates that philosophy cannot be done well in isolation from others.

But do any of these points bare against the intuition that *Critical Cal* is becoming more psychologically independent and for that very reason, a better thinker? It does seem as though his emerging awareness of his social location and the ways in which his thinking has been unthinkingly formed by it is essential to his thinking better, more rationally. What is less than clear, though, is that this means he is now thinking "independently." I think that what Cal's case shows, perhaps surprisingly, is that it is very easy to conflate thinking well and thinking independently. This is because, contingently, in the world as we know it, lots of bad thinking is the result of social influence. There are charismatic leaders and social and political and religious communities that are incredibly effective at propagating all sorts of false and unjustified beliefs. But the problem is not charisma or community; the problem arises when the content of the ideas expressed and their mode of expression constrain access to sources of information that might challenge or falsify those very ideas. Put differently, there are kinds of intellectual influences that are not conducive to rational thinking because they are prone to exclude *other influences* which would stimulate better thinking. Cal isn't thinking better because he's thinking independently, he's thinking better because he's thinking more fully or deeply, and this enriched thinking appears to be the product of exposure to what are for him new and different influences. It's not, evidently, being *influenced* that is contrary to rational thinking; it's having those influences be arbitrarily constraining in ways that preclude whole avenues of intellectual possibility.

In *Not for Profit: Why Democracy Needs the Humanities*, Martha Nussbaum makes an interesting case for a moral pedagogy that actually hinges on an important kind of psychological dependence. She argues that the kinds of moral understanding that citizens in a plural democracy must possess if our society is to function harmoniously and productively are well-produced by immersion in the kinds of arts (she focuses on dance and drama and literature) that stimulate our capacity for sympathetic imagination. In other words, moral education requires that we submit ourselves to experiences that are affectively potent and thus capable of shifting our perspectives and eliciting moral concern for those different from ourselves. Left to our own devices, left thinking for ourselves, we remain parochial, concerned only or primarily for ourselves and those with whom we have close connections. On Nussbaum's view, it is absolutely vital that we at least metaphorically "lose ourselves" in books and theatre and other arts in order to see things in some ways as others see them, which is necessary for moral understanding.[22] It turns out, on views like this, that unself-conscious immersion in forms of art, what we often think of as *suspension of disbelief*—a seeming hallmark of *un*critical thinking—is essential to the acquisition of moral knowledge. Without this capacity to submit ourselves to the influence of experiences, the power of which we do not fully understand, we would be cut off from important moral knowledge. The present point is that *if* the acquisition of such knowledge is rational, and psychological independence is an obstacle to this acquisition, then psychological independence will not be rational. One might, however, take Nussbaum's argument to show that a certain kind of irrational (or at least nonrational) experience is a necessary part of a successful moral education. For those sympathetic to this interpretation, it should be clear that the Rationality Account of The Ideal of Authenticity should be implausible from the start. After all, if we favor a moral education that comes at the expense of rationality, then The Ideal of Authenticity can't plausibly be grounded by appeal to rationality. (For those who think morality may trump rationality, The Moral Account of The Ideal of Authenticity, considered in the next chapter, may hold some appeal.)

I propose that if being a follower, as such, seems like a bad thing, it seems bad in virtue of its effects on our well-being and its potential moral implications. Uncritically submitting to others' influence *can* lead us to think and do things that are bad for us and for others (as the works of Hannah Arendt and Stanley Milgram suggest). The reason to think "for ourselves," when there is such reason, often seems better interpreted in ethical terms than in purely rational ones.[23] (I return to this idea in the last chapter of the book.) For now, the point to keep in mind is that we can and do often conflate independent thinking and good thinking. Indeed, sometimes thinking well requires critical distance from various others. But, equally often, thinking well, and rationally, requires collective, interactive, social, and immersive experience.[24]

RATIONALITY AND AUTHENTICITY AS WHOLEHEARTEDNESS

Recall Sergio, the romantic, who is ambivalent in his relationship(s). On one construal, he simply isn't sure about his feelings for David. His feelings are indeterminate. On another, he is torn between his affections for David and Geoffrey. And on a third construal, his feelings for David oscillate; he is inconstant in his love. In each of these scenarios, we can see how Sergio seems to face a practical problem: it doesn't seem clear what he should do. Should he stay with David or leave him? On the assumption of a monogamous disposition, should he choose David or Geoffrey? In any of these scenarios, we can imagine Sergio's behavior is a bit unpredictable. Depending on how he feels at the moment, he may treat David or Geoffrey differently. Says Harry Frankfurt, "[d]eficiency in wholeheartedness is a kind of irrationality, then, which infects our practical lives and renders them incoherent."[25] Frankfurt's recommendation to Sergio would be to *settle* what he wants so that he can live a coherent practical life. Unless he becomes wholehearted—of one determinate mind—Sergio seems blocked from a kind of "behavioral effectiveness" that he seems to want and need. When our passions are unclear or pulled in different directions we may be paralyzed or fickle. And this can thwart our desire to achieve various goals. Even worse, it might seem to preclude the very living of our lives. Resolving affective indeterminacy and inner conflict, identifying clearly and unambivalently with a coherent vision of ourselves and our chosen paths, thus seems essential for living practically rational lives.

Relatedly, becoming wholehearted in these ways seems essential to making narrative sense of our lives. Having a determinate and reasonably diachronically stable sense of who we are and what we want seems like it might actually be a kind of precondition for practical agency altogether. We are able to think of ourselves as persons, in part, because we are able to understand and select our choices in light of the preferences and values that define us for ourselves. With these points in mind, The Rationality Account of The Ideal of Authenticity as Wholeheartedness suggests that wholeheartedness is necessary for practical rationality because it prevents paralysis, facilitates the possibility of practical consistency over time, and enables the kind of determinate sense of self that in part constitutes us as agents. Moreover, if ambivalence disposes us to make conflicting judgments about what is good or if ambivalence precludes a kind of self-knowledge (say, about what we want), then wholeheartedness may also promote our epistemic rationality.

Bernard Williams, Wholeheartedness, and Ground Projects

In the context of love, wholeheartedness can seem like a powerfully attractive ideal. Most of us hope not to feel conflicted or ambivalent about our loves. Most of us are also deeply averse to cognitive dissonance; when our half-hearted or weak-willed behavior does not match our sense of who we are or want to be, we rationalize to try to overcome this condition. If Bernard Williams is right, I suggest, it is our "ground projects" that constitute the strongest evidence of how central wholeheartedness is to living a good life. According to Williams, our ground projects are the commitments "which are closely related to [our] existence and which to a significant degree give a meaning" to our lives.[26] These are projects, fueled by "categorical desires," which ground our identities and without which we might not even recognize ourselves as ourselves. Williams' classic examples of ground projects include a person's love for a spouse and being anti-war. These are powerful examples because it is so easy to see how commitments like these can be motivationally overriding—those who are in their grip often do not even recognize competing considerations as providing reasons for acting against them. Williams shows this by suggesting the absurdity of a husband *morally deliberating* about whether to save his drowning wife or a total stranger. Given the husband's wholehearted love, competing moral considerations do not (and Williams thinks *ought* not) even register as a basis for a practical calculation about what to do. When ground projects are in play we typically simply act. But while ground projects are often motivationally (and perhaps also rationally) overriding, they needn't be things we think about a lot nor need they be especially deep or moral. Says Williams, "The categorical desires that propel one on do not have to be even very evident to consciousness, let alone grand or large; one good testimony to one's existence having a point is that the question of its point does not arise, and the propelling concerns may be of a relatively everyday kind such as certainly provide the ground of many sorts of happiness."[27] In other words, it is our engagement in activities whose worth is simply *presupposed* and about which we are not skeptical or ambivalent that provides our lives with meaning. Putting it even more strongly, Williams claims that ground projects "are the condition of my existence, in the sense that unless I am propelled forward by the conatus of desire, project and interest, it is unclear why I should go on at all."[28] The projects that keep us from asking about the point of existence are compellingly thought of as those about which we are wholehearted. If having projects which propel us in this way is a condition of our existence, this would seem to support the thought that wholeheartedness is, in fact, an ideal. That which structures our practical lives and gives our lives meaning would seem to be something that we ought to value as an ideal.

Perhaps paradoxically, though, it looks like becoming more wholehearted about more things may actually tend to undermine wholeheartedness, and this would mean that we cannot coherently aspire to maximize wholeheartedness. As we increase the number of things we are wholeheartedly committed to, we thereby increase the possibilities for conflict among these things. I may start out unambivalent about the importance of my work and equally unambivalent about the importance of my environmental activism. But given my limited time and the potentially unlimited demands of these two commitments, I will pretty quickly start to worry about whether I am properly allotting my time, and this means thinking about how to prioritize my values. Suddenly, my wholeheartedness is in jeopardy. The more things we are wholehearted about, the greater the likelihood that we will find ourselves in situations where our ground projects contingently conflict and must be weighed against each other. Adopting wholeheartedness as an ideal to be aimed at in *every* domain of life turns out to be self-defeating.

Rather than supporting The Ideal of Authenticity as Wholeheartedness, I think Williams' account of the value of ground projects to a meaningful life suggests two quite different observations. The first is that those of us who are engaged in living our lives must already be successfully wholehearted about *something*. Most of us are lucky enough to be practically committed to various specific things in our lives. That is to say, minimally, that most of us have at least some ground project(s) that we cannot give up without serious loss to our sense of self. So, even granting that some wholeheartedness is necessary for living a meaningful life, *lacking* wholeheartedness about any *particular* thing or things does not seem to pose any general threat to having meaning in life: being wholehearted about *something* seems sufficient for having purpose and for generating meaning. So it seems that Williams' account of ground projects does not give us reason to take wholeheartedness (construed as the attitude we take toward our ground projects) as the ideal attitude to take toward all or most of our commitments.

The second observation is that, in virtue of characterizing ground projects as things we cannot step away from without in some important way losing our sense of ourselves, Williams allows ground projects, as such, to trump other apparently very important things, including moral ones. Indeed, Williams explicitly argues that we cannot be required to act on the demands of impartial moral theories like utilitarianism or Kantianism because they threaten to alienate us from the categorical ground projects that give our lives meaning.[29] Williams is thus granting us (rational) permission not to abandon our ground projects, even when doing so might have significant costs to others. This means we have a kind of freedom—the freedom to not give up what we are wholehearted about. But this kind of freedom starts to seem a bit scary unless we place some principled limits, in particular moral ones, on the value of wholeheartedness (and ground projects) as such.[30] As we shall see in more detail in our next chapter on authenticity and morality, wholeheartedness, as such, poses a threat to other important values we should not want to sacrifice.

The Rationality of Ambivalence

In chapter 1 discussion of ambivalence, I argued that we shouldn't presume that ambivalence in love must generally be *bad for* the ambivalent person. Here, a set of related points suggests that there needn't be anything *irrational* about Sergio's apparent "predicament." There is nothing evidently irrational about ambivalence, construed as affective indeterminacy. There is no logical contradiction or inconsistency in Sergio's indeterminate psychology. There is no rational requirement for us to have clear or consistent *feelings* about everything.[31] The features of David that induce Sergio's love may be genuinely affection-worthy (David is so *easygoing*) while the features that do not (David is judgmentally anti-intellectual) are not. Not only does it seem perfectly rational for Sergio to respond to these characteristics as he does, but it would seem to be irrational if he didn't, given the relative appeal, to Sergio, of the traits in question.

The same holds in the case where Sergio is torn between David and Geoffrey. His desires may not be co-satisfiable (say he simultaneously desires a monogamous relationship with each of them), but this on its own involves no contradiction.[32] It does mean he cannot get *everything* he wants, so there is a sense in which Sergio faces a practical dilemma: whom should he pursue? But the problem doesn't evidently involve a deficiency of rationality. He wants what he wants and he can't have it all. Stoics might see this as good reason to change his desires; but this seems like a point about Sergio's well-being, not about whether he is rational.

Again, if we understand Sergio's ambivalence to consist in the oscillation of his desires, there is no clear irrationality. Given this condition, Sergio is incapable of committing to David or Geoffrey, but this only seems like a "problem" if it keeps Sergio from getting something else he wants (say, a stable monogamous relationship), not because the constellation of his preferences, as such, are irrational. Moreover, it is worth noting that in the case of oscillation, Sergio's feelings are perfectly consistent at any given moment. We do not normally take changing one's mind or one's heart to be irrational, as such.

It is quite generally the case that we want various things, the attainment of which are mutually exclusive. Jesse is torn between buying a small loft in the city or a ranch house in the suburbs and wants only one house. These seem like perfectly reasonable desires even though they cannot all be satisfied. If this paralyzes her and she is left homeless, we would surely think something had gone terribly wrong. But the problem seems to be that she hasn't shown proper concern for something we take her to care about more than *where* she lives: *that* she live somewhere. If she flipped a coin to pick houses (but did not resolve her ambivalence) her practical problem would be solved. Imagine the coin toss dictated that she buy the ranch house and she did so but still felt some pangs of regret about the loft. We might think she should get over it (and be happily unconflicted about her choice), but it's not clear what mistake of rationality would be involved in her persistent feeling of regret.

That said, there are many situations where paralysis and "inaction" do not seem to be problematic at all. Some decisions may be either so trivial or so momentous that willing oneself to be wholehearted about them may seem either unnecessary or reckless. I've occasionally been unsure about what kind of ice cream to order at the ice cream parlor and, upon arriving at the front of the line and being asked what I wanted, I simply had no answer and walked away. In light of not knowing what I wanted, I got nothing. But this somehow felt like the right outcome. I couldn't choose this or that, so I didn't. Notwithstanding Buridan's ass, when we don't have a basis to choose from among a set of particular options, it can be perfectly rational not to take any of them. Suspension of judgment and of choice is rational when practical reason does not dictate any course. The point here is just that there doesn't seem to be any requirement of reason demanding that I settle what kind of ice cream I want even if it means I get none.

Let us return for a moment to the case of ambivalence where Sergio's feelings are indeterminate. We might be tempted to wonder whether Sergio's lack of self-knowledge (about *what* he wants) constitutes a form of epistemic irrationality. Knowing how we feel may often be epistemically virtuous (see the Rationality Account of Authenticity as Self-Knowledge, below) and there is a good sense in which Sergio doesn't know this. But Sergio can easily manifest the virtue of self-knowledge if he knows *that* he is ambivalent. The requirement of self-knowledge (if there is one) cannot include a requirement to know what is not available to be known. And in the cases described, there is no reason that Sergio cannot know all the relevant facts about his feelings for David or Geoffrey. There is no evident epistemic failure here.

It is also telling that we so often describe wholehearted romantic love as "blind." We glorify love by invoking its epistemic irrationality. We admire people who are not highly sensitive to the flaws of the people they love and who persist in their love through difficult circumstances that might cause lesser lovers to falter. It should be clear that such blind love poses a risk to well-being, as it makes the lover vulnerable to potentially unperceived threats. A person who is blindly in love may not notice evidence of the beloved's infidelity or of other vices that could seriously harm her. From an epistemic perspective, we should keep in mind that the person who is blindly and wholeheartedly in love may also not be able to recognize the value of other pursuits and activities.

Ambivalence as Philosophical Perspective

Let us turn, now, from the example of ambivalent love to a different, more philosophical or existential kind of ambivalence. Consider a philosophically-minded person who, in taking her life seriously, is prone to a fairly deep skepticism about, and even ironic detachment from, her life choices. Thomas Nagel seems to think that something like this attitude might actually be the solution to the "problem" of the *meaning* of life. Instead of being overwhelmed (or filled with existential terror) by the combined thoughts (a) that we are ultimately responsible for ourselves and (b) that there is no decisively correct way to live (or even to go about figuring out how to live), we may be able to lighten things up with a sort of ambivalence that comes from seeing our lives from a detached, impartial perspective. Against Camus' darker existential vision, Nagel proposes that we "approach our absurd lives with irony instead of heroism or despair."[33] "If *sub specie aeternitatus* there is no reason to believe that anything matters, then that doesn't matter either."[34] Of course, Nagel also thinks that the human condition compels us to take things seriously. So, we cannot and should not keep ourselves permanently focused, from the impartial perspective, on the absurdity of life. Inevitably, we "return to our familiar convictions," says Nagel. But we can do so with what we might think of as philosophical *perspective*, "with a certain irony and resignation."[35] As an alternative to Camus' heroic, Sisyphean response to the problem of the absurd, I am taking Nagel to be suggesting a kind of reasonable ambivalence. Nagel's proposed "ironic" stance is the stance of a person with a healthy, ambivalent, and philosophically rich life; a life that appreciates and endorses the human oscillation between conviction and comic perspective. If Nagel is right, this kind of life might, in fact, be best for us, both experientially and rationally. Though Nagel thinks (surely with Williams here) that we cannot live rich, meaningful lives while being ambivalent about everything all the time (we must *return* to our "familiar convictions"), I would go so far as to suggest that he thinks a disposition to *doubt* the importance of our projects—to be at least occasionally ambivalent about them—is a *necessary* condition of the good life.

In contrast with Nagel, Charles Taylor suggests a somewhat different relation to ambivalence. If Taylor is right, then it is the effort to struggle *through* ambivalence that is most characteristic of us as persons. According to Taylor, it is an "essential characteristic of a person"[36] to be a "strong evaluator."[37] To be a strong evaluator is to take responsibility for one's life by making choices in light of one's "deepest unstructured sense of what is important, which is as yet inchoate and which [one is] trying to bring to definition."[38] Says Taylor, "[W]e consider people deep to the extent, inter alia, that they are capable of this kind of radical self-reflection."[39] In other words, self-reflection is the process we engage in trying to move from "unstructured" and "inchoate" states to more definite ones, and it is this aim of becoming clear on what is important that gives us depth as persons. This is also how Taylor thinks we properly enact the aspiration to authenticity, so I think it is fair to see Taylor's conception of authenticity as resonating with an idea of wholeheartedness. In chapter 5, I criticize Taylor on the grounds that it is not clear how *self*-reflection functions in his account of authenticity. For present purposes, though, what matters is that Taylor himself sees our "unstructured" and "inchoate" states as partly constitutive of our personhood. And this is some reason to be concerned about the demands an ideal that asks us, ultimately, to overcome those states.

What Nagel and Frankfurt and Taylor seem to agree upon is the essentiality, to our human lives, of things being *unclear* and permanently open to radical reconsideration. The disposition to question things, to see possibilities as open, seems characteristic of lives that are both meaningful and deep. It is also worth noting that the disposition to reconsider the value of our projects in light of relevant (and especially salient) evidence is also closely related to the idea of conscience. I will argue in our next chapter that the possibility of conscience comes with the permanent possibility of alienation and fragmentation. Acting on or against conscience can involve betraying deep parts of ourselves. But we don't normally conclude on these grounds that it would be better not to have conscience. A parallel argument applies to ambivalence. The disposition to think abstractly, and from a variety of different perspectives, about what is of value and how we ought to live is a disposition that can reliably be expected to produce ambivalence. We shouldn't conclude on these grounds that this kind of thinking is, in general, bad or bad for us. We should conclude, rather, that living rationally and well can be expected to involve quite a bit of ambivalence. I suggest, in fact, that we might have reason to worry about people whose commitments are so wholehearted that they are beyond question, utterly unshakable, no matter the cost. If an Ideal of Authenticity were to encourage this kind of commitment (under the guise of the importance of being true to ourselves), we should surely be wary of it.

The Irrationality of Wholeheartedness

As we have pointed out, if Sergio is ambivalent for good reason, the ambivalence may well manifest epistemic rationality. When indeterminacy, inconsistency, or inconstancy of feeling are responses to relevant aspects of the person (or thing) about whom (or which) we are ambivalent, it seems to be eminently rational. As noted in chapter 1, Sergio's uncertainty about David *could* be the result of Sergio's clarity about David's more and less appealing characteristics. Or, if Sergio is torn between David and Geoffrey, this may be because they each have different qualities that Sergio is properly attuned to. If settling his preferences and becoming wholehearted were to require that he *ignore* these worthy qualities, this would seem to require a kind of blindness that I just argued is not epistemically rational. In other words, becoming wholehearted will be irrational if wholeheartedness depends on our seeing only one side of things.[40] (Beyond *becoming* wholehearted, *sustaining* wholeheartedness might also involve epistemic irrationality. People who believe unflinchingly or without doubt in a cause or a person or a principle may properly be called wholehearted, but they may also be prone to dogmatism or insensitivity to other causes or persons or principles.)

Because many of us desire to think there is some special justification for our choices and commitments, overcoming ambivalence might also sometimes induce *self*-deception or a kind of epistemically vicious rationalization. The possibility of rational ambivalence suggested above means that there may sometimes be no rational basis on which to become wholehearted. But if, despite this, we nevertheless manage to make ourselves wholehearted, we might well tell ourselves a story that rationalizes our "choice." We might imagine Sergio decisively picking Geoffrey in a moment of radical existential freedom (not determined by any ultimately rational judgments about Geoffrey's superiority or about their superior compatibility); but we can also imagine Sergio later falsely telling himself (or Geoffrey) that he's made the best choice because Geoffrey is just so great. To justify his new wholeheartedness, Sergio may find himself insisting that his ambivalence was irrational, when in fact it was perfectly rational (or not less rational than his new wholeheartedness).

Finally, there are cases where becoming wholehearted would seem to involve a serious betrayal of our most basic values and for this reason seems practically irrational. For example, should Sophie of *Sophie's Choice* be wholehearted in her decision about which child to save? Surely settling, decisively, which child should live or die would violate her most fundamental commitments. She may, as a moral or psychological matter, "have to" choose (though this seems contestable[41]), but choosing wholeheartedly would seem to require a radical distortion of appropriate parental affection.[42] The idea that reason might dictate wholeheartedness in such a case seems implausible. That an Ideal of Authenticity might dictate this for Sophie would be offensive, to say the least.

RATIONALITY AND AUTHENTICITY AS SELF-KNOWLEDGE

Among the conceptions of authenticity we've been discussing, The Ideal of Authenticity as Self-Knowledge might seem the most clearly grounded in a principle of rationality. If being authentic is a matter of knowing the truth about ourselves, then it looks like being authentic is backed by a strong imperative of epistemic rationality. In Sartre's explication of bad faith, he explicitly invokes its epistemic *ir*rationality. Says Sartre:

> [W]e may judge (and this may be a logical rather than a value judgment) that certain choices are based on error and others on truth. We may also judge a man when we assert that he is acting in bad faith. [I] do not pass moral judgment against him, but I call his bad faith an error. Here, we cannot avoid making a judgment of truth.[43]

In describing the bad faith of the woman on a date in the café, Sartre focused on her refusal "to realize the urgency" of the situation. "[S]he concerns herself only with what is respectful and discreet in the attitude of her companion."[44] Sartre concludes, "[W]e know what happens next; the young woman leaves her hand there, but she does not notice that she is leaving it."[45] The core Sartrean reason to avoid bad faith is that it involves an error in belief. The problem with the inauthenticity is epistemic irrationality.

Knowing the truth about ourselves also seems instrumentally necessary for being practically rational. The character of Will, from the movie *Good Will Hunting* (who we will discuss in chapter 5), undergoes a therapeutic breakthrough that essentially involves the realization that he's thwarting his own success because of low self-esteem.[46] In coming to see the truth about himself (that his behavior is the unconscious result of childhood trauma), he enables himself to act in accordance with his "true desires" (for love and professional success). Avoiding various kinds of self-deception about who we are is straightforwardly rational: by facing and accepting important truths about ourselves, we manifest epistemic virtue. As a consequence, we also enable ourselves to pursue what we really want, which is a characteristic form of practical rationality.[47]

The Rationality of Self-Ignorance

Perhaps surprisingly, though, seeking self-knowledge is not always epistemically or practically rational. There are many truths about ourselves that seem utterly trivial, and, whether or not it is intuitive to say that we *improve* our epistemic position by learning of them, there is pretty clearly no epistemic *requirement* that we do so.[48] Facts about the number of cells in our bodies or the number of hairs on our heads are not facts that we are rationally obligated to have any knowledge of. Even worse, if David Lewis is correct, seeking knowledge can sometimes undermine it.[49] We may be in possession of true beliefs, justified by having been reliably acquired from good sources. But if we begin to investigate how we know what we know, for example, by questioning whether we are in a good position to judge our own reliability, we might end up being forced into skepticism. For this reason, it might turn out that in seeking self-knowledge in some contexts, we sometimes lose it.

The case of Will Hunting suggests that the rationality of seeking self-knowledge is most clear where the knowledge in question seems important and where the alternative to self-knowledge is self-deception. Will's pursuit of self-knowledge seems rational and vital. This is because understanding the unconscious motives that are producing his self-destructive behavior enables him to make choices that have a chance of making him happy. The rationality of his self-knowledge is being explained by the importance of this self-knowledge to his *practical* life. That said, Will's self-knowledge does also seem epistemically rational. But this isn't simply because he's learned something about himself; it's because his alternative is self-deception. Will is revealed to have a set of false beliefs about himself. He thinks that his desire to do construction work (rather than mathematics) is motivated primarily by the desire for camaraderie, by his sense of the honorability of physical labor, and by his disdain for the elitism of intellectual and academic culture. But (notwithstanding the truth of all these judgments), it turns out that his primary motivation is really based on his subconscious belief that he does not deserve to live a "successful" life. So, in his circumstances, Will's hard-won self-knowledge makes him more rational than he would otherwise be. I claim, however, that when the alternative to self-knowledge is not self-deception, there is no further *epistemic* reason to prefer self-knowledge, as such. Moreover, the pursuit of self-knowledge can often be practically irrational; and its possession can also interfere with our ability to achieve our own goals.

To see how this can be so, consider Jim, who seems, overall, emotionally adjusted, functional, and psychologically healthy. Now, imagine that Jim comes to see that he lacks all sorts of knowledge about himself and he finds this very distressing. Suppose he realizes that he doesn't remember whether his mother read to him when he was two years old. Suppose he realizes that he doesn't know why he likes fishing so much. Suppose he realizes that he isn't sure exactly why he chose the career or spouse or *life* that he did. In the absence of self-understanding, he begins to doubt his choices and eventually is tormented by a pervasive anxiety. Jim goes to therapy to seek self-knowledge but it is elusive, as his questions are difficult to answer. To his friends, he appears to be having a mid-life crisis and their advice to him is to look at all the good things in his life and to stop second-guessing himself. But he is gripped by the allure of self-knowledge and the prospect that if he could just understand himself he'd be able to make the conscious choices necessary for his own happiness. But to the rest of us he seems to be irrationally fetishizing self-knowledge. Not only does Jim not need to know why he is the way he is in order to live a good life, but his concern for this knowledge is, in effect, making it impossible for him to live well. In seeking self-knowledge he thwarts the pursuit of his own practical goals.[50]

The Rationality of Self-Deception

A moment ago, I suggested that self-knowledge is epistemically mandated when the alternative is self-deception. But even epistemically required self-knowledge can come at the expense of *practical* rationality. This is because there may be painful truths about ourselves such that being deceived about them facilitates our practical functioning. There might be some truths about ourselves the knowledge of which would be so depressing or deflating or debilitating that we'd lose the motivation to pursue our life goals. Or, perhaps more compellingly, there might be forms of dissociation or bad faith that give us the ability to function despite trauma. A victim of violence might say to himself "This isn't happening to me" and might even come to deny that the violence ever occurred. Such denial may in fact be a common way that people successfully cope with abuse. This is not to say that therapies that bring such knowledge to light are not often helpful; nor is this to deny that there are unhealthy forms of self-deception. The point is just that it would be hasty to assume that conscious awareness of different facts about ourselves predictably affects our practical lives in one main way. But this is exactly what The Ideal of Authenticity as Self-Knowledge would require if it were grounded in an ideal of practical rationality. Self-knowledge might sometimes make it possible for us to make more rational decisions about what is best for us and about how we should live. But such knowledge might also make it very difficult to make such decisions. To put it succinctly, some memories might best—and here I mean most rationally—be left unrecovered. And the Rationality Account of The Ideal of Authenticity as Self-Knowledge cannot accommodate this important fact. As suggested in our last chapter (and as will be made clearer still in chapter 5), the most plausible account of what's bad about bad faith—and self-deception in general—is not its rationality, it is that it disposes us to mislead and harm others.

Interlude: Rationality versus Well-being Accounts of Authenticity

The Rationality Account of The Ideal of Authenticity that we have just rejected might be thought of as "strict" in the following sense: it holds that even though being rational may sometimes be bad *for us*, rationality is nevertheless an ideal. On this view of rationality it would, for example, be better to know a painful truth than to live in—even admittedly blissful—ignorance; it would be better to make practical decisions in light of all the relevant information, even if doing so might sometimes make us worse off;[51] and, in the interest of rational consistency, it would be better to have coherent and commensurable values even if this meant giving up some commitments that we care about deeply. On this strict version of The Rationality Account of The Ideal of Authenticity, the reason to be true to oneself is simply that it is a way of being rational. Whether rationality conduces to various other goods would be irrelevant.[52]

By contrast, according to The Well-being Account of The Ideal of Authenticity, the reason to be authentic was that being true to ourselves reliably makes our lives go better *for us*. Interestingly, champions of rationality might be inclined to make a similar case. A non-strict version of The Rationality Account of The Ideal of Authenticity might hold, then, that being *rational* in fact always, or at least reliably, conduces to the well-being of the rational person. And indeed, there is some reason to think it does. On the epistemic side, being disposed to believe the truth (about ourselves and the world), conforming our degree of credence to the evidence, and making good inductive generalization all seem to offer tangible benefits to our well-being. On the side of practical rationality, following the means-ends rule (i.e., taking the necessary means to achieve our ends), avoiding weak will, harmonizing our values and commitments, and being morally autonomous all seem conducive to making our lives go well.

But these connections between rationality and well-being are not, I suggest, enough to establish rationality as reliably best for us. The problem here is that all of these benefits of rationality accrue only contingently and inconsistently. While we can always imagine ways in which rationality might benefits us, we can just as easily imagine cases where it does not. And if this is right, then the claims above do not vindicate either a necessary or reliable connection between rationality and well-being. There may be some *conceivable* world in which being maximally rational would, without fail, be good for us (perhaps, for example, a world in which we were all thoroughgoing stoics), but this does nothing to show that rationality is an ideal for us here, in the real world, given all our quirky psychological dispositions (e.g., to be hurt by the truth sometimes) and needs (e.g., to stop *thinking* sometimes). Put differently, because we are constitutionally irrational, it is not reliably best for us to adopt rationality as our ideal. As I argued in chapter 1, it can be best for us to be irrationally weak-willed, to suffer from bad faith and self-deception precisely because the nearest possible world is not one in which our local rationality makes our lives go better; it is a world where we are strong-willed in pursuit of bad judgments and in which we suffer from knowing painful truths about ourselves.

In response to this, a strong proponent of the well-being benefits of rationality might propose two alternative accounts of the relation between rationality and well-being. A certain kind of "philosophically minded" person who wants to challenge the hypothesis that ignorance can be bliss may propose that ultimately, in the long run, it is best for us to make it a rule to be as rational as possible, even granting that doing so might sometimes lead to nonoptimal well-being outcomes in particular cases. This would be a kind of rule-utilitarian well-being-based version of the ideal of rationality on which it is conceded that, while in some particular and anomalous situations, truth or consistency might not be good for us, nevertheless, in the grand scheme of things, we do better if we adopt a policy of maximizing rationality. Now, notwithstanding some of the general problems with rule utilitarianism, it should suffice to point out that some of those purportedly strange cases where the truth is bad for us seem like they might be so bad as to undermine the appeal of a rationality-maximizing rule.

For example, in the movie *The Matrix*, the character Cypher decides to abandon the real world of suffering and death and return to the virtual world of pain-free juicy-steak-eating. While we might object to Cypher's choice on a variety of grounds, it seems counterintuitive to insist that it could not be good *for him*, all things considered, to return to The Matrix.[53] Given the evidence available to him, the chances of a good life in the real world are reasonably judged to be exceedingly bleak. If he were to follow an epistemically rational true-belief-maximizing rule, he would have no chance of bringing about what seems likely to be his best well-being outcome.

The other strategy that a defender of the well-being benefits of rationality might adopt is to insist that the truth is, noncontingently, always best for our well-being, even if we never experience the well-being benefits in any subjectively recognizable way. On this view, having true beliefs and avoiding contradiction would simply (in part or in full) *constitute* our well-being. Plato seems to have held the stronger of these views.[54] Epictetus explicitly thought that a fully rational person could not be harmed.[55] If some version of this position were correct, then rationality might turn out, *on well-being grounds*, to be a compelling and, perhaps even overriding, ideal.

But for two reasons I suggest this too won't do as a well-being defense of rationality. To insist that knowing the truth is always good *for us*, no matter the pain and suffering that it may cause, and independently of how it affects our experience of life, requires an account of well-being that is at least superficially at odds with common sense.[56] If we side with Aristotle in thinking that life's contingencies, or "moral luck,"[57] can make one's life go better or worse, then we should be inclined to think that "well-being" is not something guaranteed by the truth of one's beliefs or the coherence of one's practical life. Intuitively, for example, painful physical or mental illnesses *are*, as a rule, bad for us. This shows, minimally, that well-being is not fully under our rational control. But, more importantly, it shows that even were we to grant that rationality is an essential constituent of well-being, there would be other things that contribute to the quality of our lives that would have to be weighed against the occasional costs of rationality. If trying to be as rational as we can be would tend, at least sometimes, to make us miserable, then this prospective misery must be taken into consideration by any account of how we should live that purports to be seriously concerned with well-being. So, even were we to adopt this somewhat odd noncontingent view of the connection between rationality and a certain kind of well-being, this would not suffice to show that we should (nonstrictly) take rationality (or authenticity, on the Rationality Account) as our ideal.

THE LIMITED APPEAL OF RATIONALITY AS AN IDEAL

This chapter has argued that authenticity does not reliably conduce to rationality. Even if it did, I suggest that it should still hold only limited appeal because being rationally true to oneself can iminish well-being and conflict with morality (as I think Williams shows in the case of ground projects). But the idea that it might not be best to be rational may seem puzzling if we think that what we ought to do, all things considered, just is by definition what is rational. Put differently, the concern here is that whatever we ought to do (full stop) is what we have most reason to do. And what we have most reason to do is surely what is most rational. Or, in yet different terms, if normativity is itself to be explained in terms of reasons,[58] then it may seem paradoxical or perhaps even incoherent to say that it can be *best* for us not to be rational. After all, this sounds like an argument that there can be overriding *reason* not to be rational. The solution to this problem requires a clarification of the conception of rationality at work in this chapter (and throughout the book). I want to say that considerations pertaining to our well-being, as well as moral consideration, do provide us with reasons (and powerful ones at that) to do various things. When I claim that it can be (and probably is) best not to take rationality as an ideal, what I mean is that *the formal rules of rationality* are not themselves rules such that conforming with *them* reliably conduces across contexts to living well in the broadest sense. There is nothing mysterious about this claim. We *could* put it by saying that there are good reasons not to make it a policy to conform with the rules of rationality (whenever we are in the midst of making practical decisions). This would only have the ring of paradox if it meant that the formal rules of rationality dictate that we not adopt a policy to conform with them.[59] But this is not the point. The point is, rather, captured by claims like these:

- It can be good for us and morally best to be weak-willed (as when our best judgment is mistakenly self-injurious or requires significant personal sacrifice).
- It can be good for us and morally best to be psychologically dependent (as when our assertion of independence is morally vicious or antisocial or self-injurious).

- It can be good for us and morally best to be ambivalent (as when wholeheartedness involves imprudent commitments or self-deception that harms others).
- It can be good for us and morally best to lack self-knowledge or even be self-deceived (as when inquiry or self-knowledge would make us unreliable or unstable participants in social life).
- It can be good for us not to be morally conscientious (as when morality requires substantial personal sacrifice).

These claims all seem plausible. And what they show is that, given the kind of creatures we are, living with various kinds of local and formal irrationality is likely to be reliably best for many of us.

NOTES

1. See Lynch (2001).
2. Economists paradigmatically think that acting on self-interest of a special kind is the definition of practical rationality. This is a substantive rather than a formal conception of rationality in the sense that it is not (overtly) a matter of truth or consistency. It seems perfectly possible for a person to disregard her own interests without lacking any self-knowledge or being involved in any epistemic or practical inconsistency. I will not be focusing here on economic rationality, but in the section below on The Ideal of Authenticity as Moral Conscientiousness, I consider the structurally parallel substantive claim that rationality and morality necessarily coincide.
3. The parameters of the epistemic requirement to seek self-knowledge are, evidently, contentious and will be discussed below.
4. This qualification is added to rule out the rationality of acting on a misguided conscience.
5. In comparison to the Well-being Account and the Moral Account of Authenticity, the Rationality Account is most plausible as a grounding account that explains why authenticity is good, rather than a theory of what makes it good advice. (For a development of this distinction, see chapter 4.)
6. Arpaly (2003).
7. The phenomenology in cases like this could vary. We can imagine that Hailey feels good about exercising her strong will, as such, but also that she feels strong misgivings about neglecting her friendships. Relatedly, we might wonder whether we should say that Hailey is *subjectively* rational or not. Typically, when people do what we reflectively *think* they ought to do (even if this is not in fact what they ought to do), we judge this to be at least subjectively rational. I think this is less clear in cases like Hailey's, where there may be strong evidence available to her about what her correct judgment ought to be and where she may even be psychologically and motivationally responsive to that evidence.
8. Some might be suspicious of this analysis precisely because it seems to fit another problematic pattern that many of us are prone to: that of rationalizing our weak will. My response to this challenge is that it presupposes the sensicality of the very possibility I am proposing. The very fact that being weak-willed can so easily be rationalized (in the objectionable sense) shows that its correlate, irrational strong will, is perfectly intelligible, non-mysterious, and something we would do well to be on guard for.
9. Because evolution seems to have allowed or selected for lots of powerful immoral and nonmoral impulses, it's less clear on the sociobiological model (than on the

Augustinian/Thomistic model) why we should construe our moral selves as our true selves. I return to this point in my criticism below.

10. This case is inspired by Susan Wolf's discussion in "Moral Saints" (2011).

11. See chapter 1 on the well-being benefits of guilty pleasures.

12. See Williams (1999) and see chapter 4 for a fuller discussion of internal and external reasons.

13. This claim is also contestable. If we are internalists (see chapter 4) about practical reason (contra Aquinas and Kant), we might doubt that everyone has reason to be good.

14. Consider Annie, who wants to take her college's honor pledge seriously. On this basis she makes the moral judgment that she should not drink on campus until she is twenty-one. But this takes a huge social toll. Indeed, she is the only one she knows, other than her Muslim and Mormon friends (whom she takes to have deeper reason than she not to drink), who does not party. Does Annie's conscience rationally bind her not to drink? What the preceding has meant to suggest is that the answer to this question isn't settled by our understanding of the nature of conscience itself. Intuitively we need to make two further and independent assessments: we need to assess how wrong it is (relative to other considerations) for her to drink and we need to assess how important it is to her, generally to do what is right. If it's not that wrong, relative to other considerations, then it could be perfectly rational for her to drink. Likewise, if Annie cares more deeply and stably about various kinds of social and psychic experiences than she does about strict honor-code adherence, it could also be rational for her to drink.

15. In chapter 3, I consider and challenge the connection between this kind of independent and critical thinking and moral and civic virtue.

16. See Shapiro (2004). The political implication is supposed to be that one should never simply comply with a directive unless it is judged to be good. But if it is judged to be good, the fact that someone is telling us to do it is completely irrelevant. Says Shapiro, "[P]hilosophical anarchists delight in pointing out that the claims of authority are problematic even in situations when those in power are right. For when someone in authority commands someone to act as they should act, their directives are redundant."

17. See Goldman (2002) and Zagzebski (2003).

18. Interestingly, when we say that an argument is "compelling," we often mean that it has some pull but that we are not conclusively persuaded. Nevertheless, in calling it "compelling" I think we are highlighting the involuntary aspect of our attraction to what we perceive to be a good argument. What matters for our purposes is just that we don't hold it against someone when their argument is compelling (on the grounds that we are being coerced or forced into submission). Rather, we think that, to the degree we cannot resist the appeal of an argument, this is evidence of its merit.

19. And I think this is correct even if we are aware that we are not expert logicians. We are content to believe reliably, on the basis of simple, deductively valid arguments, even when we cannot see or articulate exactly what makes the arguments good.

20. This amounts to a defense of a moderate externalist position about justification; we are justified in holding the beliefs that are reliably produced in us, even if we cannot ourselves fully see or understand what makes those beliefs true.

21. See Kuhn (1996).

22. "Correctly" needn't be construed in a very metaphysically robust sense here, though it could be. The idea is just that sympathetic understanding of others' perspectives is enriching and tends to promote thinking and behavior that connects us with others and makes it easier to live with people unlike ourselves.

23. I make this point explicitly in chapter 5. There, I argue that the structurally parallel cases of Jamie (who is shaped by her sorority sisters' values) and Samantha (whom I introduce below and who "fits in" with her coworkers) seem to elicit very different critical judgments, suggesting that our "authenticity" judgments may be tracking moral intuitions rather than coherent intuitions about psychological depen-

dence or independence. I suggest in that context, also, that the very idea of psychological independence is somewhat metaphysically obscure.

24. It is worth mentioning here that *advising* people to be psychologically independent comes with at least an air of paradox (see chapter 4 for a full discussion of this issue). Conversely, we may not want to rule out the possibility that recommending to others that they accept the authority or expertise of another can be perfectly rational advice. The Rationality Account of The Ideal of Authenticity as Psychological Independence may do just that.

25. Frankfurt (2004, p. 96).

26. Williams (1976, pp. 208–209).

27. Ibid., p. 208.

28. Ibid.

29. Says Williams (1976, p. 116): "It is absurd to demand of such a man, when the sums come in from the utility network which the projects of others have in part determined, that he should just step aside from his own project and decision and acknowledge the decision which utilitarian calculation requires."

30. Given Williams' account of the close connection between ground projects and meaning, we might also consider whether ground projects reliably conduce to individual well-being. Interestingly, nothing in Williams' account of ground projects precludes them from requiring significant or even radical self-sacrifice. Those who commit their lives to the selfless cause of helping others may not benefit in any reliable way from their wholeheartedness (indeed, nothing seems to rule out the possibility of self-*destructive* ground projects). Those who would defend of wholehearted ground projects on grounds of well-being face a dilemma: on the one hand, endorsing the overridingness of *non*moral ground projects looks morally problematic, even potentially scary; but, on the other hand, if those projects are especially virtuous or nobly self-sacrificing, they are all the more likely to be bad *for us*.

31. If Hume is right, the only rational requirements governing any of our desires is that they are not conditioned on false beliefs (which we can stipulate Sergio's are not). See Hume (1985).

32. See Feldman and Hazlett (2010).

33. Nagel (2000, p. 23).

34. Ibid.

35. Ibid.

36. Taylor (1976, p. 289).

37. Ibid., pp. 294–299.

38. Ibid., p. 298.

39. Ibid., p. 299.

40. See James (2003, p. 524). In defending "the will to believe" (as against skepticism that seems justified by the incomplete evidence), William James seems to endorse a kind of irrational wholeheartedness (though he doesn't use either of these terms). Criticizing the skeptic, James declares, "It is as if a man should hesitate indefinitely to ask a certain woman to marry him because he was not perfectly sure she would prove an angel after he brought her home." In one interpretation, James is here advocating the importance of committing ourselves to certain things rather than allowing epistemically rational ambivalence to hold us back. This seems to resonate with Frankfurt's concerns about ambivalence (see chapter 1).

41. We might wonder whether this is a case where paralysis constitutes "practical incoherence" or proper moral attunement.

42. This might also be construed as a case where wholeheartedness about one thing (one's love for one's children) precludes wholeheartedness about another (one's moral choices).

43. Sartre (2007, p. 47).

44. Sartre (1956, pp. 96–97).

45. Ibid.

46. I return to a fuller analysis of this case in chapter 4.

47. There are important similarities between The Ideal of Authenticity as Self-Knowledge and The Ideal of Authenticity as Psychological Independence. Apparent failures of psychological independence (e.g., *Jamie, the Sorority Sister*) often appear essentially to involve failures of self-knowledge. One thing that seems to be going wrong for Jamie is that in adopting her friends' materialistic and objectionably gendered social habits, she is apparently forgetting (or not fully acknowledging) who she really is. The defender of the Well-being Account of The Ideal of Authenticity might worry that she is destined to be unhappy precisely because of the psychic costs of denying her true self. Like Jack, she's making choices that are bad for her because she is in bad faith. Recall, also, that this was one of the central problems with "double consciousness." In coming to think of ourselves as others see us, or as others want us to be, we may suppress or repress our understanding of who we really are.

Advocates of Authenticity as Self-Knowledge should thus naturally be concerned with the epistemic risks of psychological dependence of various kinds. But several points distinguish The Ideal of Authenticity as Psychological Independence and The Ideal of Authenticity as Self-Knowledge: the former focuses on failures of authenticity that have a distinctively social origin (inauthenticity involves internalizing *others'* values) and sees inauthenticity as essentially involving an inner *conflict* about who one is. By contrast, The Ideal of Authenticity as Self-Knowledge is not concerned with the causes of failures of self-knowledge, as such. Failures of authentic self-knowledge needn't essentially involve disparity between a true independent self and a false dependent self. According to The Ideal of Authenticity as Self-Knowledge, the idea is just that not knowing the truth about ourselves involves failing properly *to be* ourselves in a way that is inevitably, in some way, bad for us.

48. See Goldman (2002) and Zagzebski (2003).

49. See Lewis (2003).

50. Of course, in describing cases where self-ignorance seems rationally preferable, we are really just pointing to instances of the larger claim that ignorance, in general can be preferable. Consider the character, Cypher, from *The Matrix* who prefers to return to his previous condition of ignorance, to live in a wholly simulated environment, rather than to suffer the painful existence of the real world. His example should resonate with the argument of chapter 1 that we can't assume that knowledge is always best *for* us. Here, a lesson we might learn from Cypher's case is that his preference for the matrix may be *practically* rational, given his circumstances and his overall motivational psychology.

51. See Velleman's discussion of the right to die (1992) for an elucidation of how knowing our options can sometimes make us worse off.

52. For this very reason, I argue the Rationality Account seems to fail; most of us do not (and I claim should not) prize rationality above all else.

53. It's worth noting here that adopting this view of Cypher's decision to go back into The Matrix is perfectly compatible with Nozickian intuitions about the appeal (or lack thereof) of entering an "experience machine." Nozick's point is that most of us would not prefer to enter a machine programmable to simulate any subjectively desirable "experience" we might want (Nozick, 1974). But the reasons for preferring the real world needn't be well-being-based. So, one might consistently think that one's well-being is maximized in the machine while also thinking there are decisive ethical, aesthetic or even epistemic reasons not to get in.

54. Says Socrates in *The Apology*, "[C]ertainly, Meletus or Anytus couldn't harm me in any way: that's not possible. For I don't think it's lawful for a better man to be harmed by a worse" (Plato 2005, p. 129).

55. See Epictetus (2004).

56. This is not to say that the view is incoherent or clearly false. Rather, I think the defender of this view will simply be in a dialectical standoff with those of us who think that well-being, as such, is something that is essentially connected with subjective experience.

57. See Nagel (2000) and Williams (1999).

58. See Scanlon (1998).

59. Although, if Michael Stocker (1976) is correct, even this isn't strictly contradictory; it could be that the best way to *conform* with a rule is not to make it a conscious policy to follow it (or perhaps even to make it a conscious policy not to).

THREE

The Moral Account of The Ideal of Authenticity

If the value of well-being or rationality cannot vindicate our attraction to The Ideal of Authenticity, perhaps the Moral Account can do better. Recall the case of *Annie and the Honor Code*:

> Annie is in the grip of what feels like a moral dilemma. She's thinking about smoking some marijuana with her friends (she's never done this before, she thinks it might be fun, and she doesn't think it's wrong in itself). But she's a diligent student, attending a college with an honor code she's sworn to uphold. Annie has a great relationship with her mom and, knowing that she did some drugs in her day, decides to call her up and ask her what she thinks. Her mother, sympathetic, gives her the advice she almost always gives her: just be true to yourself. After some hard thinking, Annie sheepishly tells her friends that she's not joining them, she has too much homework (she doesn't want to sound self-righteous). The next morning, she finds out that Campus Security, having been called about noise in an adjacent room, smelled the pot and busted her friends, who are now facing a disciplinary hearing and the possibility of serious penalties.

Or imagine a version of Caitlin's case where her parents are telling her to be true to herself in making her decision about her pregnancy and it's clear that they mean that her decisions should be guided by her conscience, rather than by other practical or psychological considerations.

The Moral Account of The Ideal of Authenticity aims to show that being authentic makes us morally better or more virtuous people or, alternatively, that authenticity, as such, conduces to a morally better world. In *The Ethics of Authenticity,* Charles Taylor is clear that he thinks authenticity is a "moral ideal,"[1] arguing (against the "instrumentalism" of a well-being approach), that there is "moral force" to the ideal of authenticity.[2] Indeed, I think it is fair to say that Taylor's defense of The Ideal of Authenticity hinges on his critique of those who ground the ideal in hedonistic or aesthetic values. If we consider the five conceptions of authenticity explored in this book (we will return to Taylor's own moralized conception in chapter 5), we can see how they might resonate with the idea that authenticity is a distinctively moral ideal. If being authentic paradigmatically involves having a strong will or resisting temptation, then authenticity will seem to be something like a virtue, along the lines of temperance. We often say, by way of praise and admiration, that the strong-willed person has "integrity," or is "conscientious," words synonymous with strong moral character. Relatedly, the idea that authenticity is about thinking for oneself seems to have significant moral import. Thinking for oneself is thought by many to be an essential, if not the essential component of a good life, guided by conscience and critical independent thought. It is an assumption among many liberal arts college faculty, for example, that teaching students to think critically and independently is the basic way to foster a community of ethically engaged progressive and upstanding citizens. I have also regularly heard my college's honor code explained in terms of a moral requirement to be true to oneself, to live up to *one's own* values rather than conforming, for example, to various anti-social pressures. How plausible is it that being true to ourselves is, reliably, the best way to be the morally best we can be?[3]

In this chapter I object to the Moral Account of The Ideal of Authenticity by presenting compelling counterexamples, showing that authenticity does not reliably conduce to morality and that, indeed, inauthenticity often does. People can be authentic on the five conceptions we're considering, but also indisputably bad. It seems plausible, for example, that we can be conscientiously true to ourselves in the pursuit of morally bad ends. People who commit crimes despite widespread social disapproval may be highly psychologically independent so in that sense, authentic. But in thinking for themselves they may also think *immorally*. If one's iconoclasm involves flouting moral norms, then we should expect psychological independence to be morally problematic. Artists who may seem especially authentic may be so at the expense of moral virtue (this is an important element of Taylor's critique of an aesthetic grounding of authenticity). Similarly, as we shall see, I argue (contra Aquinas, Martin Luther King, Jr., and Kant) that thinking rigorously, consistently, and self-critically is no guarantee of thinking (morally) *rightly*. Despite liberal platitudes about the value of a liberal-arts college education, the formal skill of "critically thinking" for oneself is, as such, content neutral, so orthogonal to moral virtue. In light of examples like these, it seems that it pretty clearly can be morally better for people to be inauthentic and not be true to themselves. If we think people can be authentically bad, then surely it is morally preferable for them to betray their authentic selves.

This chapter also beings to highlight some of the moral and metaethical assumptions that must be made if one is to see a sufficiently close connection between authenticity and morality to generate a moral grounding of The Ideal of Authenticity. On the one hand, defenders of The Ideal of Authenticity sometimes seem committed to the radically relativistic idea that *whatever* one does authentically and conscientiously must be morally okay. This captures the intuition that none of us are ultimately in a privileged position to judge each other, so the only standard that remains is the standard that each of us chooses for ourselves. I agree with Taylor that this is an implausibly permissive ethical stance (and in fact may be self-defeating if authenticity is itself given a privileged or objective normative status).[4] On the other hand, others who invoke The Ideal of Authenticity do so with the assumption that it has specific and non-relativistic moral content. Some think that being authentic requires a very specific expression of one's racial identity or sexual orientation or gender identity (e.g., not "passing," or being out, or being a "real man," etc.). In contexts like this, I argue (against Taylor in chapter 5), that The Ideal of Authenticity functions to disguise various contentious and problematic moral views that would be better articulated without the distorting framework of true-self metaphysics and ideals. I claim that the Moral Account of The Ideal of Authenticity is particularly dangerous when it functions to legitimize a charge of inauthenticity against anyone who disagrees with our moral positions or with prevailing moral norms. Inauthenticity accusations are rhetorically powerful but also especially pernicious, as they direct us away from the contentful moral debates we might otherwise have. For example, one might think, apart from any authenticity considerations that there is a special political, social, or personal value in the solidarity of historically marginalized people. Or one might think that certain domestic or sexual relations are—or are not—better than others. Better to try to make the moral or ethical cases for these claims, I propose, than to resort to the morally stigmatizing and metaphysically suspect charge of inauthenticity. Better to abandon the Moral Account of The Ideal of Authenticity and instead just make the best authenticity-independent moral arguments that we can. But before turning to the details of my critique of the Moral Account of The Ideal of Authenticity, a bit of background on why the account might seem so compelling.

BEING GOOD BY BEING OURSELVES: FIVE KINDS OF TRUE-SELF MORALISM

Annie's case shows that in trying to be true to ourselves we are often trying to do what we think is right. The appeal of the Moral Account of The Ideal of Authenticity hinges on the appeal of the idea that being true to ourselves is a matter of being morally conscientious or morally good. Is there a tight connection between being conscientious, and doing what actually is right? Given the pervasive possibility of misguided conscience, it is less than clear that being authentic, as such, can be expected to conduce reliably to a moral life. To see why moral conscientiousness does seem closely connected to doing what is right, we will consider five powerful lines of thought suggesting why being true to ourselves can be expected to make us good.[5]

The first line of thought appeals to the idea that somewhere deep down within each of us is a kind of moral compass that directs us to the good, if we are just honest and vigilant enough to pay attention to it. As on Thomas Aquinas' view, this could have a theological explanation. Says Aquinas, "The natural law is promulgated by the very fact that God instilled it into men's minds so as to be know by them naturally."[6] Put differently, "[T]he light of natural reason, whereby we discern what is good and what is evil, which is the function of the natural law, is nothing else than an imprint on us of the divine light."[7] If moral knowledge is imprinted on us in this way, we can expect genuinely conscientious introspection to get us to it. Martin Luther King, Jr.'s civil disobedience theory relies heavily on this idea. Realizing that some interpreted his call for disobedience to unjust laws as "an invitation to anarchy," King explains that the person who follows conscience "is in reality expressing the highest respect for law." King's view is that a person who engages in a process of conscientious "self-purification" will be able, reliably, to discern what justice is.[8]

There might also be good *non*-theistic reasons to think that we all have access, within us, to some fundamental moral truths. Given our social nature, it is not crazy to think that we might have basic drives toward cooperation and mutual protection.[9] On this second line of thought, the proposal is that we have almost certainly evolved to be disposed to moral behavior. While an investigation of the vibrant debates about the sociobiology of altruism is beyond our scope here, what matters, for our purposes, is just the thought that our human nature might well incline us to the good if we can just get in touch with that nature.

Kant offers us yet a third possibility. If something like the Categorical Imperative (the requirement that we treat people as ends in themselves and not as mere means) can be derived from principles of reason (for example, principles of consistency or of universalizability), then being *autonomous*, or true to our own rational natures, would involve a fundamental moral constraint, guaranteeing at least minimal moral decency. On the Kantian view, we might say that following conscience, rationalistically construed, is simply equivalent to complying with the constraints of the moral law (i.e., following the Categorical Imperative).

What the Thomistic and sociobiological and Kantian views have in common is the idea that being true to our nature ultimately involves compliance with some specific contentful moral rules that are in principle accessible to all. By contrast, there are two additional lines of thought suggesting that being true to ourselves, no matter what behavior that ultimately yields, is always morally good or at least morally permissible. The first is straightforward moral relativism. For those already attracted to a subjectivist form of relativism, The Ideal of Authenticity, as such, should have evident appeal. If there is no objective standard determining what is right and wrong and if each of us is therefore, ultimately, *our own* moral measure, then it is reasonable to think that all any of us can be asked (or morally expected) to do is what *we* think is right or best. Some might find this morally terrifying on its face, but there are many reasons to be attracted to relativism. When people disagree about what is right and wrong, often there does not seem to be any way to settle the disagreement. The parties may agree on all the relevant empirical facts and it may not be obvious where to look next to settle the dispute. For example, people who disagree about the death penalty might be in complete agreement about all the relevant social and psychological facts. They might agree about whether it is an effective deterrent or not. But their *moral* disagreement may persist, neither party being swayed by the other's moral claims or arguments. If we become skeptical that there is any demonstrable standard of right and wrong that could settle such disagreements, and we are not tempted just to become nihilists or abandon our values, we might conclude that what each of us ought, morally, to do, is just what we individually, conscientiously, think is right. (How this might apply to the death penalty is beyond our current scope.) If we relativize morality to each individual, then, clearly, each of us is bound by nothing other than our own moral convictions. Being true to conscience would simply amount to complying with the only moral standard there is.[10] Correspondingly, if relativism of this kind were correct, then the only form of moral criticism that would ever be appropriate would be the charge that someone has not done what *she herself* thinks is right.[11] In Annie's case (above), if she is true to herself she follows the only moral standard that applies to her. Indeed, I think this resonates with a natural interpretation of Annie's mother's be-true-to-yourself advice; it seems to mean that if Annie is just true to herself *she cannot do wrong*.

Interestingly, this relativistic line of thought is one that is often articulated by my students in discussion of my college's honor code. At the core of the code (and many honor codes) is the pledge to "take responsibility for [one's] beliefs" and to have "integrity." It's natural to think that this means that the ethical standard in question is being *true* to your beliefs, being conscientious, doing what *you* think is right. To have "integrity" seems to mean acting on your values, not betraying *yourself*. Of course, this generates an immediate puzzle if we consider infractions of college rules that are nonetheless not violations of a student's conscience or personal integrity. We might understand Annie's predicament along precisely these lines. She doesn't think smoking a joint is wrong; she may even think it will be a valuable mind-expanding and social experience. Maybe *smoking* the joint would be the way for her to "take responsibility" for her beliefs and thereby translate her values into her choices. Of course, she also takes her honor pledge seriously, and she understands that it, at least implicitly, commits her to following the rules of the college and the law. But we can imagine her wondering whether she really did agree to all this. The pledge is a condition of matriculation, so the conditions of her honor code pledge are hardly free of pressure. Is it plausible to think that every incoming freshman is bound by "honor" or "integrity" not to have an alcoholic beverage before the age of twenty-one? In light of these complications, Annie's mother's authenticity advice starts to seem incredibly compelling as *moral* advice. It's not at all clear what moral *mistake* Annie would be making, *whatever* she decides to do. She may be violating the law and school rules if she smokes; but it is far from obvious that, in following conscience in that way, she would be doing something decisively morally prohibited.[12] Are we really in a position to morally criticize Annie if she decides to smoke a joint, thinking in all conscientiousness that it is not wrong?

Short of moral relativism, there is a fifth, related, line of thought that also supports a strong connection between being conscientious and one's moral standing. Consider this claim, which I'll call *The Culpability Constraint*: no one can be morally blameworthy for acting on her best all-things-considered moral judgment. This is meant to capture the compelling thought that no one can ask more of us, as a moral matter, than that we do our best to do what is right. Unlike the views we have been considering thus far, this is not to say that in following conscience we *will* necessarily do what really is right or permissible. Rather, the idea is that any of us who lives up to this standard is living as well as anyone can reasonably morally demand. According to *The Culpability Constraint*, we ought not to hold others culpable for doing what they *conscientiously* believe is right. We may disagree with them; we may rebuke them or constrain them if their conception of the good is sufficiently different from our own; we may even be sure they are wrong. But all this is compatible with thinking that we cannot reasonably have asked or expected anything more from them.

In support of *The Culpability Constraint* is the intuition that it is only fair to hold people blameworthy for wrongdoing if we think they knew better. This is why commonsense moral thought says that young children and the mentally ill (if they are incapable of making good moral judgments or conforming their behavior to those judgments) do not deserve punishment for their mistakes. Rather, what they need is correction, education or therapy. When we act on conscience, even when we are wrong, we can honestly say that we didn't know better and this is exculpating. According to *The Culpability Constraint*, "I used my best moral judgment," when true, is always morally mitigating, making punishment, and even reactive attitudes like moral resentment, inappropriate. If *The Culpability Constraint* is correct, we will thus also have identified yet another way that being conscientious is morally good: in being conscientious we keep ourselves in some kind of good moral standing, undeserving of blame or retributive punishment.

We've now got five different lines of thought suggesting that being true to ourselves, construed as being morally conscientious, is essentially connected with living a moral life—one theological, one sociobiological, one rationalistic, one relativistic, and one appealing to a commonsense intuition about moral culpability. If any of these is right then there will be substantial intuitive support for the Moral Account of The Ideal of Authenticity.

MORALITY AND AUTHENTICITY AS STRONG WILL

Alison, the Smoker has been our paradigm of Authenticity as Strong Will. She sticks to her resolution to quit, despite her strong desire to smoke. Is there any sense in saying that Alison is a *morally* better person for having conquered her addiction and quit smoking? On the face of it (assuming that smoking, as such, is not morally wrong), this does not seem to have any particular moral significance. But Alison does seem admirable. Her strong will is virtuous and it seems appropriate if our regard for her is raised by her exercise of self-control. In general, we probably prefer to surround ourselves with people disposed to exercise such control. Given the variety of potentially anti-social temptations we all face, we can expect strong-willed people to be better friends and citizens because such people will, by hypothesis, be able to control their anti-social or selfish impulses. Researchers have gone so far as to call the power to exercise self-control "the moral muscle."[13]

Moreover, if we think about people like Alison, we may reasonably judge that the exercise of self-control in one domain is some good evidence of a more generally reliable character.[14] Alison demonstrates a disposition to restrain herself in accordance with the dictates of her best judgment. Another observation suggesting the moral importance of strong will is that we take impulse control to be an important part of a child's psychological development and socialization. Parents and teachers appropriately reward such self-control and we plausibly take it to be an essential part of children's moral development.

Immoral Strong Will

Of course, it is also possible to exercise self-control in the promotion of morally bad ends. If a thief must overcome fear or squeamishness in order to perpetrate her crimes, this still seems like strong will. Is it admirable? Is it virtuous? Can we sensibly praise a trait of character while condemning its mode of expression? I am sympathetic to the idea that the strong-willed thief manifests some virtues of character (e.g., bravery, fortitude, etc.). But I also think it's clear that if we choose to say this, we are not committing ourselves to thinking that it is always virtuous, all things considered, to be strong-willed. Nor are we committed to thinking that it's even generally reliably morally best to be strong-willed. In order to know whether it's morally good for a person to be disposed to be strong-willed, we need to know more about the content of the person's motivational psychology. In particular, we need to know whether the person's best judgments are reliably morally good. If they are, then we can expect the person's exercise of strong will to be morally good and praiseworthy, overall; otherwise we cannot.

Alternatively, we might think that strong will is not a virtue as such, but is only admirable in a context where it functions to constrain immoral or amoral impulses. The Kantian idea that an action has moral worth only when performed out of duty, from a good will (as against passion or inclination) might seem to support the thought that strong will is, essentially, morally good. Indeed, the intuition that the person who acts from duty as opposed to inclination is more praiseworthy than the person who just "naturally" and effortlessly does good, seems to demonstrate the distinctive moral character of strong will. But a more careful reading of the Kantian point makes clear that it is not strong will, *per se,* that is morally praiseworthy; it is, rather, a strong will with a distinctively moral character. What makes strong will worthy of praise on the Kantian model is the *moral quality* of the strong will. Without such moral quality, control, as such, lacks worth.[15] Only in its presence is strong will quintessentially praiseworthy.

Against the Kantian view, but also against the moral value of strong will, is the possibility that strong will is at best a kind of necessary evil. Consider a virtue-based ethical theory on which the person with a genuinely good character does what is right as a spontaneous response to the perception of the needs and interests of others, and is correlatively averse to harming others for corresponding reasons. For the thoroughly virtuous person, properly educated and attuned to the good, strong will would be unnecessary. But in the absence of such thorough virtue, strong will would be a necessary corrective, admirable insofar as it provides evidence of attunement to the good, but not admirable insofar as its very necessity demonstrates an inclination to vice that must be corralled.

So, in assessing whether strong will, as such, is morally good, the three options we are considering are these: (a) It is morally good, as such, even in the case of the strong-willed thief; (b) It is morally good, as such, but only counts as genuinely strong will in contexts where it is exercised as a constraint on immoral or amoral impulses; and (c) It is a necessary evil, praiseworthy not in itself but only as evidence of some degree of orientation toward the good. For reasons described above, (a) will seem counterintuitive to many; and the plausibility of (b) may hinge on some suspect Kantian metaphysical ideas—for example, the idea that we cannot rationally will the bad. This leaves me inclined to (c) with the resultant implication that there is no essential or necessarily reliable connection between The Ideal of Authenticity as Strong Will and that which is morally praiseworthy.

In keeping with (c), a more plausible and much narrower claim about the connection between strong will and moral worth would be that while strong will is not morally praiseworthy as such, the strong-willed implementation of the edicts of *conscience* is praiseworthy, as such. The idea would be that it *is* reliably morally good to be strong-willed in the practical exercise of conscience. The fact that we can imagine a version of the strong-willed thief who exercises self-control precisely by suppressing her conscience suggests the appeal of the present view. A person who effortfully succeeds in doing what she herself thinks is *morally* right—and not simply what she thinks is best relative to some other, possibly selfish or nonmoral standards—seems, on the face of it, morally admirable even if what she does isn't in fact right. With this in mind, Authenticity as Moral Conscientiousness may look like a morally better account of authenticity than Authenticity as Strong Will. So to this we turn next.[16]

MORALITY AND AUTHENTICITY AS MORAL CONSCIENTIOUSNESS

Consider *Cassie and Her Conscience:* Cassie is thinking about plagiarizing her as-yet unwritten philosophy paper which is due the next day so that she can go see her favorite band with her friends. She's tempted, but after much tortured reflection decides that she couldn't live with herself if she cheated and, in accordance with her moral judgment, she stays in and writes her paper. In being strong-willed and resisting the temptation to cheat, it is natural to say that Cassie has been true to herself by acting *conscientiously* and she is praiseworthy for her decision.

Recall that *The Culpability Constraint* is a claim about the conditions in which it is appropriate to hold someone to be blameworthy or morally accountable for wrongdoing. According to *The Constraint,* no one can be morally blameworthy for acting on her best all-things-considered moral judgment. This is meant to capture the compelling thought that no one can ask more of us, as a moral matter, than that we do our best to do what is right.[17] This does not mean that in following conscience we necessarily in fact do what is right or permissible. Rather, the idea is that when we follow conscience we are demonstrating the proper concern for morality. And if we do what is wrong, out of conscience, we can truly say that we did not know better. It is because of this that, intuitively, we are not blameworthy. Others may disagree with what we have done; and it may be appropriate for them rebuke us or even constrain us (on forward-looking, consequentialist grounds) if they think we are a danger to others. But all this is compatible with thinking that no more can be morally expected of others than that they do what they think is right. If authenticity is a matter of acting conscientiously (say because the true self is the moral self), then there will be good reason to think that The Ideal of Authenticity has a moral grounding. Following conscience would be a way to ensure at least minimally decent moral standing.

The Moral Value of Violating Conscience

There are number of problems with *The Culpability Constraint*, as stated, but we will focus on one. The central problem is that some qualifications seem necessary to exclude from non-culpability those whose moral judgments seem negligently or recklessly misguided. There are people whose best moral judgment seems so out of keeping with moral common sense that we are appropriately unwilling to let them off the moral hook when they insist that they were doing what they thought was right. So, to be plausible, *The Culpability Constraint* needs to be supplemented by a requirement that the conscientious person meet some standard of reasonable moral reflection or moral inquiry. But even this might not do. In *Unprincipled Virtue*, Nomy Arpaly's central argument is that our moral assessments ought to track a person's character and not be guided (primarily) by the person's state of subjective rationality. If a person's conscience is thoroughly bad, then we have a case of the inversion of Arpaly's title: we have a case of principled vice. Looked at this way, it is anything but exculpatory to insist that though it was vice, at least it was principled.

What this line of thought suggests is that it is morally better—more praiseworthy—for a person to fail to act on conscience, if that conscience is itself distorted and especially if the failure of conscience is itself a manifestation of virtue. Arpaly uses Huckleberry Finn to make this case. Huck consistently thinks he should turn Jim, the escaped slave, in to his "rightful" owners. But Huck repeatedly fails to do so, and berates himself for his weakness. But what is clear from the story is that Huck is acting in accordance with his (unbeknownst to him) virtuous character, which is properly attuned, despite himself, to the goods of friendship and equality. Huck is thus praiseworthy for violating conscience. He betrays his best judgment, and in so doing, earns our admiration. Now, a defender of The Ideal of Authenticity as Moral Conscientiousness might reply, here, that though Huck is subjectively and phenomenologically acting against conscience, he is nevertheless evidently being true to himself. Deep down, Huck really is virtuous and we might say that he acts, authentically, in accordance with his virtue, despite the impulses that pull him toward vice. This is in fact perfectly consistent with Arpaly's virtue-based analysis.

The problem with this analysis is just that it seriously muddles our understanding of what conscience is. Should we understand conscience as that "voice" that speaks in the explicit language of morality? Or should we understand conscience as whatever motivational force in fact reliably guides us to do what is right? Though "thinking conscientiously" sounds like a highly reflective mode of thought, should we nonetheless say that a person can act conscientiously without even knowing it or even while thinking she is *violating* conscience? At least for the purpose of explicating the grounding of The Ideal of Authenticity *as* Moral Conscientiousness, it seems preferable to stick with an account of conscience that resonates with our subjective experience of it as a kind of moral voice. Perhaps a case can be made that Huck "really" is following conscience. But to make this case, it seems we must allow that a person can follow conscience in bad faith and out of apparent weak will. Whether these are even conceptually coherent claims is difficult to assess. But what is important for our present purposes is just that our understanding of the relationships between the true self, the moral self and conscience are at best opaque. When a good person does what's right, defenders of The Ideal of Authenticity as Moral Conscientiousness may want to say that she's been true to herself. But good people can still have deep and stable commitments that conflict with what is good; interestingly, some of those commitments might even be self-described as "moral" or "conscientious" by the very people who possess them. When they are, it seems *ad hoc* to claim that they are merely "conscientious" (in scare quotes) but not actually conscientious, proper. To take this route is to risk severing the link between conscience and the subjective experience of *thinking*, and this is a fairly high price to pay.[18] It also means abandoning what some think is true by definition and what was the original basis of the Moral Account of The Ideal of Authenticity as Moral Conscientiousness: that acting conscientiously is morally good.

But suppose we abandon talk of conscience, as such, and instead focus on the moral significance of *thinking independently*. Is there reason to think that being psychologically independent reliably conduces to being good or doing what is right? Many of my colleagues in the liberal arts take it to be a virtual platitude that thinking independently is a necessary component of thinking critically, and that critical thinking is at least one central way in which we become good citizens—if not good people.

MORALITY AND AUTHENTICITY AS PSYCHOLOGICAL INDEPENDENCE

We've already explored in detail two cases where it might seem that psychological independence is closely connected with moral thinking. When Caitlin is trying to decide what to do about her pregnancy, she receives a lot of strong input from her friends and family. Caitlin cares deeply about doing "the right thing" and she's been weighing any number of competing moral and nonmoral considerations. In telling her to just be true to herself, Caitlin's doctor might be construed as offering a kind of moral advice. One possibility is that the doctor thinks that thinking for herself (and not being unduly influence by social pressures) is the way for Caitlin to *figure out* what is right. Another possibility is the implication that doing what she herself thinks is right *just is* what is right. This second possibility might hinge on a generalized moral relativism (what is right is what we ourselves independently judge is right) or on a more narrow relativistic view about complex moral questions like the ethics of abortion (the view that on questions *like this*, what is right for each person depends on what that person thinks). On either interpretation, the common thread is that being independent-minded is Caitlin's best shot at doing what is right. A second case we've considered, where psychological independence seems especially morally significant, was the case of Jamie, the sorority sister. Jamie seems unduly influenced by her sorority sisters in a way that seems bad for her but also morally problematic from a feminist perspective—she changes her fashion choices and her sense of her own body because she's internalizing sexist gender norms. When her friends back home tell her to be true to herself, one thing they might mean is that if she reflects inwardly on who she "really" is, she will see that she's acceding to bad values that are not reflective of her authentic self. If Jamie succeeds in being psychologically independent, the thinking goes, she escapes a morally problematic materialism and avoids conforming with and propagating oppressively sexist values. The idea behind the Moral Account of The Ideal of Authenticity as Psychological Independence is that thinking for oneself is a kind of moral safeguard against conformity with bad—or completely absent—moral thinking.[19]

Iris Marion Young's depiction of double consciousness captures the moral significance of a certain kind of psychological dependence. Double consciousness involves "looking at oneself through the eyes of others, of measuring one's soul by the tape of a world that looks on in amused contempt and pity."[20] The result is

> fragmentation, the splitting of the whole person into parts of a person which, in stereotyping, may take the form of a war between a "true" and "false" self—or, in sexual objectification, the form of an often coerced and degrading identification of a person with her body; mys-

> tification, the systematic obscuring of both the reality and agencies of psychological oppression so that its intended effect, the depreciated self, is lived out as destiny, guilt or neurosis.[21]

Moreover, those suffering from psychological oppression of this kind "may find it difficult to achieve what existentialists call an authentic choice of self, or what some psychologists have regarded as a state of self-actualization."[22] If a person is never able to develop the capacity for authentic psychological independence, "the prefabricated self triumphs over the authentic self which, with work and encouragement, might sometime have emerged."[23] Psychological oppression thus stunts *moral agency*: in the absence of an actualized, autonomous self,[24] the psychologically dependent person is not able to *take responsibility* for her choices in a morally meaningful way.

Equally morally problematic is the cause of psychological oppression. Says Young,

> [T]hose living under cultural imperialism find themselves defined from the outside, positioned, and placed by a system of dominant meanings they experience as arising from elsewhere, from those with whom they do not identify and who do not identify with them. The dominant culture's stereotyped, marked, and inferiorized images of the group must be internalized by group members at least to the degree that they are forced to react to behaviors of others that express of are influences by those images.[25]

In criticizing the true-self metaphysics of psychological oppression, Jean Grimshaw nonetheless characterizes a version of the view in a powerful way:

> "behind this victimized female self, whose actions and desires are assumed to be not truly 'her own', since they derive from processes of force, conditioning or psychological manipulation, there is seen to be an authentic female self, whose recovery or discovery it is one of the aims of feminism to achieve."[26]

In other words, the recovery of the true self is nothing less than the realization of a self that is uncorrupted and freed to act, morally and responsibly, in accordance with its own undistorted moral vision. Achieving Authenticity as Psychological Independence, on this conception, essentially amounts to the shedding of a false and bad self and the recovery of the moral self.

Psychological Independence and Critical Thinking

For those of us in the liberal academy, there is another salient example of how psychological independence seems to have distinctly moral value: many liberal educators think that in teaching our students to think for themselves—or to be critical thinkers—we are providing them with the intellectual resources to be *good citizens*. As suggested in our previous chapter, thinking "for oneself" is often a way of gaining critical distance and this can, indeed, facilitate the kind of careful thinking that makes fallacious and sophistic arguments transparently bad. Critical and independent thinkers can sift through and identify bad arguments and be properly skeptical of claims presented without (good) evidence. And because there are many bad arguments for "bad values," this kind of independent thinking seems to have immense moral value, especially in a democracy.[27] Thinking for oneself thus appears to be an ethical and political ideal necessary for challenging our political leaders and voting from an informed perspective.

Even more radically (and this is often not stated explicitly), some liberal educators also think that developing a refined and critical intellectual independence is a central enabling condition for the construction and defense of good *progressive* arguments (I've seen this most clearly in campus discussions of climate change and abortion). Of course I do not mean to imply here that politically conservative educators do not also think that critical and independent thinking is an essential precondition for good moral thinking. On the contrary, conservative public intellectuals like David Horowitz make a case of a comparable kind, *against* their liberal counterparts: the problem with "elite" educational institutions, on the conservative view, is that they are sites of indoctrination, not education. The liberal hegemony within academia is, on the conservative view, precisely what is keeping young minds from thinking freely and presumably, also, from properly valuing intellectual and political and economic freedom. What the liberal and conservative perspectives have in common is the shared assumption that *independence* of mind facilitates a clarity of thought that can be expected to have a particular moral or political bent. Of course it is not a "bent" at all if it is simply the product of critical independent thought. And therein lies the appeal of the Moral Account of Psychological Independence: psychological independence seems like a formal, not a contentful feature of thought so (apart from the value placed on psychological independence itself) invoking it looks value-neutral and intellectually open-minded. If a certain way of thinking, which many agree is conducive to or partly constitutive of *rational* thinking, yields particular moral conclusions, then those conclusions may be accorded a special moral status. Of course, to the degree that independence of thought *is* a formal feature of thought, to just that degree we might be skeptical (*pace* Kant) that it can yield any particular moral conclusions.

The Moral Costs of Psychological Independence

In the last chapter, we discussed various ways in which independent, iconoclastic thinking can be irrational. Here I want to highlight the observation that these ways of thinking can also easily be immoral or amoral.

Thinking "newly" and "independently" (if that is even possible)[28] in a moral context is often synonymous with (and, perhaps by definition, entails) the subversion of conventional morality, as such. In some contexts we identify such people as revolutionaries or visionaries or liberators. What this shows is that psychologically independent moral reformers are, by their nature, socially disruptive. When "society" is in moral need of disruption, these nonconformists may hopefully and appropriately be hailed. But if conventional morality has much that is good about it, we can also expect moral iconoclasm to be morally risky or even downright dangerous. When we think of moral iconoclasts, we should be just as likely to think of Gandhi or Martin Luther King, Jr., as we are to think of Nietzsche or Heidegger.[29] [30]

While the experiments of social psychologists like Stanley Milgram and Philip Zimbardo[31] are paradigmatically taken to show the moral risks of obedience and insufficient psychological independence, the more general social-psychological lesson to be drawn from their work is about the moral significance of social influence, as such. Studies like Milgram's highlight some scary moral consequences of a failure of psychological independence. But there is also overwhelming evidence that forms of social influence and control can just as well be harnessed toward good moral ends.[32] Perhaps most intuitive is the thought that our values are *quite generally* propagated and instilled through socialization and acculturation. And this is not, evidently, something to be lamented on the grounds that those of us who internalize good values from good parents and good teachers have been the unwitting dupes of authenticity-subverting brainwashing.

Interlude: The Paternalism of True-Self Feminism

As we shall see in chapter 5, making good sense of the metaphysics of psychological independence is not easy. And in a moment, I will argue that even if there were always *some* reliable moral benefits to being psychologically independent, it is not reliably best, all things considered. But before turning to those arguments, it is worth observing some of the morally problematic rhetoric that can sometimes accompany The Ideal of Authenticity as Psychological Independence. While discussions of double consciousness and psychological oppression undoubtedly sensitize us to an important and truly terrible psychological dimension of institutionalized racism, sexism and homophobia, there can also be something distinctively patronizing and paternalistic about the project of revealing to others that their values and commitments are not really their own. In more extreme cases, descriptions of the "victims" of psychological oppression can be strikingly dehumanizing. As Grimshaw observes: "Any view which sees self-affirmation in terms of an 'authentic' inner self arising from the smashing of a socially conditioned 'false self', or which sees autonomy as a question of the origin of actions from 'inside' rather than 'outside', is almost bound to adopt, however implicitly, a derogatory attitude towards those who are not yet 'authentic.'"[33] She continues:

> Mary Daly's picture of the way in which women's selves are invaded by patriarchal conditioning is even more striking. She describes women, for example, as "moronised", "robotised", "lobotomised", as "the puppets of Papa". At times she seems to see women as so "brainwashed" that they are scarcely human; thus she describes them as "fembots", even "mutants".[34]

The attitude that these descriptions evince certainly seems ill-suited to improving the lives of the people so characterized.

Now, it should be acknowledged that the most well-meaning (or subtly manipulative) authenticity advocates may be able to refine their language in a way that is sensitive to these problems. Many people think that Oprah Winfrey succeeds on this score. Her evident empathy, even love, for her audience is rarely perceived as patronizing or demeaning by those who are receiving her encouraging embrace. But the structure of Oprah's relationship to her audience in many ways belies this apparent sensitivity. As Kathryn Lofton puts it, when Oprah says, "Girls, I'll guide you to your total originality," she is, paradoxically, communicating that the way to be original is to be just like her.[35] Putting aside Oprah's plausibly noble motives, then, the point is that the form and content of her helpful suggestions often end up being doubly self-defeating. First, simply in virtue of being an advice-giver, presumed to have wisdom, she is functionally introducing a further set of "external" values, and this, in itself, seems in tension with an ideal of psychological independence. (See chapter 4 for a full development of the paradoxical implications of the advice to be independent.) But second, and even more paradoxically, the content of her authenticity advice, the purported key to one's own "total originality," seems to be to be *like* Oprah—not in being true to oneself, but in consuming what she promotes, reading what she reads and thus *buying* into her cult(ure) of self-fulfillment. This nontransparent and self-defeating commodification of authenticity advice should seem especially morally pernicious to those who think that "genuine" psychological independence is a condition of full moral agency.

Of course, the question of what kinds of rhetoric are most conducive to various kinds of liberation is a difficult one. But if the preceding line of criticism is correct, one conclusion we can draw is that there are a set of distinctive moral issues that arise for those who think it is their job to liberate *others* from their false selves.

The Moral Value of Psychological Dependence

As noted in the last chapter, good (rational) thinking is often collaborative, intersubjective, and deeply social. If we were convinced of a close connection between rational thinking and morally good thinking, we might also draw the conclusion that good moral thinking must be collaborative, intersubjective, and social, rather than fundamentally independent. This might be an especially plausible account of good moral thinking if we assume that morality has, essentially, to do with negotiating interpersonal difference and disagreement. But we might, alternatively, be skeptical of any necessary connection between the relative (in)dependence of thought and its moral quality. It seems as if it is a contingent matter—and a highly variable one at that—whether conformity or iconoclasm conduces to moral thought and action. Imagine, for a moment, whatever you in fact take to be a virtuous society; I imagine it is marked by values like equality, respect, and collective welfare, construed in their ideal forms and properly balanced against each other. In such a society, I propose, we should be glad to have our young people acculturated with a sense of communal pride[36] and a collective moral identity. In such a society, we might reasonably think that thinking, morally, *like others*, will be a morally good thing. The visions of the ideal state that both Plato and Aristotle propose are ones in which "the people" are to be formed, morally by parents, teachers and social institutions that have themselves been properly formed in accordance with justice and virtue. Notwithstanding the model of Socrates (or perhaps in light of Socrates and his fate), most of us would not want to live in a society of free-thinking philosophers or iconoclasts.[37] With Aristotle and Martha Nussbaum, many of us would prefer to live in a society of citizens molded by the immersive experiences (with family and friends; with art and sport, etc.) that shape our moral emotions, often and sometimes even most effectively, without our conscious or deliberate awareness.

But at the same time, many of us are acutely aware of the ways in which our society is unjust and of the ways in which these injustices are perpetuated by social and political and religious ideologies that depend for their continued success on populations of "uncritical" citizens who experience the status quo as natural or unchangeable or good. When we focus on this sad observation, the appeal of psychological independence is undeniable because it seems like the first necessary step to moral resistance and reform. And this may in fact be so. What I have tried to show is just that it is not psychological independence, as such, that can be reliably counted on to produce a moral citizenry. The Moral Account of Authenticity as Psychological Independence thus fails as a general account of the value of psychological independence. If what we care about is morality, we will need to investigate the moral quality of our society, our culture, our institutions, and only then make a judgment about how it would be morally improved and whether such improvement is best brought about by promoting something like "independent thinking" or by modes of inquiry, discussion, education, and influence that explicitly recognize and even exploit our fundamental psychological and moral interdependencies. There is some reason to think that this interdependence is actually a fundamental precondition for the cultivation of moral conscience. And if this is right, it might turn out that thinking morally cannot normally be done at all in the absence of psychological dependence on others and perhaps even forms of psychological alienation that are characteristic of double consciousness. I turn to that more radical possibility now.

The Moral Value of Conscience as Double Consciousness

In chapter 1, I argued that certain kinds of guilty pleasures may actually depend upon a kind of double consciousness. Here I argue that conscience itself may have the structure of double consciousness and that we should not lament this. On many theories of psychological development, the capacities for abstract ethical thought and even for conscience itself, arise as the result of complex forms of socialization, where the key process is the internalization of pro-social norms.[38] With this in mind, a structural parallel between paradigm cases of psychological oppression and cases more naturally described as conflicts of conscience emerges. Consider a fleshed-out version of *Cassie and Her Conscience:*

> Cassie has been a fan of the band Quantum Doldrum for years. Her roommate, Jessica, informs her that they will be playing a one-night gig at Angst, a club about an hour away from campus. Unfortunately, Cassie has a huge philosophy paper due the next morning and it's nowhere near done. Cassie knows that Jessica has, in the past, turned in a paper that she downloaded from philosophypapersthatdontsuck.com. She didn't get caught and in fact got a B+. Cassie, who has never done anything like this before, is seriously considering it. She knows the practice is pretty rampant on campus and none of her peers think it's really such a big deal. Ironically, she's been reading Nietzsche for this very class, and she's kind of convinced that all this morality stuff is really just a vast hoax perpetrated on the naïve and weak-minded. Also, she tells herself, it's just this once and it's not like you get a chance to see Doldrum every day. But there is a nagging voice in her head telling her that it's wrong. In fact, she's pretty sure it's her mother's voice, and though she wishes she could be as carefree as her friends are, the voice just won't go away. Frustrated at her mother for the morally puritanical upbringing she put her through (and at herself for not being able to overcome it), Cassie tells Jessica that she can't go to the concert. She's got to write her paper.

Let's stipulate that Cassie's conscience is in fact the product of her socialization and that she is aware of this in a way that upsets her. As a matter of her phenomenology, Cassie is alienated from her own conscience. She experiences it as in some way "external" and oppressive, but she is nevertheless motivated to comply with the ethical norm. The case seems to be structurally the same as paradigm cases of psychological oppression (cf. *Jamie, the Sorority Sister*). But are we inclined to think that it would be better for Cassie to overcome her socialization and cheat?

There is a sense in which it might well seem better *for her*. If it weren't for the nagging voice in her head, Cassie might have gone to the concert and had a blast, felt no anxiety or guilt, and gotten a B+. In fact I'm inclined to think there are some serious prospective costs to Cassie if she tries to, or succeeds in, purging herself of her conscience. The process of undergoing such a change would, undoubtedly, be painful. She would presumably suffer from a degree of moral anguish as she tried to habituate herself to wrongdoing. And if we think there are also more general benefits to well-being that come from complying with moral rules, Cassie stands to forgo these as well. She might get caught and face resulting penalties; she might lose the respect of her teachers and her more conscientious peers. She also might end up, after her transformation, as the kind of person who is simply not trustworthy—and it's very hard to keep friendships and other mutually beneficial relationships in good standing if people don't trust you. So there is at least some good reason to think that it's not going to be good for Cassie to overcome her conscience.

But even granting the short-term benefits *to Cassie* of her overcoming her conscience, doing so does not seem worth it when compared with the salient ethical considerations. My own response to the thought that Cassie has internalized a norm that manages to constrain her and subject her to the looming threat of moral guilt is—thank goodness! Neither the fact that her conscience has an "external" origin nor the fact that she experiences it as alien and oppressive does the least bit to make me think it would be better if she did not have a conscience.

What this suggests is that we need to reflect more deeply on what is supposed to be bad about double consciousness. The problem, evidently, is not simply (1) that it consists in the phenomenology of a fragmented self or (2) the fact that the constraining norm has an external origin. (3) It is not the fact that the norm is self-imposed by the "victim" herself. And (4) it is also not the fact that the internalized norm causes the oppressed person psychological pain. All four of these features are present in Cassie's case, yet none of them makes us think it would be best for her to escape her conscience. If we think that *Jamie's* psychological oppression is to be lamented and overcome, but not Cassie's structurally similar condition, then one good hypothesis is that our judgments are tracking salient *moral* differences between the cases, not anything related to the self, as such, or The Ideal of Authenticity, in particular. It appears to be the *content* of the internalized norms that we care about and not whether they result in fragmentation, alienation, or pain. We only judge psychological oppression to be bad, and something to be overcome, when we think the "oppressive" norms in question are themselves bad ones. But if they are good, I suggest we are all too pleased to see people "submit" to them in the way Cassie does.

The case of conscience thus shows that seeing ourselves through the eyes of others and internalizing what are hopefully collectively beneficial values is plausibly among the most important ways we become morally educated. Ideally, such socialization becomes the basis of empathy, intersubjective understanding and generous fellow-feeling. But it also serves as a psychological constraint we should normally be grateful for. Psychological independence, as such, can be amoral and anarchical. The preceding suggests that double consciousness is a standing possibility for those with a properly functioning conscience. Double consciousness may thus be an predictable feature of reliable moral thinking itself.

MORALITY AND AUTHENTICITY AS WHOLEHEARTEDNESS

Recall, again, our romantic counter-hero, Sergio, our paragon of ambivalence in love. While many might think that his life would be improved if he were to become wholehearted (chapter 1) and others might think that norms of practical or epistemic rationality dictate that he do so (chapter 2), some, including myself, might think that the best reason for Sergio to become wholehearted is a moral one: Sergio's ambivalent relationship with David could involve Sergio's mistreating him. As we originally described the case, Sergio is prone to get frustrated with David when David exhibits some of the traits that are the source of Sergio's ambivalence. If Sergio's ambivalence consists in a kind of indeterminacy of feeling—there is no fact of the matter about whether Sergio loves David—this might also be confusing to David. Sometimes he is treated by Sergio with the deep affection characteristic of a person who takes another's well-being as seriously as his own;[39] but sometimes he is treated in a way that makes him wonder where he stands. The same problem may hold if Sergio's feelings for David are constantly oscillating or if Sergio is romantically torn between David and Geoffrey. In all these scenarios, Sergio's behavior may appear fickle and David (and Geoffrey) might have a legitimate moral gripe against him. How can David form reasonable expectations about how he will be treated when Sergio's behavior is inconstant and it is either indeterminate or unclear how Sergio in fact feels.

According to the Moral Account of The Ideal of Authenticity as Wholeheartedness, when we are less than wholehearted about others (or about other life projects), we are prone to just the kinds of behavioral and communicative inconstancies that Sergio demonstrates. For a case of ambivalence outside the romantic context, recall Jordan who has cycled through many careers over the course of his life and settled on none.

Now imagine the uncertainty and vulnerability of the people who might need to rely upon him. His partner may not know whether to rely on his paycheck. His kids can't be sure that his new job won't have different work hours that might change their daily routines. And if his colleagues know about his restless professional pattern they might have doubts about giving him certain longer-term responsibilities that normally come with his job. The point is that when there is no fact of the matter about what we "really" want or who we "really" are or, as the language of wholeheartedness suggests, what we are really committed to, we become unreliable partners, parents, colleagues, and friends. Settling who we are, by becoming wholehearted, thus seems essential to our becoming stable and reasonably predictable people, capable of being appropriately trusted and relied upon.

Frankfurt says: "[C]onflict within the will precludes behavioral effectiveness, by moving us to act in contrary directions at the same time."[40] I've argued thus far that we cannot assume that such "behavioral ineffectiveness" must be bad for Sergio or Jordan and that we cannot assume it is in any way irrational. What seems more compelling is the thought that it is morally risky to be ambivalent and that it is our morally best bet, as far as treating *others* is concerned, that we aspire to wholeheartedness. In short, when we are wholehearted, we are predictable and reliable, and these are essential to treating others well; in the case of wholehearted love we even go so far as to take the beloved's ends as our own.

The Moral Costs of Wholeheartedness

While there may be a variety of prospective moral benefits of wholeheartedness, there are also a number of moral risks that should be given equal attention. Two first kinds of risk are ones we mentioned in our discussion of the Well-being Account of The Ideal of Authenticity as Wholeheartedness. If Sergio feels compelled to act wholeheartedly in love, he may feel compelled to break off his relationship with David, rather than continue it in a less than wholehearted fashion. As a matter of moral luck this could turn out to be bad for David because it's possible that Sergio might have "naturally" shifted from ambivalence to wholeheartedness in the course of their continuing relationship. If Sergio is in the grip of an Ideal of Wholeheartedness he might not give the relationship the time it might take to become a wholehearted one. And in doing so, he potentially prevents David from experiencing the joys of what could have been a full and loving relationship. And if we add the possibility that David might be perfectly happy to take this risk, it looks objectionably paternalistic for Sergio to break off the relationship (on moral grounds). Now, if Sergio does not end his relationship because of a lack of wholeheartedness, an alternative is that he somehow wills himself *into* wholeheartedness. But this carries its own moral risks. On the one hand, it might turn out to be bad for Sergio to be wholehearted about David. Perhaps his ambivalence was for good reason (say it was responsive to evidence of their incompatibility).[41] If this is possible, then in becoming wholehearted, Sergio commits, fully to a relationship that might be bad for him.[42] But it could just as easily be bad for David, and for the very same reasons. If Sergio is wholehearted in his love and the two are nevertheless incompatible in significant ways, Sergio may be inclined to insist on the continuing of the relationship even if or when David is inclined to move on. If romantic ambivalence results in a kind of behavioral fickleness, wholeheartedness may manifest as a kind of monomania or romantic zealotry. It may not be easy to get *out* of a relationship with someone disinclined to ambivalence and this difficulty can itself sometimes be quite dangerous. A similar point holds with respect to wholeheartedness outside the romantic context. When we are wholehearted we can be expected to have trouble with change. Constancy and stability seem good, but when they come at the expense of flexibility, open-mindedness and a capacity to recognize when it is time to move on, these may seem less like virtues than like pathologies.

The Morality of Ambivalence

Initially it seemed that Sergio and Jordan treat people better if they became wholehearted. They would seem newly able to embody virtues like loyalty and trustworthiness. And because of this, when they become wholehearted, others are able to know where they stand in relation to them and make prudent choices in light of this vital information. But (even granting that wholeheartedness has its moral risks) is it clear that David or Geoffrey must be put in moral danger by Sergio's ambivalence? Is it clear that the people in Jordan's ambivalent life must be at risk? And, finally, is it clear that Sergio and Jordan must be disposed to disloyalty or untrustworthiness if they remain ambivalent? I think the answer to all of these questions is "no."

The intuition that David is put at risk by Sergio's ambivalence seems to rely upon two unnecessary presuppositions. The first is that David is either not aware of Sergio's ambivalence or that Sergio has somehow misled him about his feelings. But neither of these are any part of the ambivalence as such. Indeed, by description of the case, David has good evidence of Sergio's ambivalence: Sergio's inconstant behavior. Even if Sergio were not completely up front about his ambivalence (and, again, there seems to be nothing about the ambivalence that precludes absolute honesty about one's ambivalent feelings), David seems to be in a pretty good position to make informed and prudent judgments and decisions about the relationship. Of course, all relationships that lack completely transparent communication (i.e., all relationships) subject their parties to some moral risk. But is there any special risk incurred by David in virtue of Sergio's ambivalence? It's not clear what this could be, so long as David is in possession of the relevant information concerning Sergio's feelings and likely behavior. And this suggests the second important and unnecessary presupposition supporting the intuition that Sergio's ambivalence is especially morally risky: the concern about moral risk to David seems to presuppose that what David wants or needs is a very specific kind of romantic constancy. But we can easily imagine that while Sergio is the tormented ambivalent romantic, David is content to have some short-term fun with someone he's attracted to and finds interesting. In other words, unless we assume that David really wants or needs to rely on Sergio for wholehearted, committed, loving attention, it seems badly paternalistic to think that he is being put in danger by Sergio's ambivalence. So long as both parties make reasonable efforts to be honest about how they feel and what they want (and the difficulty and moral stakes of this requirement should not be underestimated), being in a relationship with a romantically ambivalent person poses no special moral dangers. Unlike the transparently romantically ambivalent person, there might, however be another kind of person who does pose a special moral danger to others: the person disposed to *act as if* he is wholehearted, when in fact he is not and misrepresents himself and thus wrongly incurs the trust and expectations of others. If romantic conventions or a certain romantic disposition inclines some people to profess their love when in fact they are ambivalent, this comes at a potentially significant moral cost. But note that the problem here is not with ambivalence but with dishonesty. And, perhaps less charitably, it is a problem with The Ideal of Authenticity as Wholeheartedness *if* that Ideal induces people—well-intentioned people who value wholeheartedness—to appear wholehearted when they are not.

There is one further moral concern with Authenticity as Wholeheartedness (outside the romantic context) worth mentioning. This concern stems from the thought that it may be morally appropriate to be ambivalent about some deep and intractable moral questions. Wholehearted moral activists may often earn our admiration but they can also run the risk of seeming (or being) ideological in ways that ignore or deny moral complexity. For example, those who see no moral ambiguity about the ethics of abortion may be missing some moral understanding that might properly induce a degree of ambivalence. The problem here derives from the possibility that an Ideal of Wholeheartedness can be at odds with seeing things clearly as they are. Ambivalence, as a form of skepticism, may thus reliably be the *morally* best attitude to take toward a set of difficult moral issues where reasonable disagreement seems possible. Ambivalence about such issues can be a manifestation of an open mind and open minds are modest, receptive of criticism, and less likely to indict others hastily. Contrary to the Moral Account of The Ideal of Authenticity as Wholeheartedness, ambivalence, in context, is itself a manifestation of moral virtue.

MORALITY AND AUTHENTICITY AS SELF-KNOWLEDGE

We said a moment ago that if Sergio subjects David to a moral risk, it is only if Sergio is not honest with David about his ambivalence. The moral dangers of dishonesty suggest the clear moral value of self-knowledge. Unless Sergio is aware of his ambivalence, he will not be able to communicate effectively with David and, indeed, it is even possible that Sergio will evince wholeheartedness in bad faith and thus potentially "lead David on." If he does so, Sergio's failure to know the truth about himself seems especially pernicious. With this in mind, defenders of the Moral Account of The Ideal of Authenticity as Self-Knowledge hold that the importance of self-knowledge is to be located in its obvious importance to our treatment of others. Allan Hazlett and I have argued in this vein that what is bad about bad faith, when it is bad, is the moral risk it poses to others.[43]

In chapters 1 and 2, we discussed Sartre's paradigm case of bad faith. In that example, the woman on the date refuses to acknowledge certain important facts about herself and her situation and in so doing fails, in existentialist terms, to take responsibility for herself. I have argued thus far that her bad faith may well not be bad *for* her; I have also argued that it can be rational, all things considered, to ignore or even repress certain facts about ourselves or our experiences. Here the concern is one that I find more compelling: that when we lack important knowledge of ourselves we run the risk of misleading others and incurring reasonable expectations that we will not be able to satisfy. In failing to acknowledge the truth about the man's romantic intentions and in failing to recognize herself as a facticity, as an object of his desire, Sartre's character, like Sergio, runs a risk of misleading another. If she "thoughtlessly" "allows" him to rest his hand on hers, he may reasonably think that she is romantically interested in him, even if she is not. If, through a lack of knowledge of ourselves, we are disposed to hurt others, this is a strong moral reason to take self-knowledge as an ideal.

Plausibly, there is an even more general moral duty to be epistemically responsible. If this is right, the value of self-knowledge might be a special case of the moral value of knowledge in general. In *The Ethics of Belief,* William Clifford proposes that "[I]t is wrong always, everywhere, for everyone, to believe anything upon insufficient evidence."[44] Why might this be? Clifford's answer is this:

> No real belief, however trifling and fragmentary it may seem, is ever truly insignificant; it prepares us to receive more of its like, confirms those which resembled it before, and weakens others; and so gradually

> lays a stealthy train in out inmost thoughts, which may some day explode into overt action, and leave its stamp upon our character forever . . . And no man's belief is in any case a private matter which concerns himself alone.[45]

On the face of it, Clifford is offering a consequentialist argument for adopting a very demanding epistemic standard. He continues, "[I]f I let myself believe anything on insufficient evidence, there may be no great harm done by the individual belief; it may be true after all, or I may never have occasion to exhibit it in outward acts. But I cannot help doing this great wrong to Man, that I make myself credulous."[46] By contrasting the "individual belief" with credulity, I take Clifford to me highlighting the standing moral risk of believing without evidence.

There are thus two salient moral benefits of self-knowledge: as a species of knowledge, self-knowledge contributes to well-being; possession of self-knowledge also prevents us from deceiving others on account of our own self-deception or bad faith.

The Moral Costs of Self-Knowledge

But neither the possession of self-knowledge, nor its pursuit are guaranteed to reliably promote proper treatment of others. Indeed, there seem to be perfectly normal circumstances in which valuing self-knowledge too highly might predictably corrode or undermine certain kinds of interpersonal intimacy and even trust. This is true, in part because in seeking self-knowledge we may sometimes (or perhaps, often, depending on various psychological contingencies) become skeptical about how we feel about others or about what we want from our relationships with them. On the first possibility, the pursuit of self-knowledge might reveal to us that we don't in fact have the emotions that our behavior seems to evince. And on the second, the discovery involves the realization that we may have false beliefs about our own social, interpersonal, romantic or moral values. Or, alternatively, ambivalence might sometimes be a quite natural product of introspection. Upon reflecting on our feelings we may discover (or indeed determine) that we are conflicted about how we feel or that we don't ultimately know how we feel at all. All of these possibilities pose some moral risk to those who may depend upon us. Of course, as we have noted already, whether ambivalence is morally risky is itself a contingent matter. If the people with whom we are engaged or the projects in which we are involved do not require any sustained expectation of commitment, then ambivalence might be unproblematic. But often, those with whom we are cooperatively connected do depend on our sustained and even passionate engagement and such dependency means that there will be a standing moral risk if we engage forms of reflection that might undermine our commitments.

Relatedly, the pursuit of self-knowledge can sometimes involve a morally problematic form of self-involvement. Here we need only imagine a kind of neurosis that involves a need to understand oneself that is heightened to such an extent that it comes at the expense of a concern for, or sensitivity to, others (pretty much all the characters that Woody Allen has played come to mind here). And, finally, when moral philosophy is taught well to those who have not thought hard about their values, the result can often be a kind of moral disorientation that has real interpersonal consequences. I have had students who, after reflecting inwardly about what they really believe, have declared themselves, Nietzscheans, Randians (indeed egoists of all flavors), relativists, and even on one occasion, white supremacist.[47] My guess is that this may be a more common occurrence in a certain kind of classroom that we might expect.[48] When we press ourselves to be clear about our own moral beliefs, there are no guarantees about what we will find. And whether we discover truths about ourselves, or whether our inquiry leads us into self-deception, either way there can be significant moral costs.

The Moral Value of Self-Ignorance

In light of the preceding account of the potential moral costs of self-knowledge, the possibility arises that we might be morally better people in the absence of self-knowledge. Digging deeply into one's sense of self and or one's values can change one. For precisely this reason, many of us think these activities are important. If we do think that psychotherapy and philosophy are morally important for this person, then they can also be morally dangerous. In this chapter's section on psychological independence I argued that we should be skeptical of any particular contentful theory of the relationship between critical thinking and moral thinking. The point is relevant here: whether seeking or acquiring self-knowledge is likely to make us better people or is likely to conduce to our treating others well, will depend upon what we discover about ourselves and how this newfound knowledge is integrated within our motivational psychology. Some might treat others better if they are in the grip of certain delusions or certain kinds of bad faith. I have a (nominally) religious friend who has told me that in his most honest moments of introspection he confronts the truth that he does not believe in God. But the thought terrifies him—on moral grounds. He claims that if he submits to his atheism he is afraid of the moral monster he will become because he believes that if there is no God, then all is permitted. Interestingly, none of my observations about his moral psychology quell his fears. I point out that he is a wonderful friend and husband and teacher and that none of these things would be different if he accepted his atheism. His compelling response is that his affections run only so far. His circle of concern is not as expansive as the domain to which his religion dictates his moral behavior must extend. While I cannot imagine what he would become if he "officially" lost his faith, his description of his own psychology is frightening. I, for one, will be glad if he continues to deceive himself, in his waking hours, that he believes.

ARE YOU YOUR CONSCIENCE? THE LIMITED APPEAL OF MORALITY AS AN IDEAL

If the preceding has been convincing, I will have established, contrary to the Moral Account of The Ideal of Authenticity, that it may often, and in many normal kinds of situations, be morally best *not* to be true to ourselves. Being strong-willed, psychologically independent, and wholehearted can, in all sorts of circumstances, make us morally worse people and dispose us to hurt others in a variety of ways. So can the pursuit or possession of self-knowledge. Perhaps more surprisingly, even if being true to ourselves is a matter of acting on conscience, it still isn't clear that this reliably makes us morally better because conscience may be distorted or misdirected. We should also keep in mind the reasons to be skeptical of the idea that being true to yourself is essentially about doing (or trying to do) what is morally right; it seems like there are many examples where, intuitively, we'd want to say that a person has been perfectly true to herself but has not even tried to do what is right.

Fortunately, most of us have been raised to take moral considerations seriously, so when we are in doubt about what to do, and we try to figure out what our "true selves" really think, most of us are guided, or at least constrained, by morality. For this reason, when Annie asks for her mother's advice, and the reply is "Be true to yourself," that advice is straightforwardly interpretable as *moral* advice. Annie is a morally conscientious person; this is why she experiences her situation as a moral dilemma in the first place. But surely not everyone is like this. If we imagine that Annie were very different, would we be able to assume that in trying to be true to herself, she'd be trying to do what was *morally right*? Some people may lack an attunement to moral considerations altogether; others might simply experience conscience as a nagging internal voice that is given some, but not overriding, or even special weight in decision-making.[49] It seems that people like this could be true to themselves *without* acting on moral conscience or even thinking about what would be morally right. Indeed, it seems that acting on conscience could even be a *betrayal* of a person's true self if that self were sufficiently devoid of moral commitments.

Perhaps even more problematically, there is also good reason for those of us *with* substantial moral commitments to doubt that being true to ourselves is essentially a matter of acting on conscience. To see why, consider a question of Susan Wolf's: Is it "always better to be morally better?"[50] Wolf argues that we *do* not and *should* not take morality to be the "comprehensive guide to conduct."[51] This just means that what is *morally* best is not always necessarily what is best, full stop. Wolf compellingly contends that various other good things in life, like friendship or having a sense of humor, can and should sometimes trump moral considerations. If you think it could be "okay" to help a friend who is no more deserving than others get ahead, or if you think it is "okay" to tell an hysterical but somewhat snide joke that comes at someone's expense, then you think that morality provides only some of the many practical considerations relevant to decision-making. You may think to yourself, "telling this joke is a bit morally problematic, but all things considered, it's so funny that it's worth it!" In Wolf's estimation, "[A] person may be *perfectly wonderful* without being *perfectly moral*."[52]

Of course, Aquinas, Kant, and others have significant replies here. To put it somewhat anachronistically, Aquinas might insist that those for whom conscience is not overriding are in some way alienated from their true selves, blind to the moral truth imprinted within them. Kant will insist that those who fail to see the rationally binding force of the Categorical Imperative are therefore practically irrational and heteronomous. On the Thomistic or Kantian view, the proposal would be that the failure to engage or act on conscience (perhaps the result of corrupting passions), constitutes a failure to engage our most important and defining capacities as persons. Rather than exploring the complicated metaphysics of these replies here, I'll just note that in order to convince those of us who are skeptical of them, these theories need to show exactly what kind of mistake is being made by people for whom moral conscience is not always decisive in practical deliberation.[53] We may simply *define* a properly functioning, rational, autonomous, or authentic person as one who thinks in a certain distinctively moral way, or whose thinking yields certain moral content. But in the absence of an independent compelling reason to adopt such a definition, we may reasonably continue to think that people can be fully "themselves," fully autonomous (in an admittedly non-Kantian sense), while not caring much about morality, either as such or in substance.

If, for most of us, morality is not our *comprehensive* guide to conduct, then the very idea that being true to ourselves is a matter of being morally conscientious is called into question. If we think about the relationship between our moral and nonmoral values in this Wolfian way, our "perfectly wonderful" selves are not overridingly committed to morality. If being true to ourselves is a matter of being true to our all-things-considered best judgments, then authenticity is not plausibly a matter of being *morally* conscientious at all. This is just what it means to say that neither morality nor moral conscience is our "comprehensive guide to conduct." If this is right, then we ought to doubt that conscience is the core of the true self, even for average, morally adjusted people. But even if it were, there would still be reason reject the Moral Account of The Ideal of Authenticity. And this is because, as Wolf compellingly puts it, it is not "particularly reasonable or healthy or desirable" to aspire to be as morally good as one can be.[54]

NOTES

1. Taylor (199, p. 15).
2. Ibid., p. 16.
3. Keep in mind, again, the three claims that I suggest defenders of The Ideal of Authenticity should be committed to: (1) Authenticity is about how one relates to oneself; (2) Being authentic is the most reliable way to live the best life one can; (3) The Ideal is inescapable and thus is normatively binding on all. Claims (2) and (3) seems especially plausible on the Moral Account of The Ideal of Authenticity because it is a particularly compelling idea that living morally is an ideal in the relevant sense and it is also quite appealing to think that morality is binding on all. Claim (3) is the least compelling and this is because it is not evident that morality as fundamentally about how we relate to ourselves—indeed many think it is analytic that morality is about how we treat *others*. But this is not incompatible with an account of authenticity that makes it distinctively moral. If the Moral Account of The Ideal of Authenticity is correct, this would mean that *in virtue* of standing in some proper relation to ourselves, we are either disposed or determined to stand in some proper relation to others. So the two conditions would either be coextensive or reliably connected (See chapter 4 on the distinction between a good-making theory and an action-guiding theory).
4. Taylor (1991, p. 13).
5. The list is not meant to be exhaustive.
6. Aquinas (2008, p. 11).
7. Aquinas (1913, Q 90).
8. See King (2008, p. 234).
9. This is not to say that our biological natures do not also dispose us to violence and aggression or that these drives are not truly "us." One possibility, though, is that to the degree that such drives are aimed at preserving our own families or communities they might themselves be understood as moral instincts. Of course this raises the difficult question of how to characterize the scope of the moral. I return to this question in chapter 4.
10. Of course this formulation itself raises some serious problems for relativism. There seems to be a dilemma: the view that it's *really, objectively* right for each of us to do what we, individually think is right, is evidently *not* relativistic. But if the view is just that it's true from *some perspective* that it's right for each of us to do what we, individually think is right, then it is also false from some perspective. Indeed, it will turn out to be just as true that we should not all do what we, individually think is right and this seem to fall short of what would seem to be required for a robust, metaethically relativistic defense of The Ideal of Authenticity.
11. By "criticism" here I mean rational criticism. As Gilbert Harman (2011) points out, there would be nothing inappropriate in simply condemning moral views and behavior that we think despicable.
12. Let's assume here that smoking the joint would not contribute to a violent drug trade or demonstrably harm anyone.
13. Mead et al. (2009).
14. Notwithstanding, here, arguments and evidence that there is no such thing as character at all. See Doris (2005).
15. Of course, Kant may deny that there could be such control of a *rational* kind in the absence of the motive of duty. If acting rationally entails acting morally and these

coincide with acting from a strong and good will, then it will be impossible to act with strong will but wrongly. I argue against this view, below.

16. Interestingly, the exhortation to *be* strong-willed is itself often morally fraught. The idea that being strong-willed is a key to well-being is something like a cornerstone of what we might think of as a libertarian, "tough-love" approach to self-help (see McGraw 2001). According to a version of the tough love ideology, our troubles in life are, paradigmatically, the result our own failures to live up to our own deep sense of how we know we should be living. On this view, the key to living a good and happy life is, first, to be brutally honest with ourselves about what we "really" want and, then, to exercise the self-control necessary to become those better, truer versions of ourselves. This means that the proper response to the personal failures of others is not primarily sympathy, but criticism. And, correspondingly, the proper attitude to take toward our own failures is not self-acceptance, but critical judgment and the taking of "personal responsibility." On this model of self-help, feelings of guilt and regret are there to spur us to change—they are the true self's call to action. When tough-love advocates exhort us to be true to ourselves, they are calling us to recognize that the exercise of goal-directed strong will in the pursuit of our deep values, is the essential means to achieving success in life. If we "let" our families and friends, or the media, or our addictions control us, if we take the "easy" path, it is our own fault for allowing our lesser, "false" selves to rule, and in failing to be strong-willed we have no one to blame but ourselves.

17. Note the incoherence of advising someone, on moral grounds, to act against conscience: "don't do what you think is right" is not a suggestion that can be conscientiously followed. Correspondingly, it seems morally appropriate not to hold conscientious but morally wrong behavior against the conscientious agent.

18. See Arendt (2006).

19. Ibid. These cases also highlight how slippery our everyday notion of psychological independence can be. Consider, for example, how the concept of "cool" implicates our ideas about self and other: smoking is often thought "cool" precisely because it is perceived to be countercultural, a symbolic act of transgressive independence. Of course, the countercultural appeal of smoking is also the product of advertising and our association of it with people who seem, themselves, to represent an ideal of iconoclastic cool (Humphrey Bogart, James Dean). As we discussed in chapter 1, *not* smoking has been made marginally more cool by slickly produced government-sponsored ads crafted to look like funky iphone videos made by hip teens "thinking for themselves" about manipulative cigarette advertising. The point is that, often, what looks or feels like authentic nonconformity, is just conformity of another kind. We might think of this, more broadly, as the paradox of cool: coolness is always associated with an air of iconoclastic authenticity but it is also something that draws us to emulate it. We want to be authentic *just like the cool people are*. The result, of course, is whole subcultures of people who dress alike, listen to the same music and project a collective "we-don't-care-what-anyone-thinks-of-us" air of pseudo-authenticity. The difficulty of thinking of these "followers" as suffering from a form of psychological oppression might begin to make us suspicious that there is anything wrong, per se, with a substantial degree of dependent-mindedness. I argue for this point in the remainder of this chapter.

20. See Young (2005, p. 101).

21. Bartky (p. 106).

22. Ibid.

23. Ibid.

24. See Arpaly (2003) for a discussion of eight different conception of autonomy.

25. Young, p. 101.

26. See Grimshaw (2005, p. 331).

27. See Nussbaum (2012).

28. See chapters 1 and 5 for discussions of the obscure metaphysics of psychological independence.

29. Notwithstanding the merits of Nietzschean or Heideggerian arguments, it should be clear that whether or in what sense Nazism resonated with of any particular conception of authenticity is a matter of important debate. The present point is just that there is reason to expect a connection, in some circumstances, between rejecting the moral thinking of others and the rejection of pro-social or egalitarian moral values—or even the rejection of morality itself.

30. Says Nietzsche, "[t]he noble type of man regards *himself* as a determiner of values; he does not require to be approved of; he passes the judgment: 'what is injurious to me is injurious in itself'; he knows that it is he himself only who confers honour on things; he is a *creator of values*." (2011, p. 123)

31. Milgram (1963) and Haney, Banks and Zimbardo (1971).

32. See Rosenberg (2011).

33. Ibid., p. 332. See also Frye (2005) and Millet (1977).

34. Grimshaw (p. 330).

35. See Schneider (2011).

36. Such communal pride needn't be parochial or exclusive—except in so far as it is based on a particular set of by-hypothesis good moral values.

37. See chapter 1 for a discussion of Tina Rosenberg's *Join the Club*, a powerful account of the social benefits of psychological dependence.

38. See Piaget (1965), Kohlberg (1984), and Gilligan (1993).

39. Recall that on Frankfurt's view (2004, p. 79), what it is to love someone is to be wholeheartedly committed to the promotion of the ends of the beloved. The ambivalent person is not so committed and for this reason does not express love. To evince only half-hearted concern for someone's well-being is, intuitively, not to love them.

40. Frankfurt (2004, p. 96).

41. This is another example of how wholeheartedness can be in tension with epistemic rationality (See chapter 2). For those who think there might be a reliable connection between rationality and morality, this would provide yet another reason to be skeptical of the moral value of wholeheartedness.

42. Should we count this risk as a *moral* risk for Sergio? We might think it is really just a matter of imprudence. But if we think of The Ideal of Authenticity as itself something with moral power, then we might be inclined to say that The Ideal itself is potentially harmful to those who hold it and that therefore The Ideal itself is morally dangerous. Alternatively we might restrict ourselves to the claim that promoting an ideal that is prospectively bad for those who hold it is itself morally problematic.

43. Feldman and Hazlett (2010).

44. Clifford (2003, p. 518).

45. Ibid p. 516.

46. Ibid p. 518.

47. In moments of optimism I have faith in the moral value of critical thinking. But my critique of the Moral Account of The Ideal of Authenticity as Psychological Independence returns me to a state of painful pessimism.

48. It should be clear that I don't think these shifts in perspective are necessarily justified. So the claim here is not that these students' beliefs about themselves necessarily constitute self-knowledge. Rather the idea is that if we take the pursuit of self-knowledge as an action-guiding ideal, these are some of the reasonable consequences; and these consequences are themselves morally problematic.

49. See Williams' discussion of Gauguin in *Moral Luck* (1999). In the example, Gauguin is described as someone who has moral concerns but simply opts to neglect them in order to pursue artistic success.

50. Wolf (2011, p. 482).

51. Ibid., p. 480.

52. Ibid., p. 481.

53. There seems to be abundant evidence from everyday life suggesting that people cannot be bootstrapped into moral thinking simply by appeal to natural or practical reason. Admittedly, this evidence does not establish that Thomistic or Kantian meta-

ethics are indefensible. But those of us resistant to the theological assumptions of Thomistic Natural Law and sympathetic to the idea that formal principles of rationality will not yield substantive principles of morality, are on good grounds to be skeptical of the success of these replies and skeptical of the idea that conscience, properly activated, is a guarantee of good moral judgment or behavior.

54. Wolf, p. 479.

FOUR

Bad Advice: Action-Guiding Rules and the Nature of Normative Failure

The Ideal of Authenticity is held by many to be the guiding principle essential for navigating ourselves through moral and practical dilemmas, for maintaining and promoting our (physical and psychological) health, and even for giving life its meaning. Because of this, it is unsurprising that it is also often invoked by its adherents as *advice* to those trying to make difficult decisions. Interestingly, one could endorse a version of The Ideal of Authenticity without thinking of it as essentially action-guiding. One could think that while we in fact live best if we live (or strive to live) authentically, nevertheless we should not adopt authenticity as our practical guiding principle. We might say that, on this kind of view, The Ideal of Authenticity would be a *good-making* theory of life, but not an *action-guiding* theory. To say that an ideal is part of a good-making theory is to say that, as a matter of fact, living in accordance with that ideal at least in part explains or constitutes what a good life *is*. More generally, good-making theories offer an account of what makes something good, for example, what makes a life good, or what would make the world a good place, or perhaps even what makes a cake good. Utilitarianism, construed as a good-making theory, offers an account of what makes the world a good place—its being a place where utility is, in fact, maximally promoted. Utilitarianism correspondingly provides an explanation of what the best world would be—a world in which there is as little suffering and as much well-being as possible for every sentient being.

It is natural to think that good-making theories will generally coincide with action-guiding theories because, once we know what *is* good, it will typically seem wise to adopt the promotion of that good as a practical policy. But good-making theories are, as such, entirely silent on the practical question of how best to *go about* promoting the good (e.g., making one's life good or making the world a good place). Knowing what makes a cake good does not obviously tell us how to make a good cake. With this in mind, we can see that the best way to go about living a utility-maximizing life (a life that is good, *qua* utilitarianism, as a *good-making* theory) may *not be* to adopt utilitarianism as an action-guiding maxim.[1] It might turn out that, given the world as it is, the best way to maximize utility is (rather than consciously aiming to maximize it) by cultivating a virtuous character, or treating some people preferentially rather than treating everyone impartially (contrary to classic act-utilitarianism taken as an action-guiding theory), or perhaps even following the Golden Rule. Correspondingly, if The Ideal of Authenticity were construed solely as a good-making theory, it is possible that the best way to go about *being* authentic might be *not* to think about authenticity much (or even at all) in our practical deliberations, let alone take it as our guiding principle.

This possibility—that the best way to achieve authenticity might be *not* to aim at it—should be especially plausible to those who think that a certain kind of spontaneity is essential for living authentically (call this The Ideal of Authenticity as Spontaneity). The idea here would be that thinking about authenticity and consciously trying to be authentic might produce a kind of self-consciousness that is in fact antithetical to authenticity and actually characteristic of *in*authenticity. On this conception of authenticity, the truly authentic are those who unself-consciously—without planning or orchestration—just naturally live in accordance with their true selves. By contrast, certain kinds of self-conscious people or those who experience significant uncertainty about who they "really" are (and these things may turn out to be connected) will be disposed to appear (and be) anxious or neurotic. The behavior of such hyperself-conscious people may thus appear and also, from the first-person perspective, *feel* phony or pretentious precisely because these people are trying so hard to be "authentic." This book has not thus far explored The Ideal of Authenticity as Spontaneity precisely because it is not a conception of authenticity that seems easily adoptable as an action-guiding ideal. This book focuses on The Ideal of Authenticity as a something that is thought to have practically guiding value, and for this reason it is something that is so salient in our normative discourse. But, again, for those who think that we have true selves and that living spontaneously, in harmony with those selves, is what makes our lives good, The Ideal of Authenticity as Spontaneity should be appealing as a good-making theory of life. But if thinking much about our own authenticity tends to undermine it, then The Ideal of Authenticity as Spontaneity will not be an ideal that it makes sense to take for oneself as practical guidance and it will not be an ideal that it makes sense to advise others to adopt as a way of approaching practical or moral questions and dilemmas. In the terms I develop below, advising someone to be spontaneous by advising them to think deeply about what to do seems *self-defeating*. The purpose of this chapter is to investigate whether the five conceptions of authenticity that we have been focusing on make sense when taken as action-guiding principles or given as advice. To this end, I proceed to develop some constraints on what makes advice, in general, *good advice*.

To get our thinking started, consider this *Grandmotherly Advice* given to an apparently happily single man:

> You're in your forties, Corey, and I really think it's time for you to settle down, get married, and have a family. Family is the most important thing in life and if you don't have your own, you'll regret it later. Raising kids with someone you love is the most meaningful thing you can do in life. You don't want to be alone when you're my age; you need someone to take care of and to take care of you. I know you think you're young but you've got to get your priorities straight. You need to keep in mind that no one is perfect and no relationship is perfect but you can't let that stop you from finding love. I had sixty years of wonderful marriage to your grandfather and I want that for you—and you don't have much time if I'm going to dance at your wedding.

Let's imagine that Corey reacts badly to the advice. Not only is he entirely unmotivated by it, but he's heard it all before; he feels like his grandmother is being presumptuous about his psychology and his needs; he feels that she is not recognizing his commitments; and he substantively rejects some of the values that the advice seems to presuppose. But is the advice bad advice? What makes it good or bad, *as advice*? In this chapter, I assume that advice can be assessed on a sliding scale: there can be better and worse advice and better advice, we shall say, satisfies more of the conditions on "good advice" that I will develop here. "Good advice" will thus be our gold standard for advice. In accordance with the idea of the sliding scale, then, we can say that advice can be right or useful or successful in certain respects without being fully "good advice" in our ideal sense. To the degree that advice is not "good" it will be deficient with respect to one or more of the conditions to be proposed. To help think about what the conditions on good advice might be, in what follows, we will be considering: whether and how good advice must be sensitive to the particular and contingent needs, interests, and values of the advisee; whether good advice must always be recognizable as such by a rational advisee; whether good advice must motivate a rational advisee; and whether there are any objective normative facts or truths that determine whether advice is good advice.

In exploring these questions, I start from the analytic assumption that good advice must, minimally, provide us with *normative reasons* for taking a certain course of action. This means that advice is, by definition, meant to provide advisees with reasons that justify a proposed course of action. When advice is good, these reasons do in fact justify that course of action.[2] With the above questions in mind, I propose seven criteria for good advice. Ultimately, the aim of this chapter is to argue that The Ideal of Authenticity, in its various forms, generally fares badly, and for clear principled reasons, with respect to these criteria. But before turning to that argument, first two preliminary discussions, one on the nature of norms, reasons and imperatives and one on the question of what advice is, as contrasted with things that may appear similar to advice but that I suggest are not best understood as advice.

NORMS AND REASONS

I've said that I will be assuming that if advice is good, it must provide the advisee with practical *reason(s)* to take a certain course of action. This is to say that I take practical normativity—the domain of normativity concerned with what we ought to do—to be explicable in terms of reasons. One thing this means is that it can't be the case, for example, that Corey *ought* to follow his grandmother's advice even though he has no *reason* to do so. Now, what the conditions are that determine when a certain consideration provides a reason for a person to do a certain thing is a large and thorny question. We might wonder, for example, whether there are any norms that are rationally binding on all of us, independent of our particular and contingent interests, concerns, or patterns of motivation. Put differently, are there are any categorical imperatives or are all imperatives merely hypothetical? In J. L. Mackie's terms, we might wonder whether there are any normative judgments that are "objectively prescriptive."[3] And this closely overlaps with the question of whether there are any reasons that are "external" or whether there are only "internal" reasons.[4] Do good practical reasons depend, for their normative force, on preexisting facts about particular agents' psychological make-ups? Must all practical reasons (and hence all good advice) somehow derive from, or "tap into," the psychologies or personal interests of the people to whom they apply?[5] Does Corey only have reason to follow his grandmother's advice if he *happens* to have commitments that will be best promoted by doing so?

While I will not be delving too deeply into the literature on these questions, they are important to ask here because the normative force of authenticity advice and its intuitive appeal as advice or practical guidance may hinge on various ambiguities relating to these questions. To see how, let's briefly compare two cases of authenticity advice. First, remember Caitlin, who is trying to decide whether to have an abortion. Her best friend, Batya, who just wants what's best for her, advises, "Just be true to yourself." Second, imagine Joe, a struggling filmmaker, who is considering taking a job at an advertising firm. His friend and fellow artist, Tamir, who happens to be a Marxist, advises, "Be true to yourself." In context,

Batya's and Tamir's advice may be of quite different kinds, invoking different normative frameworks. It is natural to interpret Batya's advice as encouraging Caitlin to figure out what *she*, Caitlin, thinks is best and do whatever that is. So, what Batya thinks Caitlin should do is implicitly taken to hinge on Caitlin's desires and values. By contrast, it might be natural to interpret Tamir's identical words as invoking a particular set of social and political values and advising Joe that it would be wrong to "sell out" and take the advertising job, even if he's tempted by it and even if it might well be good for him in various ways. The point here is that the kinds of considerations that authenticity advice tacitly invokes can vary widely and this variation may elicit different intuitions about the normative grounding of good advice. In order to figure out whether Batya's or Tamir's advice is good, we will need to identify what values they appeal to; but we will also need an account of what (if anything) makes those values *reason-giving* for Caitlin or Joe. As we shall see, Batya's advice could be bad (if it is bad) in various ways—for example, it could fail to be informative to Caitlin (it doesn't provide her with any new considerations to assess). But Batya's advice might fail for different reasons than Tamir's advice (if it does fail). For example, Tamir's advice could be informative to Joe but fail to motivate him. The most general lesson here is that advice can fail by failing to provide reasons at all; or it can fail to provide *motivating* reasons. This is important for our discussion of authenticity because it suggests, again, the diversity of constraints on good advice in general; it suggests that in different contexts authenticity advice can invoke a plurality of normative considerations each of which will require critical attention;[6] and it suggests that how and whether advice taps into the motivational psychology of a rational advisee is important to our assessment of the quality of advice.

So, returning to the *Grandmotherly Advice* for a moment, it will be instructive to inquire into what kind of imperative it seems to constitute and what kinds of reasons it seems to or aims to invoke. Let's assume that Corey's grandmother is genuinely concerned for his well-being, that she wants what is best for him. But, as noted above, one of the reasons her advice bothers Corey is that it feels to him insufficiently sensitive to his unique particularities. His grandmother's arguments seem to assume that *everyone* in a certain general position ought to marry and have children. He reads her advice as presuming that these activities are essential constituents of a good life and he hears her to be saying that if he doesn't see this, then he is simply failing (in her view, due to his immaturity) to appreciate a fundamental normative truth. This, we may presume, is what his grandmother means by telling him to get his priorities straight—the implication is that they are mistaken.[7] But when Corey reflects on what he has reason to do, given his current preferences, commitments, and values, his grandmother's implicit claims about the good life have no pull for him. If she could nevertheless be right about what he should do, then this fact about him (that the advice has no psychological pull) would be irrelevant to the quality of her advice. If she is right, then we can assume that if he were thinking properly, *if he were fully rational*, he would see the truth of her words and heed her advice. On this construal, we can say that the grandmother's advice has the form of a *categorical imperative* because its normative force is not meant *by the advisor* to depend on the particularities of Corey's motivational make-up.[8] Interestingly, the *Grandmotherly Advice* about marriage and kids does not obviously seem to be rationally inescapable in this way. Instead, it seems to me that its force appropriately depends on what Corey actually wants or cares about. If this is correct (and, as we shall see below, Corey's grandmother might dispute this), then the advice, to the degree that it is good advice, can only comprise a *hypothetical imperative* (in that its normative force depends upon the existence of certain contingent features of Corey's motivational psychology).

In saying that "family is the most important thing in life," Corey's grandmother may be interpreted as saying that he ought to desire marriage and kids because they are good. Let's assume that Corey's grandmother thinks that if he were to think about it honestly, he would recognize the good of having "his own" family and this would bring about in him the appropriate desire. This doesn't mean that Corey's grandmother thinks he should get married and have kids *even if* he doesn't want to. Rather, she thinks that if he were rational, he would desire what is good and see that her view of the good is correct. Of course, this may sound objectionably patronizing to many of us, so perhaps it would be more charitable to interpret the grandmother's advice as hinging on certain plausible observations about Corey: in fact, he doesn't want to feel lonely in later life; he does want to pursue meaningful activities; and he doesn't want to regret his choices when he looks back at them with the benefit of hindsight. And it's *possible* that all of these considerations could provide him with reasons to take his grandmother's advice. In Bernard Williams' language, there might be a "sound deliberative route" from existing elements of Corey's motivational psychology to a motive to get married and have kids. On this conception, any reasons he has to do these things would in fact depend upon and stem from certain antecedent desires he has and would be, in this sense, "internal."[9] The grandmother's advice might *look* categorical because she seems to be recognizing that his current desires do not support marriage and children. But the "charitable" proposal here is that she is attributing to him a set of desires and values that, at least to her, seem reasonable to attribute, in context. On the assumption that Corey does have those concerns and values (even while this fact might not be obvious to *him*) the grandmotherly advice could well be good. Indeed, Corey's grandmother might take the advice to be useful precisely because it directs him to introspect more thoroughly and carefully about what he "really" wants and in so doing he might come to identify what he has "really" cared about all along. Of course, it might turn out that he doesn't and if this is how things in fact turn out, then, because the advice is, on this construal, only hypothetical, the advice would fail to have rational force.[10]

So, to clarify the distinction between hypothetical and categorical imperatives we can say that hypothetical imperatives have this form:

> Supposing that you desire X, and given that by Φ-ing you can promote the occurrence of X, you ought to Φ.

And categorical imperatives have this form:

> You ought, rationally, to desire X, and given that by Φ-ing you can promote the occurrence of X, you ought to Φ.[11]

Advice of the former kind is common. I may suggest, for example, that you have dinner at Angelo's because I think you're in the mood for pizza. But there are also more subtle examples where the hypothetical antecedent is less evident: I suggest, for example, that a student of mine quit smoking but I do so on the (tacit) assumption that he prefers long-term health to the short-term pleasures of smoking and I think that my advice might provoke his reflection on this fact. But I grant that it is at least possible that he doesn't actually care about his long-term health or his future self and that this could, in principle, be perfectly rational (say, if he has a degenerative disease that he reasonably expects will end his life in his thirties). On the model of hypothetical imperatives, my advice to him to quit smoking would be less than good if it is based on a false assumption about the desires of my advisee.[12] By contrast, categorical advice is not retracted (or considered mistaken by the advisor) if it turns out that the advisee does not care about the normative considerations being invoked. Moreover, if there are in fact categorical norms, then one cannot get off their hook simply in virtue of contingencies about the content of one's motivational psychology. Now, there is a sense in which, in virtue of their contingency, hypothetical imperatives are in some sense weaker than categorical imperatives. It makes no sense to say, in response to a categorical imperative, "But why should I do what reason categorically demands?" But hypothetical imperatives are equally inescapable when the (sometimes suppressed) conditional antecedent is satisfied. So, it makes equally little sense to ask "But why should I take the necessary means to promote the satisfaction of the desires I endorse?"[13]

As we shall see, The Ideal of Authenticity, invoked as action-guiding advice, might sometimes be construed as expressing a categorical imperative. Indeed, on the Rationality Account of The Ideal it might be true by definition that it is—for example, if the advice to be true to yourself is tantamount to the advice to be strong-willed. If being strong-willed were a necessary condition of practical rationality, and if the rules of rationality were themselves categorical (because they are binding on us no matter our particular ends and no matter our preferences[14]), then authenticity advice would constitute a categorical imperative. In other words, the advice to be true to yourself would be required by an inescapable normative rule of rationality. Put differently yet, whether to be true to yourself (construed as a mandate to follow your own best judgment) would not be rationally optional.[15] The assumption would be that the authenticity advisee *must* follow the advice if she is to continue to be justified in thinking of herself as rational.

In light of the preceding, I will in argue that advice in general is prone to fail in two main ways: (a) by being so indifferent to the actual concerns and interests of those in need of guidance that it fails to motivate them or (b) by being so sensitive to those concerns that it turns out to be trivial or contentless. (Very plausibly, the true-self advice that Caitlin takes to be supportive and validating is bad *advice* precisely because it had no action-guiding content that she could conceivably disagree with.)

So, to sum up, I will be taking advice to be reason-giving and good advice to be motivating. Given these assumptions, it will be useful to distinguish between some things that might look like advice but that might be better characterized in a different way. By drawing these distinctions we will be able to see why invoking authenticity might sometimes have the appearance of advice when in fact it is not even advice at all. So, as we proceed through examples of things that look like advice but aren't, we should remember to ask ourselves whether and when the exhortation to "be true to yourself" really amounts to one of these, non-advisory declarations.

WHAT ADVICE IS NOT

Cheering Is Not Advice

"Go team, you can do it!" is a cheer but is not advice, in part because it does not aim to inform the "cheeree" of anything. Its purpose, rather, is *simply* to motivate or *simply* to demonstrate support for the person being cheered. One indicator that an exhortation is a cheer and not advice is that the cheeree will already be engaged in the pursuit of the goal whose achievement is being cheered for. This is, of course, evidence that that person is not asking for advice and also evidence that the "cheerer" endorses the goal that the cheeree has antecedently adopted. By contrast, advice is paradigmatically given when the advisor independently thinks the advisee needs direction (or redirection) or when a prospective advisee asks for advice. Advice offers something up for the advisee's consideration; cheering does not.

Collaborative Deliberation about Our Internal Reasons Is Not Advice

So, advice is usually given when an advisor thinks the advisee is in need of direction or in response to a request. But not all practical help offered under these conditions is best thought of as advice. Suppose, at restaurant, I ask a fellow diner, "What's good?" or even, "What should I order?" and the response is, "Are you in the mood for something spicy?" I may be asking for help in figuring out a course of action, but the reply (in this case explicitly) does not tell me what the advisor thinks I should do (though it does presuppose that I ought, presumptively, to satisfy my cravings in the broadest sense). The "advice," rather than directing me toward any particular choice, facilitates my own reflection on some possibly relevant criterion of choice. The advisor need not be invested in what I do, but is prompting me to think more concretely or more creatively or thoroughly about my own desires. The suggestion that I think about the appeal of a certain thing can very well help me figure out what to do. And, unlike a case of cheering, the suggestion does engage my faculty of practical deliberation and thus has the capacity to bring reasons to light. But what it does not do, and what advice paradigmatically does do, is aim to propose a course of action that is normatively approved of by the advisor. The help offered in this case can be translated to fit this schema:

> If it turns out that Φ-ing will promote the occurrence of X, and *if you desire* X, you ought to Φ.

I suggest that this schema does not in fact prescribe Φ-ing. Corey's grandmother could have said to him "*If* you don't want to be alone when you're my age, you should plan on getting married and having kids." This formulation is evidently much less patronizing precisely because it explicitly refrains from making any assumption about the "advisee's" actual desires and thus leaves it open to what (the advisor thinks) the advisee should actually do.

Implanting Desires Is Not Advice

"Are you in the mood for something spicy?" can be helpful in the above situation because it can direct me to reflect on my preferences, and introspection of that sort can reveal to me what I want and hence it can help reveal to me what I should order. But the same question might be helpful for a different reason—it might in fact *induce in me* a desire for something spicy, a desire which may not have been antecedently present. Sometimes thinking about possibilities that we haven't yet considered changes our desires and even the patterns of our preferences.[16] Just thinking about the spicy options might make my mouth water and instill in me a desire, say, for a plate of kimchee. (This contrasts, importantly, with the "internalistic" construal of Corey's grandmother's advice, above, where we imagined that her advice prompts him to *discover* a sound deliberative route from his already-existing desires to the practical outcome she is substantively proposing.)

Browbeating Is Not Advice

The suggestion that I think about something spicy might have the helpful effects of inducing self-reflection and of shaping my preferences. But sometimes suggestions aren't helpful at all because they amount to mere browbeating. There are cases where what might look like advice (because the advisor is invested in directing the advisee's decision and is recommending a clear normative position) is nonetheless not advice because the recommendation does not appeal to the advisee's deliberative faculties. Unlike prospectively helpful cases of desire-implanting suggestions (like the suggestion of something spicy), the present kind of "advice" falls short of being real advice because it does not offer any proposal for practical deliberation. If I simply tell you what to do, over and over, it becomes implausible to think that I am trying to redirect you to *think* about relevant normative considerations. You may ultimately do what I say simply to stop me from badgering you, but this, in my sense, would not be an example of your "taking my advice." If I only care about *what* you do and not *why*, I may be fine with your compliance with my directive, but this is itself evidence that my exhortations may not have been aimed at prompting your practical deliberation. Browbeating you to Φ may induce you to Φ, but it fails to be advice insofar as browbeating does not respect (or is simply indifferent to) your rational agency. After providing you with what I take to be the best reasons for you to Φ, and observing that you have reflected on those reasons and appear indifferent to them, I may continue to encourage you to Φ; but, if I do so without adducing new considerations in favor of Φ-ing, there is good reason to think this is no longer advice.

Demands Are Not Advice

It's also worth distinguishing between browbeating exhortations and *demands*. I might declare, simply, "You must Φ" or "I demand that you Φ." As in cases of browbeating, one thing missing here is evidence of reasons for Φ-ing being offered for the consideration of the "demandee." But what is distinctive about demands is that, rather than offering normative considerations that bear in favor of the merits of Φ-ing as such, they tacitly or explicitly invoke a form of authority intended by the "demandor" to legitimize the demand *as a demand*.[17] So, if a parent says to a child, "Eat your spinach because I said so and I am you father," this is not, intuitively, *advice* about spinach eating, even though it may well provide the child with a reason to comply with the demand. In the case of demands, the essential reason provided for compliance (if there is one) is that the party making the demand has the legitimate authority to do so.[18]

Commands Are Not Advice

Sometimes what looks like a demand comes with the tacit implication of a threat. Unlike demands, *commands* are backed by threats for non-compliance.[19] If, holding a gun, a mugger says, "Give me your money," this is properly understood as *creating* a powerful prudential reason for compliance. As with demands, the reasons provided for compliance in the case of commands are not reasons having to do with the distinctive merits of the commanded action. As with both browbeating and demands, commands, quite evidently, do not respect the deliberative autonomy of the commandee. Commands produce the very normative situation that makes it rational (if it is rational) for the commandee to comply with the command.[20] By contrast, advice aims to direct or redirect the advisee to the antecedently present features of the practical situation that are proposed as having special normative weight. As a test for whether a particular exhortation could be a case of advice we can ask whether the exhortation would be compatible with the addendum, "Of course it's up to you." If that addendum is added to demands or commands it clearly sounds facetious. Consider, "I advise you to give me your money; if you don't, I will shoot you in the head; of course, it's completely up to you." While we might think that it is in fact *true* that it is still up to the commandee to decide whether to comply with the command, what makes a command distinct from advice is that the commander is not aiming to *facilitate* the commandee's good reasoning, but to *limit* the parameters of such reasoning.[21]

Laws Are Not Advice

Related to demands and commands are laws which, on the basis of some legitimate authority, direct citizens or subjects to comply with certain edicts. I propose that laws do not constitute advice because they too are not (normally) compatible with the "Of course it's up to you" addendum. If laws are, by definition, binding,[22] in the sense that there is some (possibly defeasible) legal duty or obligation to comply with them simply because they are laws, then, by hypothesis, we have some reason to comply with them. But if the reason for compliance ultimately has to do with the legitimate authority of the lawmaker, then individual laws do not solicit compliance primarily in virtue of our rational recognition of the normative justification of their content. If laws constituted advice, appropriately assessed by each citizen for their normative merits, then (as some philosophical anarchists claim), laws would lose their obligatory status.

They would turn out to be more akin to suggestions whose normative force would be properly determined on the basis of each of our individual rational deliberations.[23]

The proposal, thus far, then, is that advice, as such, must be aimed at appealing to the deliberative faculties of the advisee, must be reason-giving, and must be practically helpful. On the basis of the preceding contrasts with what is not advice, I add that advice must not be mere encouragement, must not merely induce further thinking or implant new desires; it must not browbeat or simply appeal to legitimate authority or to brute power. In light of these observations, I suggest seven conditions of good advice. The aim in what follows, remember, is to show how, in different contexts and on our five conceptions of authenticity, The Ideal of Authenticity fails to meet one or more of these conditions of good advice. I will suggest that the ways in which The Ideal of Authenticity fails as action-guiding advice—or fails to be advice altogether—sheds significant light on why the advice is so seductive and also gives us strong reason to be suspicious of the advice's often hidden content and the often hidden motives of those who proffer it.

SEVEN CRITERIA OF GOOD ADVICE

We're now in a position to suggest a set of specific ways that advice can fail. Corresponding to each type of failure, we can identify a feature of advice that would make it good. As noted at the start of this chapter, I do not claim that valuable guidance must avoid all the pitfalls of bad advice to be important or worth giving. Nor do I claim that each of the good-making features of advice is a necessary condition on successful or ultimately worthwhile advice. Rather, the thought is that advice can be assessed overall, with respect to these dimensions. After exploring each of the seven proposed conditions on good guidance, I consider how each of our five conceptions of authenticity fares with respect to each condition.

1. Contentfulness (contrast with Triviality)

   "You gotta do what you gotta do." Taken in a certain way, this might seem to be a piece of philosophical wisdom. But, at least literally, it doesn't offer any actual suggestion about *what* you "gotta" do. If you sought advice about what to do and received this stoical bromide as a reply, it might make you feel some relief but, on the face of it, if a directive fails to propose any course of action at all, it is deficient in a fundamental way. We shall say that advice has *content* if it directs the advisee to take some course of action rather than some other live alternative. By contrast, when "advice" lacks content it is trivial or empty.

   One way that a claim, in general, can lack content is by being tautologous or true by definition. The aphorism, "It is what it is," is true by definition so lacks content in this way. But, like "You gotta do what you gotta do," it still may be pragmatically meaningful. Asserted in certain contexts, for example, "It is what it is" might express a kind of steely resignation to the way things are. It might mean, for example, that there's no point stressing out about something you can't change. "You gotta do what you gotta do" is similar in this way. Though literally contentless, it is generally invoked as a way of recommending acceptance of the best of a set of bad practical options. Correlatively, a piece of advice may look contentful but nevertheless lack content. Suppose a person in the midst of trying to resolve a moral dilemma is told to "do what's right." "What's right" is substantive in the sense that it rules out important (say, immoral) alternatives; but in context, the advice may be empty if it offers no guidance toward figuring out *what* is right.[24] Of course, there are also contexts in which "do what's right" is not trivial. If the advice includes a tacit specification of what *is* right, or if the advisee is considering doing what's *wrong* rather than right, then the directive would have substance.

Applying the criterion of contentfulness to Corey's grandmother's advice, it is clear that the advice is not trivial. She's telling Corey to take one course of action rather than the one he is in the midst of taking; so if her advice is bad, we will have to locate its badness elsewhere. We should not, however, confuse the contentfulness of a piece of advice with the question of whether it is informative.

2. Informativeness (contrast with Obviousness)

Suppose a teacher says to a lazy student, "You should really study more if you want to improve your grades." This may well be very good advice in a variety of senses: it specifies some course of action rather than another, so it has content; if followed, it might well produce the desired outcome and that outcome seems valuable, so the advice may be normatively correct (see criterion 7 below)—but the advice may also be completely unhelpful. It may be unhelpful for more than one reason (see criterion 5 below), but here our focus is on the presumption that the advice fails to *inform* the advisee of something not already known by the advisee. The advice lacks usefulness on this account. We can picture the student in question, quite clearly, thinking to himself, "Duh! I'm perfectly aware of my lazy habits!" The "Duh" reaction perfectly captures the failure of informativeness. The advisee is given no new information from which some better deliberations or choices can prospectively emerge. So, we shall say that a piece of advice is *obvious* if it fails to provide any new information to the advisee.

Is Corey's grandmother's advice obvious in this way? In one sense, yes. While receiving the advice he may be thinking, impatiently, to himself, "Yes, Grandma, I know you think this is what I should do." So his grandmother would not be newly informing him of an idea with which he was unfamiliar. She would be telling him something he'd heard before (likely from her, in which case the "advice" may look like browbeating), and this may account for a part of his frustration. But in a deeper sense, the advice is not at all obvious to Corey. Because he doesn't agree with the advice, the content or truth or correctness of the advice is not obvious to him. We can imagine, in fact, that this is precisely why his grandmother feels the need to offer it—in the hope that he will come to *appreciate* the force of an already familiar idea. When we hear familiar advice, but *see* it for the first time as *good* advice, it might appropriately be thought of as informative.[25] So we might say that if Corey's grandmother's advice is normatively correct (see 7 below), and if he is thinking properly, it would have the potential to be informative. This suggests that advice can be informative in at least two different ways: it can successfully articulate practical considerations that the advisee is not already aware of, or it can assert something that is known by the advisee but not yet understood to be correct.

3. Potential Usefulness (contrast with Superfluousness)

Advice is useful, in a general sense, if it can be employed by an advisee to some good or desirable end. Here I want to suggest a slightly narrower idea; we shall say that advice is *useful* only if there is a reasonable likelihood that the prospective advisee would *not* act in accordance with the content of the advice if it were not proffered. Consider, by contrast, advising a germophobe with obsessive compulsive disorder, "Don't forget to wash your hands," or a teacher saying to a type-A student, "Don't forget to do your homework!" There is, quite simply, no point in issuing the advice—it is superfluous—because there is essentially no chance the suggested course of action is not already among the advisee's overriding practical commitments. (Other examples of superfluous advice would be advice that directs activity that is already in progress or that is impossible not to do.) So, advice is only potentially useful—it only has a practical *point*—when the advisee is not already expected to do (or doing) what the advice recommends.

Corey's grandmother's advice fares well with respect to this criterion. He is clearly able not to comply with it; he is not predisposed to comply with it; and indeed he is in the midst of not complying with it. The advice is thus reasonably aimed at redirecting his behavior, so it is not superfluous.

4. Ought Implies Can (OIC)

Advice whose content will inevitably be carried out is superfluous; advice that *can't* be followed is equally pointless. Because advice is normally meant to recommend a course of action as that which ought to be done, advice aimed at someone who cannot do it violates that Kantian "ought implies can" principle: "[T]he action to which the '*ought*' applies must indeed be possible under natural conditions."[26] The Kantian idea is that it cannot be the case that one ought to do something if one is not capable of doing it. In a moral context this is, intuitively, a matter of the unfairness (and potential injustice) of holding each other to standards that we cannot meet. For present purposes, what matters is the apparent pointlessness of giving advice that can't be followed. In the middle of a squabble, a partner in a relationship yells, "Don't be mad!" The natural reaction to this is "You can't tell me how to feel." Over and above the fact that telling someone not to be mad usually has the reverse effect, advising people how to feel is generally bad advice because the advice normally can't *be* followed in any direct voluntary way.[27] If our emotions are not under our control, then the advice to change them on demand would violate OIC.

OIC is certainly contentious, perhaps especially so in the context of *ideals* where we might think it appropriate to aspire to and recommend certain standards even knowing that we, and others, may not be able (fully) to achieve them.[28] But there are also good reasons to endorse the principle. As noted, the principle explains the unfairness of blaming people for what they couldn't but do ("I couldn't help it," when true, seems to be an absolute defense against moral criticism); it also explains why we take small children, some mentally ill people and most non-human animals not to be subject to moral requirements. (There's no sense in saying to the lion, "Please don't tear apart that wildebeest.") These intuitions make good sense in light of OIC.

Could Corey take his grandmother's advice? There's certainly no logical or physical obstacle to his doing so; whether he is psychologically able to do so, given his current motivational set is less clear. There are three implications here: to assess whether various kinds of advice violate "ought implies can," we will need to determine the modal status of the "can"; we will need to determine what it means to say that certain courses of action are or are not psychologically possible for us; and we will need to consider how much evidence of a person's ability to comply is necessary for advice to be reasonable, in light of OIC.

5. Motivational or Practical Efficacy (contrast with Motivational or Practical Inertness)

Imagine that as you walk by a hardened meth addict on the street you say, "You really shouldn't smoke that meth." While it's not *impossible* that the addict might register the advice, be sparked into the epiphany that he ought to get clean, and go straight to rehab, the more likely result is none at all. This is the likely result even if the addict hears the advice and agrees with it. The problem with the advice is that it can't reasonably be expected to have motivating power. The advice isn't the kind of thing suited to elicit compliance in this situation.

Imagine, alternatively, that you are working on a Rubik's Cube but you don't know much math. A math professor walks by and, seeing you struggling, says helpfully, "Just work it out using combinatorics and basic geometry." As with the advice to the crack addict, let's assume that the problem is not that you are *incapable* of complying with the advice. If the professor sat you down for an extended tutorial, let us suppose you'd be able to get it. But as things stand, you have no way of translating the advice into any action-guiding rules that would actually help you achieve your goal of solving the puzzle. Corey's grandmother's advice seems bad in a way somewhat more similar to that of the crack addict than the puzzle solver. If we assume that Corey is fully engaged in life projects that are orthogonal to and incompatible with the advice, we should expect the advice to be motivationally inert. No matter how much he thinks about it, his circumstances dictate that it won't motivate him take corresponding action.

6. Self-Consistency (contrast with Self-Defeat)

So, advice can fail by failing to motivate or by failing to provide usable action-guiding rules. It can also fail by inducing action that is contrary to the very content of the advice. When this happens, advice is *self-defeating*. If I say to you in a snotty tone "Don't be pissed at *me*" I may thereby induce in you the very feeling that is being recommended against. The "advice" is logically consistent but the issuing of the advice is pragmatically in tension with the likelihood of its being successfully followed. "Don't think of pink elephants" is self-defeating in a more direct way; the advice can't be followed, as such, without at least initially violating it. Advice can also be self-defeating in a third way. If I tell you not to follow *anyone's* advice then, if you follow it, you violate it; if you don't follow it, you (perhaps) comply with it in the local case but you may run afoul of it more broadly. (As should be clear—and as we shall see in detail below—The Ideal of Authenticity as Psychological Independence faces this problem head-on.)

Though Corey's grandmother's advice seems acceptable with respect to this condition, we can imagine a scenario where her advice could be pragmatically self-defeating. Suppose that Corey turns out, upon reflection, to be disposed to marry and have kids but is also, for some complex psychological reason, deeply averse to taking his grandmother's advice. In that case, her *giving* the advice might be the perverse cause of his not following it.

7. Normative Rightness (contrast with Normative Wrongness)
   Perhaps the most salient way that advice can be bad is when its content is mistaken or false (normatively wrong). This happens, paradigmatically, when the values that the advice expresses or is aiming to promote, are themselves bad values. *Pace* Wolf, many would consider advice that is patently *morally* wrong to fail in this way. But advice needn't be morally wrong to be normatively wrong. If Corey's grandmother is wrong that the good life requires marriage and kids, this makes the advice bad in the present sense. Advice can also be mistaken in virtue of directing someone to take means not conducive to perfectly good ends (for example, "You should gargle sand to quench your thirst"). If we suppose that Corey's grandmother really just wants him to be happy, but that she's wrong in thinking that his getting married will make him happy, then the advice is wrong in virtue of a false empirical prediction about Corey. What these cases all have in common is that the *content* of the advice is problematic in one way or another.

To sum up, we can say that advice can be sub-optimal in a variety of ways. Advice is deficient:

1. when it lacks content;
2. when it has content but isn't informative to the advisee;
3. when it has content but is superfluous or redundant;
4. when it can't be followed;
5. when it fails to engage rational motivation conducive to its own purposes;
6. when it induces action contrary to those purposes;
7. when its content is mistaken.

How do our five conceptions of The Ideal of Authenticity fare with respect to these features of bad advice?

THE IDEAL OF AUTHENTICITY IS BAD ADVICE

The Ideal of Authenticity as Strong Will

Recall Alison, who has resolved to quit smoking and who experiences her strong will in resisting temptation as a way of being true to herself. If we imagine a good friend reminding her, when she's tempted to smoke, of her resolution to quit and encouraging her to be strong and true to herself, this sounds like pretty good advice. But is it? On the face if it, this authenticity advice is directing Alison not to smoke, so it seems to have clear content (1). The advice may also contribute to Alison's resolve, so it is potentially well-suited to motivating her (5).[29] In virtue of this (and notwithstanding controversial claims about whether addictions are literally compulsive), the advice clearly *can* be followed (4) and is not evidently self-defeating (6). Moreover, given the clear prospect that Alison might still choose to smoke, the advice is not superfluous (3). The advice will also seem normatively correct to most of us if we agree that smoking is, all things considered, bad (7); if we think health is a component of the good life, then we will agree with the underlying value that the advice is promoting; and even if we think that health isn't objectively valuable (but only has value if it is part of what Alison cares about), the advice still seems good because it is directly sensitive to Alison's own practical commitments. The advice is aimed at helping Alison achieve her own goals. So, whether we think the advice constitutes a categorical or hypothetical imperative its content still looks good.

The remaining question is whether the advice is informative to Alison (2), and here the answer is, pretty clearly, not. By our description of the case, Alison is trying to stick to her guns and not smoke, so the advice—to be true to herself and stick to her guns—could not be more obvious to her. Alison is *already trying* to do what she has antecedently judged to be best. And her friend is simply reaffirming this aim. What I think this suggests is that what might look like eminently good advice in this situation *is not really advice at all*. As noted above, there is an important difference between motivating someone in a certain direction by cheering them on and motivating them by offering up considerations intended to promote practical deliberation about what to do. But Alison's problem here is not that she doesn't know what to do; it's that she's having a bit of trouble motivating herself to do it. And while her friend's encouragement to be true to herself might well help Alison with exactly what she needs (that is, strength of will), that encouragement is not evidently functioning by appeal to her rational faculties; her faculty of practical reason has done all it needs to do; she's made her best practical judgment; what's left is just for her to translate this judgment into action. And my suggestion here is that if the encouragement "works," it is not because Alison is newly appreciating the importance of any consideration she was not already aware of (including the value of being strong-willed or true to herself).[30]

Recall that The Ideal of Authenticity as Strong Will amounts to this thought: to be true to yourself is to do what you judge best, all things considered. This was thought to be a basic requirement of practical rationality. Notice that, from the first-person perspective, one can't sensically say to oneself, "Don't do what you think is best," or coherently ask oneself, "Ought I do what I think is best?" *Advising* Alison to be herself by being strong-willed is thus tantamount to the advice to "Be rational." And if being rational in the practical domain just amounts to doing "what should be done," then contrary to what was proposed two paragraphs ago, the advice turns out to be trivial (1). To put the point more bluntly: Alison has reflectively judged what she thinks is best; Alison's friend knows that Alison thinks quitting is best and the friend is then "advising" Alison to do what she thinks is best. So, the "advice" reduces to this: "Alison, do what you explicitly know you should do." This is patently uninformative because it's partly constitutive of being a practical reasoner that one is disposed to strive to do what seems right from the first-person perspective. By hypothesis, Alison *is* a practical reasoner, so the advice, if it is advice at all, is trivial, uninformative, and obvious. It means, essentially, "You ought to do what you ought to do, given your nature."[31]

There are four further reasons to doubt that the advice to be strong-willed is generally useful, motivating, or normatively correct: the first is that in cases where there is no fact of the matter about what a person judges to be best, authenticity advice, construed as advice to be strong-willed, will violate OIC (4) and thus be practically inert (5). In Alison's case, there is a fact of the matter about what she thinks is best, so by hypothesis, there is a fact of the matter about what it would mean for her to be strong-willed and true to herself. But in other kinds of cases, there may be no determinate fact of the matter. For example, when Caitlin's doctor tells her to be strong-willed in her abortion decision, but Caitlin has no idea what she thinks is best, then there is no way for her to follow the advice. A second, more interesting issue has to do with the obscure metaphysics of weak will and this correlative question: why would anyone consciously and deliberately act contrary to her occurent best judgment?[32] If there is no good answer to this question, then we might be tempted by the thought that it's actually psychologically impossible (contrary to the evident phenomenology) to act contrary to our best judgment. This may be construed as a charitable (from the perspective of rationality) interpretation of apparently "weak-willed" behavior. Given that weak will is evidently (locally) irrational it might seem preferable to assume that people's choices do correspond to their best judgments and that when their choices appear not to, this is evidence that they've changed their minds or that what they report to be their best judgment isn't necessarily so. We thus might want to resist attributing irrationality to people who are making perfectly intelligible decisions.[33] At any rate, for those who think this approach is plausible, then the advice to be strong-willed might be superfluous (3) for a quite general and principled reason and that reason is (on the current proposal) that weak will is, strictly speaking, impossible.[34]

A third issue worth considering is whether advice to be strong-willed might ever be self-defeating. I'm inclined to think that, though reflecting on the importance of one's resolve can often be motivating (and helpfully cheered), it can also sometimes be dispiriting. Reflecting on the state of one's habitually weak will can fill a person with doubts about the power of one's will; moreover, repeatedly telling ourselves to be strong and not do certain things that we have a strong desire to do keeps those things salient in our minds and can threaten resolve. A too frequent reminder to be true to my resolutions might convince me that it's just too hard and I might as well give up. Fourth, and finally, it should be kept in mind that it's possible to be strong-willed in pursuit of what is bad or wrong (this was a central argument of chapter 3); so while the advice to Alison seems normatively correct, there is no general reason to think that advice to be strong-willed must fare well with respect to our seventh criterion of good advice, normative rightness. A person can comply with The Ideal of Authenticity as Strong Will and be thoroughly terrible—if the person's best judgments are terrible. So there is no particular reason to presume that the advice to be authentically strong-willed will generally be good advice, as far as its *content* is concerned. That said, I think the most difficult challenge for the advocate of Authenticity as Strong Will is to explain how the advice could possibly be informative or rationally useful. If a person is in the midst of trying to stick to her resolve, it's hard to see how the advice to be true to herself could provide any new information relevant to her practical decision-making, so the "advice" looks like mere cheering and thus not like any kind of advice at all.[35]

The Ideal of Authenticity as Psychological Independence

Recall *Jamie, the Sorority Sister.* In response to the social pressure of her sorority sisters (about which she is conflicted), she quits shotput, starts dressing differently, and generally changes a variety of behaviors to conform to these new friends' gendered social expectations. When Jamie goes home to visit her old high school friends (who loved her the way she was), she is somewhat unrecognizable to them with her long hair and her new clothes and they tell her that she should be true to herself. We can imagine that what they mean is that Jamie should have more confidence in herself; that she shouldn't feel the need to conform with other people's standards; that she should resist their undue influence and be who she really is, not who *they* want her to be. They are advising her to be herself by being psychologically independent. Like the "advice" intended to help Alison quit smoking, this authenticity advice may look pretty good at first glance. The advice directs Jamie to think for herself about her choices and it directs her toward a substantive course of action that is different from the course she is currently taking. So the advice evidently has content (1) and is also not superfluous (3). Given some reasonable feminist intuitions, the advice also looks, normatively, very, very good (7).[36]

Is the advice informative (2) to Jamie? Well, that will depend on how she feels about the changes she's been making. If the changes have happened slowly and somewhat unreflectively, the advice might come as a bit of a surprise to her. She might be jolted to look at herself through the eyes of her old friends and realize, then and there, that she has not really been true to herself. On the other hand, it is also possible that Jamie is deeply aware of the significance of the choices she's been making and that she feels torn about them and even somewhat resentful of her sorority sisters for putting all that pressure on her. Suppose she feels a bit alienated from her recent choices because they don't feel "like her" from the inside. If this is the case, then her old friends' advice to her may be obvious (and perhaps for this very reason also frustrating and a bit offensive).

Should we expect the psychological independence advice to be motivationally efficacious for Jamie (5)? Again, the answer will presumably depend on Jamie's actual concerns and commitments. Jamie might feel good about making new friends and she might be coming to like her new look or the way people now look at her; or she might be a kind of pragmatist and judge that it will be best for her social life if she does conform with her sisters' conventions, even if she doesn't herself endorse them, as such. Or, alternatively, it's possible that Jamie might just be so influenced by her new friends that no amount of admonition to "think for herself" would change the way she's thinking. In all of these scenarios, the true-self advice can be expected to be motivationally inert and thus fall well short of good advice by failing to tap into any rationally motivating elements of Jamie's motivational set.

The most difficult problem for advice that exhorts us to be psychologically independent, of course, is that it runs an obvious risk of being self-defeating (6). And, if it is self-defeating in a certain way, it may also violate OIC (4) and thus constitute advice that cannot be followed at all. The question, here, is whether and in what sense being authentically psychologically independent is compatible with following advice. If Jamie is generally quite susceptible to social influence, and if she cares a lot about the opinions of her high school friends, it's possible that she'll feel shamed by their disapproval and she might now take steps to conform with *their* view of how she should be presenting herself. Intuitively, if this is how Jamie responds, then she is not succeeding in being authentically psychologically independent by the very standards that her old friends would seem to be endorsing; she is just being buffeted by different winds. If she "complies" with her old friends' advice to be true to herself *because she cares about their estimation of her,* then she'll pretty clearly fail to be true to herself in the relevant "independent" way, and the advice will be self-defeating. But could the influence of her old friends be of a different sort than that of her new ones and thus escape the present criticism?

Let's stipulate that the two groups have different values and that Jamie is attracted to aspects of both friend-groups. Let's suppose, on one scenario, that Jamie is prompted by the authenticity advice of her old friends to think hard about the nature of autonomy and about her fundamental or "deep" values and that on that reflective basis she comes to judge that she should be less influenced by others in her sports and fashion preferences; if this is what happens it looks like she can both take her old friends' advice and remain pretty robustly psychologically independent. The advice does not seem self-defeating. But if Jamie follows the advice even in part on the basis of the social influence of her old friends, then the advice does look self-defeating. If we try to imagine the plausible "real world" psychologies of people like Jamie's old friends, we might become further suspicious of the motives behind this kind of authenticity advice: these friends are invested in their friendship with Jamie; given the changes that Jamie appears to be undergoing, they might be understandably fearful of losing her friendship. Or, equally likely, they might be offering a referendum on the gendered values that she seems to be endorsing by her recent changes. The authenticity advice, directing Jamie to focus on certain aspects of her relatively stable earlier self, is a powerful cover for these concerns that are not really about Jamie's psychological independence at all.

I suggested a moment ago that we should allow the possibility that Jamie can *follow* her friends' authenticity advice and still be psychologically independent. She can do so, it seemed, by reflecting on the advice and deciding, after meaningful deliberation, that she should not be so compliant with her sorority sisters' standards. If Jamie does this, it seems unfair to say that she has *not* thought for herself. But there are two worries that arise from this line of thought. The first is that if we grant this, it might start to seem pretty unclear what would count as Jamie *failing* to think for herself. We said that Jamie might be susceptible to social influence and that she might care deeply about her old friends' opinions. But, given our description of the case, Jamie also cares about the judgments of her sorority sisters. Presumably, she will now be experiencing some significant tension or ambivalence about her choice of self-presentation. She's not sure what she should do. She's received strong input from different sides and she's now got to figure things out. Should we say that Jamie has failed to be psychologically independent only if she decides to conform to her sorority sisters' values? This seems *ad hoc*. Her degree of psychological (in)dependence seems orthogonal to the outcome of her deliberations. Should we only count Jamie as psychologically independent if she *thinks* of herself as deciding for herself what to do? On the one hand, this sounds unreasonably demanding if it means that to be authentic we must constantly have in mind the meta-thought that our decisions are "our own." This requirement would exclude paradigm cases of reflective decision-making from the realm of the genuinely authentic. But, on the other hand, the standard may seem impossibly easy to meet. I'm not sure it's possible to think of ourselves as persons (as "strong evaluators" in Charles Taylor's sense)[37] *without* thinking of ourselves, in some way, as the "authors" of our lives. Even if an impartial observer were to judge that Jamie is especially vulnerable to social influence, it's not clear what Jamie could be doing *other* than thinking for herself about what to do. The charge of undue psychological dependence seems like a criticism of the weight that Jamie is giving, *in her deliberations*, to her peers' opinions. But this is surely not a manifestation of failure to think for herself; it is rather a particular *train* of thought that Jamie is engaging, one that ascribes value to her friends' opinions. The implication here is that authenticity advice, taken as advice to be psychologically independent, may in fact be impossible for a person *engaged* in practical deliberations *not* to follow and so would fail as advice on grounds of being superfluous (3). A person who is thinking about what to do *is* thinking for herself. Who else could be doing the thinking?

Conversely, a parallel problem emerges if we look at things from the opposite direction. If it's not clear how a practical reasoner can fail to think for herself, we might also wonder (now on the assumption that such failure is possible) how to characterize a properly independent response to the advice of others, especially when that advice directly concerns matters of friendship or, generally, our relationships with others. Where friendship is concerned, mutual psychological interdependence would seem to be essentially involved. Jamie is being advised to make a decision that will directly affect her friendships, so her quality and degree of concern for her various friends thus seems like a crucially relevant consideration for her. If she were to make a decision that was not in some way deeply sensitive to her friends' concerns (and, correspondingly, her concern for their concern), we might be confused about what she was thinking about altogether. In other words, if Jamie's old friends successfully invoke for her the importance of psychological independence, they will thereby succeed in inducing her to think about the role of her relationship with them in her decision-making. On the one hand, this might reintroduce a problem of self-defeat if it causes Jamie to resist their advice on grounds of psychological independence. But, on the other hand, it raises the specter of an *ought implies can* problem (4). It might be impossible to make a good decision about the proper influence of our friends without being influenced by the *fact* that they are our friends—and not simply by the content of the considerations they may adduce when they give us advice. Being properly responsive to the goods of friendship may essentially involve being influenced by them in nonrational ways—that is, in ways that are not *solely* the product of careful consideration of the merits of their views but are also in part the product of the *fact* that they hold them. And if this were to be incompatible with the advice to be psychologically independent, then this advice would be impossible to follow, at least in the context of friendship-related decisions (where The Ideal of Authenticity as Psychological Independence is very often introduced). So, it remains unclear what it could mean for Jamie to be properly psychologically *in*dependent in this case and that should make us further suspicious of authenticity advice of this kind.

The Ideal of Authenticity as Self-Knowledge

Sometimes, authenticity advice seems best interpreted as suggesting that the advisee seek self-knowledge as a means of resolving a practical problem or question. When Caitlin is advised by her doctor to be true to herself, it is natural to read this as a call to do some difficult soul-searching. On this construal of the advice, its intent is to communicate that in making hard decisions we do well to make sure our choices reflect important truths about ourselves. So the advice is a kind of epistemic prescription with practical value. (We could interpret Jamie's friends' advice, above, in this light, as an exhortation to achieve this kind of self-knowledge. Taken this way, the implication would be that her conformity with her sorority sisters' values manifests a kind of self-deception or bad faith and the suggestion would be that if she were to investigate the truth about herself, she would see that truth and make different choices, accordingly.) We can begin our investigation of whether authenticity advice, construed as advice to seek self-knowledge, is good advice by asking whether the advice to seek self-knowledge is contentful, informative, or useful.

Suppose that Caitlin, before she receives the advice from her doctor, does not think that the way to go about deciding what to do about her pregnancy is to *introspect*. Caitlin might think, for example, that the way to figure out what to do is to think about the moral status of her fetus; or she might think that the way to figure out what to do is to reflect on the teachings of her religion; or she might think that what really matters is how her decision will affect her educational trajectory or her friendships or her family relationships. None of these lines of thought are, at least obviously, forms of self-inquiry. So, if the doctor's advice is meant to direct her away from any of these lines of thought and toward the pursuit of self-knowledge, then she is being advised to approach her dilemma in a different way, namely by thinking about aspects of her own psychology (as opposed to various other things), and this might be quite a novel suggestion for Caitlin. If she takes the self-knowledge prescription, it might well redirect her thinking and her decision-making. Interpreted along these lines, the advice is certainly non-trivial (1), informative (2), in the sense that it proposes a substantive course of deliberation that was not yet under consideration by Caitlin, and potentially useful (3).

But it's equally possible that the advice could be uninformative and superfluous. We can imagine Caitlin reacting differently to her doctor's advice, with frustration, thinking: "I'm *trying* to figure out what I think—you're not helping my deliberations at all by telling me *to* figure out what I think. What I need is help figuring out what that is!"[38] If this kind of reaction can make sense, this is some evidence that the advice is uninformative (2). In this scenario, Caitlin is already thinking about what she thinks is best and the suggestion she receives is, essentially, to figure out what she thinks is best. Moreover, because she's already seeking self-knowledge, the advice to seek it is superfluous (3). The advice is functionally useless because it offers no particular guidance that could get her closer to the achievement of her goal. Another potential reason to doubt the usefulness of the advice is that there may well be no fact of the matter about what Caitlin "really thinks." Indeed, if we suppose that Caitlin has already thought long and hard about her decision, the less reasonable it will be to assume that self-inquiry is the solution to her "problem." Her values and preferences may be indeterminate and even if she discovers this fact by introspection, this won't help her figure out what to do. What she needs in this context, in order to make a decision, is not to *discover* what she thinks but rather to *settle* what she thinks. If this is her situation, no amount of advice to introspect will help because there is no relevant fact about herself awaiting discovery. The advice to achieve self-knowledge, when there is no fact about the self to be found, seems to violate OIC (5).[39]

Interestingly, even when the advice to seek self-knowledge has the potential to be informative and useful, it may also run a significant risk of being self-defeating (6). Sometimes the activity of seeking self-knowledge actually destroys its very possibility by inducing various kinds of doubt. Asking ourselves what we "really" think or feel characteristically has the effect of raising the bar of self-knowledge and in so doing can generate skepticism.[40] If we imagine Sergio, for example, thinking about whom he "really" loves, this might undermine any stable or intuitive sense of how he feels. Or, if we imagine Jordan wondering whether the new job he took really lines up with his deepest values, we can also imagine him *coming* to doubt that it does. But beyond just generating reasonable doubts about ourselves, introspecting with the aim of gaining self-knowledge can also change the very facts about ourselves that we were trying to discover. Consider that a possible effect of successful philosophizing (or indeed of scientific inquiry) can be that we change our beliefs in the domain of inquiry. Before we begin to scrutinize those beliefs, they might be quite stable. But once we start wondering, critically, what we really believe (and if we are in doubt about the *what* we naturally turn to the *why*), we may often find our beliefs changing. So too with introspection: the moment it is revealed to us what we "in fact" think or feel we might come to think or feel differently. This idea is in fact a kind of cornerstone of various psychoanalytic therapies. Seeking self-knowledge can change us—and this, paradoxically, can make self-knowledge very difficult (and perhaps sometimes even impossible) to achieve. There is something like an observer paradox in play, where the very act of revealing certain psychological facts about ourselves may alter or subvert them altogether. When this possibility is a live one, The Ideal of Authenticity as Self-Knowledge runs the risk of being either self-defeating (6) or permanently elusive (4).[41]

If we assume, contrary to various lines of thought just proposed, that the advice to gain self-knowledge *can* be informative and useful and is *not* self-defeating or impossible to follow successfully, the remaining question is whether the advice looks normatively good or correct (7). In chapter 2, I argued that while seeking self-knowledge in a variety of contexts is epistemically rational, there is no plausible *ideal* of self-knowledge; there are plenty of trivial facts about ourselves that there seems to be no rational requirement to know (for example, the number of cells in our bodies or hairs on our heads). The epistemic value of self-knowledge seems better illuminated by contrasting it with self-deception. It seems good, *qua* epistemic rationality, to have true beliefs about ourselves *rather than false beliefs*, but there is no rational imperative to maximize our true beliefs, either in general or specifically about ourselves. What does seem rational—*practically* rational—is to seek forms of self-knowledge that are expected to help us live good and flourishing lives. And here, too, the empirical evidence suggests that whether any particular item of self-knowledge or the activity of seeking self-knowledge conduces to our living well will be a contingent and variable matter. When self-inquiry reveals to us what will make us happy or fulfilled, it can be instrumentally valuable to promoting our well-being. But, as argued in chapter 1, it can also be paralyzing and detrimental to our mental health—when self-inquiry produces self-doubt or corrodes our commitments or undermines our self-confidence. So there is no generally warranted presumption that seeking self-knowledge is a good idea (7). Finally, it is worth recalling our discussion in the last chapter of whether seeking self-knowledge is generally morally good. What is important to remember, for our present purposes, is that being directed to seek *self*-knowledge as a practical strategy for making morally good decisions is tantamount to being directed *not* to think about other people, except insofar as it is revealed to us via introspection that those others matter to us. If moral thinking is characteristically other-directed (and this will be a central point of my concluding chapter), then the advice to seek self-knowledge might function to lead us away from distinctively moral considerations. And if we think practical advice ought generally be sensitive to moral considerations, this is reason to think that advice to seek self-knowledge will not be reliably normatively right, all things considered (7).

The Ideal of Authenticity as Wholeheartedness

We have said that the advice to seek self-knowledge, as a means of figuring out what to do, will only be useful if there is some fact of the matter to be discovered about what the advisee really thinks or wants or cares about. In such cases, the advisee might be able to identify, by introspection, what she thinks is best. But often, when a person is trying to figure out what to do, there is no antecedent fact, embedded in the person's psychology, that rationally determines what she ought do. Sometimes a person is genuinely ambivalent or unsure about what course is best. Sergio, recall, is unhappy in love and in one version of the case, torn in his affections between David and Geoffrey. Suppose that Sergio *wants* to pick one of them and build a stable relationship but is simply unclear about how to go about this. Or recall Jordan, who has floated among different jobs over the course of his life. He's been a lawyer, a teacher, and a nature guide. Both Sergio and Jordan are advised by family and friends to be true to themselves and "settle down," Sergio in a relationship, Jordan in a career. On one interpretation of this advice, the implication is that those giving the advice believe that further reflection on what they really want would provide a solution to their "problems." But if Sergio and Jordan are really ambivalent in the sense just described, then this advice simply can't be successfully followed (4). But on a more charitable and less paternalistic interpretation of the advice, it might mean that the *way* to be true to oneself in cases like this is to settle what one wants—to make it a determinate psychological fact that one wants *this* rather than *that*. By hypothesis, the kind of person we are considering can't *discover* what to do by looking inward; rather, this person needs to (re)*constitute* himself so that the structure of his motivational psychology usefully provides some practical direction. Overcoming ambivalence and becoming "whole" can thus be a way to resolve practical uncertainty about what to do. The person who is true to himself is, on this conception, the person who is determinately wholehearted in his commitments.

Suppose for a moment that in Jordan's case, the advice is unsolicited. Imagine that Jordan thinks his life is going fine and he doesn't feel himself to be in need of advice. If this is his situation, then the advice, by hypothesis, is proposing a substantive course of action that Jordan is not currently pursuing or even considering. It is thus contentful (1), informative (2), and not superfluous (3). It tells Jordan what to do and suggests that his ambivalence is problematic. By contrast, imagine that Sergio has sought out advice about what to do. In this case, the advice looks either uninformative (2) or like no advice at all. If Sergio asks Bethany what she thinks he should do—should he pick David or Geoffrey?—and the answer is "Just decide and pick one," this doesn't seem to provide Sergio with any normative considerations to guide his decision. It looks more like encouragement *to* decide, rather than advice on how to go about this.

"Decide what you want" offers no informative content to someone trying to decide what he wants. The "advice" offers Sergio no directive or redirective guidance. For this reason we can presume it will be obvious to Sergio and, for this very reason, the "advice" seems utterly superfluous (3). In explaining why advice "fails" if it is superfluous, the idea was that advice has no point if it is already being followed; or if it is already expected to be followed; or if it is impossible not to follow. If Sergio is already trying to settle his choice, then it fails by the first two standards. It might "succeed" by the third, in the sense that the exhortation to choose might knock him out if his static state and *cause* him to choose. But, if it in fact does this, it does so on the basis of something other than rational considerations, so is not advice, by our definition, at all. If one were to insist, nevertheless, that exhorting Sergio to choose is a kind of advice, it looks like advice that is impossible, rationally, to follow. That is, there is no proposed line of practical deliberation that Sergio can activate simply by having the thought "I ought to be wholehearted." If he ends up wholehearted, his behavior may be properly described as "in conformity" with the advice, but because the advice does not invoke any considerations that could help Sergio choose, any eventual choice cannot plausibly be described as the rational product of the advice. Put differently, it is constitutive of the kind of ambivalence we have been describing that it cannot be overcome by practical deliberation about considerations that are already present in one's existing motivational set. Sergio's "problem" is that his beliefs and desires and values do not settle what he should do. We can say, formally, that when a person is ambivalent in this way about whether to Φ, this just means that the person's internal reasons do not yield a determinate practical verdict about whether to Φ.[42] What would be needed to overcome ambivalence *in a rational way* would be the adducement of some new considerations that would provide the ambivalent person with a new line of practical thought. In the absence of such considerations, all that can be hoped for is some kind of nonrational change in the motivational states of the agent, which might then yield some determinate practical choice.[43] So, the "advice" to settle what one wants is, as such, *rationally* impossible to follow, so seems to violate OIC (4). And if the advice cannot, rationally, be followed then it is, at least *rationally*, motivationally inert (5).[44]

So, we can formulate the problem for anti-ambivalence authenticity advice as an interesting dilemma: either the advice to settle what one wants and who one is is superfluous (because the advisee who has sought the advice is already trying to settle this); or it is impossible to follow *as advice* (because the genuinely ambivalent person cannot *rationally* overcome ambivalence). If the second horn of the dilemma is plausible, then we might, perhaps charitably, choose not to see the "advice" to Sergio or Jordan as genuine advice at all, but rather simply as conveying the advisor's judgment that wholeheartedness is better than ambivalence.

This is a substantive position but one that faces a set of challenges explored in chapters 1, 2, and 3: specifically, we have seen that wholeheartedness is at best orthogonal to well-being, practical rationality and morality and sometimes actively counterproductive to each. I have argued that Sergio and Jordan can be better off ambivalent; they can also live, ambivalently, without any practical inconsistency and while treating everyone in their lives honestly and respectfully. Unless it can be made out why we should think "authentic wholeheartedness" is a good in itself, it is unclear why it should be recommended as a practical guiding maxim at all, so the admonition to be wholehearted is simply not compelling, as far as its normative content is concerned (7).

The Ideal of Authenticity as Moral Conscientiousness

Recall *Annie and the Honor Code*: Annie is a thoughtful college student agonizing about whether to smoke marijuana with her friends, in violation of the law and her school's honor code. When she shares her dilemma with her mother, her mother advises her to be true to herself and follow her conscience. The advice evidently does have content (1). It directs Annie to a certain *kind* of consideration rather than to various others.[45] Whether the advice is informative to Annie will depend on what kind of inquiry she's been engaged in thus far. If, somehow, she hasn't construed her dilemma as a moral quandary at all, the advice might have the effect of directing her to think about her moral values. But if, as the description of the scenario suggests, the situation pretty obviously raises moral questions, then it is likely that Annie will already be in the midst of engaging conscience, so the advice would be uninformative to her (2). It would thus also fail to provide any useful consideration for her deliberations so appears superfluous (3). And, as suggested above in the case of wholeheartedness advice, when "advice" fails to adduce any reasons for its proposed course, it either fails to be advice at all, or fails to be advice that can be rationally followed (4). If Annie's conscience isn't fully formed or is simply silent on this question, listening to it will be of no help. The advice could, however, induce Annie to take a particular course of action; if Annie is very responsive to her mother's wishes, and if Annie senses that the advice really means "Don't smoke the marijuana," then it could produce a motive to comply with it. One thing to note about this scenario is that in context where advisees are under the significant influence of advisors, we might wonder whose conscience is really being followed, the advisor's or the advisee's. If Annie, in effect, follows her mother's conscience rather than her own, the advice may be self-defeating (6).

Alternatively, if Annie's relationship with her mother is fraught in a different way, the advice could also be self-defeating in a different way; it's not hard to imagine Annie as having a rebellious streak and in that case her mother's advice could lead her to decide to smoke the marijuana

(6). The more interesting and difficult question, though, is how we should assess whether advice to be morally conscientious is generally normatively good advice at all (7).

Consider the possibility that Annie's mother is generally conservative and has taught Annie to follow rules. If this is the case, the advice to be conscientious will naturally be interpreted as implying that Annie should not smoke the marijuana. There is a sense in which advice to act on conscience is disingenuous when the advisor really has a substantive moral agenda and is trying to induce compliance with that agenda by way of recommending conscientiousness. In order to assess the normative merits of this kind of advice, we may need to know a lot about the advisor's values. But if the advice is given without any agenda other than to induce moral thinking, as such, it seems we can draw one of two conclusions about the advisor's views: either the advisor thinks that conscientious introspection, by its very nature, reveals to us what is right (say, on a version of the natural law model discussed in chapters 1 and 3) or that the verdicts of conscientious introspection are always right (or permissible), *whatever* their content. We have already suggested that both of these positions are problematic. The first is empirically implausible, given the evidence of people possessed of (or by) misguided conscience. Imagine the case of a person, whom we judge to be thoroughly bad, in the midst of a practical or moral quandary. Would we advise such a person, without further clarification, to be conscientious and follow *his* conscience? I presume not. The content of the advice we'd want to offer this person would be morally substantive—it would aim to offer a particular account of what we think is right or good in the situation; we would not be content to leave this person with the thought that conscientious introspection from considerations within his own moral psychology is the best course. What this shows is that even if we were convinced that the true self were the moral self and that that self had a determinately good moral orientation (somewhere deep down), this belief would not generally justify authenticity advice as moral advice, given the apparent difficulties many people have in unearthing that hidden self. But the second interpretation of the advice to follow conscience is no more satisfying because it is implausibly relativistic. Notwithstanding a variety of difficult metaethical questions, we don't normally think that moral decisions are justified simply in virtue of being consistent with the agent's own moral judgment. Simply admitting the possibility of misguided conscience is to acknowledge as much. Of course, there are contexts where a version of the relativistic position may seem appealing and Annie's case (as well as Caitlin's) may be good examples of this. We may think that the moral question of whether it's okay to smoke marijuana (or in Caitlin's case, have an abortion) is sufficiently opaque that it should in fact be left to individual conscience. When moral questions seem to have low stakes or are open to reasonable disagreement we are often happy to advise people simply to do what they think is right, no matter what that is. For those of us who think, for example, that there is no clearly decisive principle by which to decide the abortion question, we might agree that simply following conscience is the best thing to do. But this is far short of endorsing moral relativism, as such. What makes the conscientiousness advice plausible in cases like these (if it is plausible), I propose, is that in the absence of any decisive moral decision procedure, deciding in accordance with one's own best judgment seems rationally and morally permissible (indeed, that is something like a platitude in a liberal society). And if we consider the psychological costs of making decisions from which we might end up feeling alienated, the well-being benefits of acting on conscience in cases like those are clear. The critical point, however, is that the normative merits of the advice to be conscientious seem to hinge on moral judgments that are independent of the value of authenticity or conscience as such. Our substantive intuitions about marijuana use or abortion and our intuitions about the reasonability of disagreement about these issues, are what guide our assessment of the merits of authenticity advice in cases like these. We are not content simply to accept that following conscience and thus being (or trying to be) true to our moral selves is the reliably best moral course.

Caitlin's and Annie's cases also highlight another moral problem with authenticity advice and that is its apparent self-directedness. Suppose Annie was thinking about what to do by thinking about the meaning of honor or the moral status of marijuana laws or about the value of having a new experience. None of these thoughts explicitly involve her asking herself "what her conscience is telling her" (though they may well be manifestations of the functioning of conscience). What this highlights is the fact that the exhortation to search one's conscience (like the exortation to seek self-knowledge) is, by definition, an exhortation to think about *oneself* rather than various other things. Paradoxically, in contexts of moral decision-making, this advice may seem especially problematic (I return to this in the next chapter). The proposal that the way to approach difficult moral questions is, in general, by thinking about oneself, is a proposal that would seem to lead us away from the kinds of moral considerations that we would be better off considering. Asking oneself, "What do I think is right?" is very different from asking oneself, "How will my choices affect others or my relationships with other people?" If the answer to the first kind of question is unclear, it *could* lead a person to questions of the second kind. But it is these latter questions that constitute *moral thinking*; the former, if taken as the determinant of what is right (and not for independent metaethically relativistic reasons), is evidently narcissistic.

SUMMING UP: THE IDEAL OF AUTHENTICITY AS ADVICE

Our goal in this chapter has been to consider how The Ideal of Authenticity, in its various forms, fares as action-guiding advice. I suggest that the variety of ways in which it fails reveals why The Ideal of Authenticity is so seductive in so many contexts. When the advice to be true to oneself is trivial or obvious or superfluous it often seems the most appealing—precisely because it makes no sense to reject it. By directing us to think for or about ourselves, authenticity advice, in essence, asks us to affirm what we already think or what we are already committed to or what we are already doing; authenticity advice suggests that so long as we are true to ourselves, we cannot be wrong; in such cases the advice is often, quite literally, irresistible. But as the arguments in this chapter have suggested, these are precisely the conditions that make advice bad, as advice (if it is advice at all). If the point of advice, as such, is to adduce practical reasons that can help direct or redirect a person to a good course of action, then "advice" that simply ratifies the advisee's preexisting beliefs, desires, values, and motives has no point as advice. Sometimes, however, authenticity advice does have normative content but when it does, we have seen two significant causes for suspicion of it. The first is that the content of the authenticity advice seems to be largely contingent upon the context in which it is proffered and more specifically, on the particular values of the advisor. As we have seen in this chapter, depending on the context, our five kinds of authenticity advice can mean any of the following:

1. It's best to act on your all-things-considered best judgments.
2. You shouldn't allow yourself to be too influenced by other people.
3. Self-knowledge makes your life go better.
4. Wholeheartedness is better than ambivalence.
5. So long as you follow conscience, you'll do what is in fact right.
6. Whatever you do is morally acceptable so long as it's what you really think is right to do.

I have suggested that we cannot, with sense, even question whether we should do what we ourselves think is best. So the advice to be strong-willed is trivial and superfluous. The idea that we should make "our own" decisions is equally empty and uninformative. Who else's decisions would we be making? So advice to be psychologically independent, as such, fails to provide substantive practical direction. The advice, to the ambivalent, to achieve wholeheartedness is likewise motivationally useless, at least as a rational strategy for deliberating about what to do. And the directives to seek self-knowledge or follow conscience presuppose that the self is the place to look for the answers to our deepest questions and this, we have seen, seems quite generally empirically implausible (because there may be nothing of relevance to be found within ourselves), normatively suspect (because we may not be good on the inside) and unduly self-centered (because good practical thinking, especially moral thinking, is often characteristically other-directed). Put simply, when the advice to be true to ourselves is not trivial it reliably fails for one or more of these reasons:

1. It is often terrible to follow our best judgments.
2. It can be morally good and good for us to be deeply influenced by others.
3. Self-knowledge and its pursuit can be unattainable and also debilitating.
4. Ambivalence is often perfectly appropriate and cannot normally be overcome by rational deliberation.
5. Conscience can be corrupt.
6. Thinking about oneself is not a reliable way to figure out what is morally right.

The larger point that I turn to now, in chapter 5, is that we would do better—ethically, rationally, and morally—to think about these substantive and controversial claims (and many others) than to let ourselves be sidetracked by the seductively empty or implausibly self-directed Ideal of Authenticity.

NOTES

1. See Stocker (1976).
2. To say that reasons justify an action is to say that the action would be rational to perform. An action which is rational is, minimally, rationally permissible. Some might think that good advice, of the gold-standard variety, must provide rationally overriding reasons that determine that a course of action is rationally required. I will not be assuming such a high threshold for the justifying standards of good advice.
3. See Mackie (1977).
4. See Williams (1999).
5. Or should we perhaps be error theorists or nihilists about normativity? This book does not defend a view on this question, but for the purposes of this chapter I assume that good advice is possible, so I assume, at least, that there can in fact be *good* reasons to do certain things.
6. If this second point is right, it might appropriately make us further skeptical of authenticity advice in general, given its nontransparent plasticity.
7. On this interpretation, Corey's grandmother would be, in Derek Parfit's terms, some version of an Objective List theorist. See Parfit (2011).
8. See Foot (1972).
9. See Williams (1999).
10. Interestingly, even if the advice does fail in this way, it still might remain reasonable for the grandmother to offer it if she has good reason to think Corey has have the relevant internal reasons or if she has good reason to think he should.
11. The first "ought" here should not be taken to imply or presume that bringing about the relevant desire is something that is under our direct control. Rather, the idea is that the value of Φ-ing is conditioned not on the presence of a desire for X, but on the value of X itself. This suggests that the advisor takes there to be an unconditional reason to desire X (say, that X is intrinsically good). Of course, as we shall see, if it is

not in our power to determine that we desire X, then the advice to Φ might run afoul of the "ought implies can" principle (see below).

12. See Foot (1972).

13. Though it can make perfectly good sense to ask, "But should I endorse these desires?"

14. See Dreier (2001).

15. Consider, again, the oddness of denying that you ought to do what you yourself think is best.

16. Suppose my dining partner replies to my "What's good?" inquiry with "Have you tried the whole red snapper poached with ginger and onions?" If my friend is an objectivist about culinary goods he might think that reflecting on this dish will rationally induce in me the desire to order it. If this is the case, it might be more like Corey's grandmother's advice construed categorically (see note 7 above).

17. The basis of the authority could be any number of things: it could be grounded in the responsibility of the authority *for* her subjects (as in the case of parents or guardians) or, perhaps, on the basis of their legitimate political or religious sovereignty.

18. Demands may also be backed by threats; but insofar as they are complied with, not out of respect for the authority of the issuer of the demand, but out of a fear of sanction, the demand is being treated as a command. So demands and commands can, in cases like this, overlap. I am proposing that we understand the parent's exhortation in this double case, along these lines: "As your father, I legitimately demand that you eat your spinach, but if you wrongly refuse, I back up my demand with a threat of punishment, and thus also *command* you to eat your spinach, or else!"

19. See Austin (2008).

20. See Hart (2008).

21. Of course, there is a sense in which all advice is meant to limit the advisee's reasoning—to the parameters of the appropriately adduced practical considerations. In the case of categorical advice this is most clear as the advice is meant to be binding independent of the particular needs and interests of the advisee. But unlike in the case of commands, in the case of categorical advice, the normative authority of the command is normally settled by "normative facts" that are not created by the advisor but that are in principle always present and accessible to a rational advisee. This is somewhat complicated by the possibility of cases where the normative facts themselves have to do with the relative statuses of the advisor and advisee. Consider: "You ought to Φ because of X; I am an expert on X-related things and you are a novice and there is no time to learn all the relevant things about X right now." In such a case, the reason provided to Φ does not have to do with the particular merits of Φ-ing so, on the analysis I have provided should not be construed as advice to Φ. But the advice can be properly construed as advice *to take my advice* on the grounds of my expertise—the relevant expertise about X is meant to be the normative grounding not anything to do with the fact that it is *my* advice, as such.

22. This is, of course, a matter of significant philosophical debate. See Plato (2005), Hart (2008), King (2008), and Smith (1994).

23. See Wolff (1998).

24. Alternatively, if one thought that morality were overriding, one might think that "what's right" is just equivalent to "what should be done," in which case the advice reduces to "Do what should be done," which is patently trivial.

25. If I am aware of a practical consideration but I do not recognize its normative weight, it may be natural to say that I don't understand my reason to act on that consideration. For those who endorse a version of judgment internalism (the view that our practical judgments normally go along with a corresponding motivation to act in accordance with them), this will also explain why the consideration is not motivating for me.

26. Kant (1933, p. 473).

27. And this seems true even of the advice is normatively correct (i.e. even it is true), on the case under consideration that it would in fact be better not to be mad.
28. The Sartrean ideal of avoiding bad faith might be like this: on the Sartrean conception, it might be (virtually) impossible to be perfectly vigilant in appreciation of both our facticity and our transcendence, but we might nonetheless be responsible for avoiding bad faith. We will consider whether there is a comparably plausible thing to say about The Ideal of Authenticity, below.
29. That said, the advice is not clearly practically useful because it doesn't seem to offer any actual strategy for being strong-willed that can be adopted by the advisee. In this way it is somewhat like the advice to the meth addict to quit.
30. Though, in special circumstances this could happen. If we imagine that Alison has a philosophical view (or rationalization) about the acceptability of weak will (see chapter 1) then perhaps the advice here might function by getting her to re-evaluate the importance of being strong-willed.
31. An interesting wrinkle: it is sometimes best for a person not to do what she thinks is best (for example, when the person's "best judgment" is mistaken). Of course, the advice "Don't do what you think is best" is rationally *impossible* to follow. This suggests that it might be impossible (for a rational person) not to be motivated to do what she thinks is best, so the advice might also turn out to be superfluous (3).
32. See Mele (1976) and de Sousa (1976).
33. Many smokers who appear to be trying to quit rationalize their intermittent smoking on the grounds that, in those moments, they really don't think it's wrong to smoke those few cigarettes.
34. See Davidson (1984).
35. Perhaps we can imagine someone who has never thought about the true self, as such, in the midst of trying to be strong-willed. Might advice to such a person to be strong-willed be informative in this context? Could the idea that in being weak, we betray our true selves, provide one with additional reason, from the first-person perspective, to act in accordance with one's best judgment? My own sense is that the experience of being tempted to act against one's best judgment is so connected with our sense of our own rational integrity that the addition of the language of the true self wouldn't constitute any additional motivating consideration. But I don't think we can rule out the possibility that thinking about strong will in the terms of the true self might be especially motivating. So I think cheering of this kind (not construed as advice) could, under some circumstances, be effective.
36. Indeed, I will propose that it is the moral appeal of the content of the authenticity advice that directs us away from its problems, *qua* advice.
37. See Taylor (1976) and chapter 4.
38. Imagine the doctor responding to this line of thought with, "Of course I can't tell you what to do. Just try to be true to yourself." If this is the reply, then it's clear that either the "advice" is no advice at all (but is rather just a supportive bromide) or it is an exhortation to become wholehearted, which we will consider next.
39. The advice simply to continue *seeking* self-knowledge under such circumstances would not strictly violate OIC, but it would nonetheless still be pointless (3) and might be impossible to motivate if the person became aware of the indeterminacy in question.
40. See Lewis (2003).
41. The exhortation toward authentic self-knowledge might also violate OIC for an entirely different reason: if being true to ourselves means something like avoiding Sartrean bad faith (never forgetting that one is both a facticity and a transcendence), then the advice may in fact be impossible to follow. Of course, as suggested above, this might also be a reason to doubt OIC. If we understand the existentialist ideal as essentially aspirational, we might be drawn to the idea of binding norms that we cannot fully comply with.
42. As above, I am here construing ambivalence not simply as a phenomenological or epistemic state of uncertainty but as a metaphysically indeterminate state.

43. This issue is parallel to a problem that libertarians face in the context of explaining free will: if an action is free, then by hypothesis, no facts antecedently determine what a person's will shall be; but in the absence of such facts there seems to be no rational basis for the will to be settled, so responsible action (action guided by practical reason) seems ruled out.

44. Though the possibility does remain open that, like a case of cheering, encouragement to settle oneself and become wholehearted could induce a nonrational motivational change in the "advisee."

45. Interestingly, if an advisee thought that morality were normatively overriding, the advice might lack content. To hold that morality is overriding in this way is to hold that the all-things-considered normative perspective just is the moral perspective. So, thinking about what to do would be equivalent to thinking about what is morally right or best (or at least morally permissible) for this person. I argued against this view in chapter 4. Of course, if morality were overriding in this way, and if conscience were a reliable guide to morality, then the advice to follow conscience (if possibly contentless and uninformative) would at least be normatively correct (7).

FIVE

Ethics without Authenticity: Looking Outward, Not In

The primary aim of chapters 1, 2, and 3, of this book was to establish that authenticity is not ultimately well-grounded *as an ideal* because it is not plausibly the reliably best (or even a reliably good) way to promote human well-being, rationality or a moral life. Indeed, I argued, in many common circumstances, inauthenticity is more conducive to these goods. The aim of chapter 4 was to establish that The Ideal of Authenticity fails as action-guiding advice for a variety of structured and principled reasons: it is often trivial or uninformative; it can be superfluous or impossible to follow; it is in many cases motivationally inert or self-defeating or simply normatively wrong.

I argued that, ironically, some of the reasons that The Ideal of Authenticity is bad advice actually explain its widespread appeal. Who, especially in our "liberal society," would deny, for example, that we ought to do what we think is best or right, that we ought to value our independence, or that we ought to have integrity and know ourselves? These are ethical and political platitudes for most of us and each is captured by a particular conception of The Ideal of Authenticity that has been explored in this book. In this concluding chapter, I argue that the apparent *uncontroversiality* of these ideas makes The Ideal of Authenticity a seductive cover for a set of other specific ideas and values that are far more difficult to support with good undisguised arguments. By using the language of "cover" and "disguise," I mean to raise our collective suspicions of invocations of The Ideal of Authenticity. I do not mean to suggest, however, that people typically make authenticity arguments or offer true-self advice disingenuously or in any kind of intentionally sophistic or deceptive way. On the contrary, I think The Ideal of Authenticity is usually invoked in good faith, with good intentions. It is partly for this reason that I think the corrective of this chapter might be of practical use. I want to convince those who believe in the Ideal that we ought to seek other ways of thinking about the good life and that, correspondingly, we ought to adopt other discourses when we are trying to help others live well or convince others of our own visions of the good life.

The corrective I suggest is that we actively seek to identify the values that may be obscured from view while we are idealizing and advocating authenticity. I will argue for four main claims in this concluding chapter: (1) that authenticity advice typically has the structure of a cover because, even in its most nonpaternalistic forms, the appeal to authenticity tacitly invokes other values that, upon closer scrutiny, are usually the ones carrying the philosophical weight; (2) that authenticity talk often confusingly displaces talk of relatively uncontroversial values, like the value of health or conscience or knowledge; (3) that, correlatively, authenticity advice also often disguises more controversial and politicized values, like monogamy and expression of the sexual self; and (4) that we have much to gain by replacing our talk of authenticity with discussions of the (I claim) underlying values that are not primarily about our individual relations to ourselves at all but about what how we think the social world that we live in and that we are inseparable from should best be arranged.

To establish the claims above, in what follows, I reconsider paradigm cases of each of our five conceptions of authenticity and diagnose what *non*-authenticity-based values may implicitly underlie our talk of authenticity. And to model the corrective approach I am suggesting, I highlight some of the alternative conversations we might have if we abandoned talk of the true self.

Finally, I apply the reasoning of the book as a whole to authenticity-based arguments for LGBTQ rights and respect. I argue that three different kinds of authenticity arguments fail us as moral thinkers and agents and I suggest how the proposals of this chapter might set us on a better discursive path. In doing so, one of my further aims is to shed some light on the merits and flaws of Charles Taylor's moralized, "horizons-based" conception of The Ideal of Authenticity. I argue that by embedding an essentially intersubjective and moral element within his ideal of authenticity, he pushes the idea of authenticity past its intuitive conceptual limits and also exemplifies the use of authenticity as a cover in just the way that I find most troubling.

RE-DIAGNOSING THE APPEAL OF AUTHENTICITY AS STRONG WILL

Most of us would encourage people like Alison, who is trying to quit smoking, to stick to their resolve and be strong-willed in overcoming an addiction.[1] Likewise, most of us would encourage Cassie, who was contemplating plagiarizing her philosophy paper, to be strong-willed, follow her conscience, and not cheat. What these cases have in common is that we agree with Alison's and Cassie's best judgments, in turn, about what is good for them and what is right. Most of us think, for example, that it is best, for health reasons, not to smoke; and if we are friends with Alison, we will have a special stake in her well-being. So when we encourage her to be true to herself we are endorsing what we take to be her proper concern for her well-being. In Cassie's case, those of us who would encourage her to resist the temptation to cheat so that she can go have fun with her friends are endorsing the moral imperative to be honest and to do one's own work. The point to note here, is that in encouraging Alison and Cassie to be true to themselves, it is natural to see oursleves as encouraging them to take specific courses of action that we ourselves think are substantively best and right. This is important because, I claim, we are not normally disposed to endorse Authenticity as Strong Will when we don't agree with the course of action that the strong-willed person would presumably take.

To see this, we need only consider cases where a person's best judgment is that he ought to do something that is by our lights (and possibly even by theirs) unhealthy or self-injurious or morally wrong, and where it would take strong will to enact that judgment. In chapter 1, we considered the case of an anorexic person for whom not eating requires the exercise of strong will. If we saw this person about to dig into a large and healthy-looking sandwich we wouldn't normally say, "Wait! Stick to your resolve! I know you don't really want to eat that!" There seems to be no intuitive pull to the idea that she should stick to her abstemious resolve. Or imagine, again, the amoral thief who is trying to motivate himself to overcome his fear of being caught, so that he can implement his brilliant criminal plan. We are presumably not inclined in the least to be concerned with this person's ability to be guided by his best judgments. In both of these cases, our first inclination may in fact be to consider taking action that would discourage the strong will of the parties in question. If we are inclined to facilitate the anorexic's recovery or stop the thief from carrying out his plan, what this means is that we are in favor of interfering with their exercise of strong will on prudential or health-related or moral grounds.

Now, some may react to this analysis by arguing that the anorexic's true self is distorted by her disorder and that the amoral thief's true self is equally corrupted, though in a different way. This response indicates a reluctance to see the true self as *anything but* healthy and good. What this suggests, as I've argued throughout, is that those attracted to The Ideal of Authenticity are likely to tailor their conception of the true self to fit various other powerful intuitions (say, about health or morality). But the effort to make The Ideal of Authenticity conform to those other intuitions should make us wonder whether the conception of authenticity is being constructed *ad hoc*. More importantly, though, it suggests that the "higher" values in question are really health and morality and the aim of the authenticity defender, here, is simply to establish that if we do what is healthiest for us, or what is good, this will turn out, also, to be in accordance with our true selves. This will be a happy result for those who believe in a true self, but so long as the argument goes *from* one's conception of the good, *to* one's conception of authenticity, it should be clear which values are better candidates for being the more basic ones, driving the philosophical position.

The cases of Alison and Cassie and the anorexic and the thief seem to provide strong evidence that what we care about in contexts where we invoke The Ideal of Authenticity as Strong Will is our own conception of the well-being of the person we are advising or our own conception of what is morally right or good. When our advisees' best judgments conflict with our own, the appeal of *their* being strong-willed seems to be altogether lost. Better for them to *heal* or to change than to do what is unhealthy or wrong, independent of whether that is best understood as a mode of authentic living. There are two observations to make here. The first is that The Ideal of Authenticity as Strong Will is being used, in the above contexts, as a tool for encouraging people (or cheering them on, as I argued in the previous chapter) to do what *we* think is best on non-authenticity grounds. The Ideal thus looks like a rhetorical cover for inducing people to adopt certain substantive conceptions of the good life. The second observations is that instead of telling Alison or Cassie that they should be true to themselves, we might do better to be open and honest about the conceptions of the good life that we are endorsing. Instead of saying "Be strong-willed," let's say to Alison, "Be healthy because I care about you and want you to live a long time" or to Cassie, "Don't cheat because it's wrong to deceive people about who you are and what you've done." Neither of these ways of talking to Alison and Cassie have anything to do with authenticity or their standing in a certain proper relation *to themselves*.

INTERLUDE ON OBJECTIVISM, SUBJECTIVISM, AND THE DANGEROUS PLASTICITY OF THE IDEAL OF AUTHENTICITY

As might have emerged in the course of this book, I am inclined toward a subjectivist view of well-being. This means that we should normally allow a (rational) person's own judgment about what is good or bad for her to settle the question of what really is good or bad for her. If this is right, then it is possible that self-injurious thrill-seekers (e.g., the "jackasses" of television and movies) who overcome their own fears and draw their own blood and break their own bones are not really harming themselves in the sense relevant to our discussion of well-being. This might seem to have the implication that whenever a person succeeds in doing what she herself thinks is best, she really is promoting her own well-being. To deny this would seem to commit us to an (in my view objectionably) objectivist view of well-being. Indeed, I think we are often hasty in our judgments that by hurting themselves, or doing "unhealthy" things, people are necessarily detracting from their well-being, *tout court*. We tend to project our own conceptions of the good life onto others and draw the conclusion that it is bad *for them* to do what we ourselves think is unwise or imprudent even if they don't share our views about what is worth doing.

The Ideal of Authenticity, with its exhortation to each of us to live in accordance with our own values, seems to resonate with this pluralistic kind of subjectivism. As Charles Taylor compellingly argues, it is for this very reason that The Ideal often appeals to liberals of a certain stripe, who are committed to being nonjudgmental about a spectrum of competing conceptions of the good.[2] As we shall see below, Taylor thinks this reveals a significant flaw in a popular cultural conception of The Ideal of Authenticity and his project is to develop a version of The Ideal that avoids what he takes to be a dangerous kind of value relativism. For now, though, the crucial point is that value objectivism seems to be in some intuitive tension with The Ideal of Authenticity. After all, on the objectivist view, what a person thinks is good or right for her, or what she really, even upon reflection, wants to do, does not settle what *really is* good for her or right for her to do (though these individual judgments and desires may be thought to have some objective weight). So, the objectivist about well-being (who takes well-being to be an ideal), for example, should be happy to criticize the authentic person if she is not doing what would, in fact, objectively, promote her well-being. The objectivist view can seem especially attractive in the context of functional definitions of health-related well-being. A person who drinks or smokes to the point of organ failure or cancer seems, indisputably, to be diminishing her own well-being. And if the person with the unhealthy habit says that she has thought about her choices, reflectively endorses them and is willing to live (or die) with the consequences, we may well not think this settles the question of what is best for her. We may persist in thinking the person is just plain wrong about what's best. Even if we imagine that the person gets cancer and does not complain or even seems genuinely to have no regrets, we may still think she is deeply misguided about her own well-being. This is some evidence that we have at least some objectivist intuitions about well-being; it's hard to give up the idea that a person can sometimes be just plain wrong about what is good for her. Objectivism about well-being, then, would seem to weigh against the Well-being Account of The Ideal of Authenticity. If being true to yourself can be bad for you, the objectivist might reason, then so much the worse for authenticity. Better to *change* and do what's best.

If we share the intuitions that it is not necessarily best for the jackass to harm himself, or the pro-smoking addict to smoke (despite their best judgments), does this mean we must abandon subjectivism in favor of objectivism? Should this challenge to The Ideal of Authenticity (that it seems to resonate with an implausible subjectivism) incline us toward objectivism? On both counts, I think the answer is no. All we need to make sense of the possibility of criticizing the authentically self-injuriou, is to acknowledge that sometimes our "best judgments" can be mistaken. And this is something that seems quite true *from the subjective, first-person perspective.* If we've ever seen, with hindsight, that our conscientious attempts to figure out what was best nonetheless led us astray, then we should agree that it is not always best for us to act on our own best judgment. Commonsensically, this is what justifies paternalism toward the very young or immature, or those who are cognitively impaired due to drugs or alcohol or mental illness (as we may presume in the anorexia case). We can justify protecting such people from themselves on the *subjectivist* grounds that they are not in a position to see what *they themselves* would judge best if they were in conditions more conducive to clear, prudential thinking. The idea, then, is that we need not supplant others' judgments about what is best for them in favor of our own reified judgments in order to maintain, for example, that strong will is not always best for us. Rather, we need only make the reasonable assumption (based on observational evidence) that sometimes our "best judgment" about what is best for us is not in fact best.

It is important to remind ourselves here, though, that while I've given some reason to think that objectivism is in some tension with The Ideal of Authenticity, defenders of objectivist views (of well-being or of morality) may be just as strongly drawn to The Ideal of Authenticity as subjectivists are. The objectivist may be inclined to say that any time a person's judgment about what is best for her conflicts with what really is, objectively, best for her, the person fails to be *true to herself.* If the person who makes herself sick, say, in accordance with her "best judgment" is wrong about her own well-being then, quite clearly, she does not know some important things about herself. In failing to identify her own objective interests, a defender of an objectivist view of well-being may simply say that she has failed to be in touch with her true self. The conception of authenticity in play now is one according to which a person is not authentic unless she knows what really is, *objectively,* good for her. So, in acting on mistaken judgments about ourselves, we would be failing to be true to ourselves.

One crucial lesson to draw here is that the concept of authenticity is flexible enough to function as a framework for articulating and propagating subjectivist value systems (that are often characterized as liberal and pluralistic) as well as objectivist ones (which often look more moralistic). Both subjectivists and objectivists are drawn to The Ideal of Authenticity.

For present purposes, the important thing to keep in mind is that whichever of these two accounts one has of what makes life better or worse, The Ideal of Authenticity can be used as a tool to leverage people into doing what is thought to be good for them or good, full stop. As I will argue below, Charles Taylor is especially subtle in his project of tailoring his conception of authenticity to meet the philosophical demands of his objectivist metaethical view. What this shows is that Ideal of Authenticity is an alluring pretext for convincing people to adopt quite varied visions of the good life. With the aim of getting people to embrace difference or liberal pluralistic thinking, the subjectivist may encourage people to be their authentic selves.[3] The objectivist, by contrast, tells us that in seeking authenticity we seek some determinate truth about what the good life is. If this diagnosis is right, we should be suspicious that it is authenticity, as such, that either subjectivists or objectivists really thinks is good.

RE-DIAGNOSING OF THE APPEAL OF AUTHENTICITY AS PSYCHOLOGICAL INDEPENDENCE

Our paradigm case involving authenticity as psychological independence was the case of *Jamie, the Sorority Sister*. Jamie's friends from home see that she has internalized the gendered values of her new peers (which they find objectionable) and advise her to be true to herself. Let's suppose that it is an open question whether Jamie herself feels as if the changes she has undergone involve any betrayal of her true self. For now, our focus is on the attitudes of her old friends. And here it is clear that they are likely to have a set of concerns that are very plausibly independent of any concern for Jamie's true self. These friends may be worried that they will lose Jamie's friendship if she changes her values or even if she just changes how she likes to spend her time (say, listening to Katy Perry and reading *Cosmo* instead of listening to Janis Joplin and reading Kerouac). Alternatively (or in addition), Jamie's friends may have some deep moral concerns; they may think that Jamie is becoming too materialistic or that she is actually being oppressed by the sexist culture in which she finds herself immersed. The point is that if Jamie were changing in ways these friends *approved* of, they might not find themselves so concerned with her being authentically psychologically independent.

This may be clearer if we compare Jamie with a new case, *Samantha, the Adaptive Friend.* Comparing these cases will suggest two things. The first is that our judgments about the value of Authenticity as Psychological Independence are, again, substantially *ad hoc*, tracking concerns about things that are pretty clearly unrelated to authenticity. Second, the comparison should make us skeptical that there is any definition of "psychological dependence" that applies to all and only the cases we would intuitively want to describe as a failure to be true to oneself.

Good vs. Bad Psychological Dependence

Recall that Jamie starts out as an un-self-conscious athlete, uninterested in fashion or the conventional norms of femininity, but comes to internalize the gendered norms of her sorority sisters. She quits the sport she loves, grows her hair, changes her clothing and her body. Even her sense of self begins to change. The case was initially meant to elicit the intuition that Jamie would do better to be true to herself, to stick with the activities she originally loved, and to resist, somehow, the oppressive standards that are making her quite literally uncomfortable in her own skin. But now consider *Samantha*:

> Samantha has always loved baseball, having played little league and attended more Red Sox games than she could possibly count. Her favorite possession is the ratty, worn Red Sox cap she's had since she was nine. She subscribes to the MLB League Pass cable channel so she doesn't ever have to miss a game. But when Samantha moves from Boston to Providence to work at a new job, she finds that her new colleagues don't care about baseball at all. Instead, they are obsessed with basketball, and they repeatedly invite her to join them at college games, to go out to watch the NBA on TNT, and to the bar after work to talk about basketball. Samantha, wanting to fit in and make new friends, decides to go along: she buys some Celtics gear and joins her colleagues watching games, all the while pretending to like basketball.[4]

There is some clear sense in which we might intuitively judge that Samantha is not being true to herself. After all, by description of the case, she is pretending to be something she is not. We tend to think that a person is phony or inauthentic when we know that the person is in some way posing, or evincing an affectation that seems at odds with our sense of who she "really" is. As Lionel Trilling puts it, being authentic requires "a congruence between avowal and actual feeling."[5] So, in this case, some (myself not included) might be tempted to think it would be better if Samantha didn't fake an interest in basketball, but instead tried to find some baseball-loving friends or (notwithstanding the paradoxical nature of this suggestion) recruit her new acquaintances to adopt her interests.[6]

But suppose Samantha's story continues like this: After a few months of watching basketball games with her new friends, and after her friends explain a few things about the game to her, Samantha finds herself enjoying it, and appreciating aspects of basketball she hadn't understood before; eventually, her interest in baseball fades and she becomes as genuinely passionate about basketball as any lifelong Celtics fan. I think it would be bizarre to insist, at this point, that Samantha has wrongly betrayed her "true" baseball-loving self. It would be equally odd to say that she has finally *found* her true basketball-loving self. The natural thing to say is that Samantha has changed. Now, what are we inclined to say if we extend Jamie's story analogously?

Suppose Jamie fully takes on board her sorority sisters' values. She comes to like the more effeminate way she dresses, the approval she gets from her sorority sisters, and the attention of a set of newly interested young men. We can imagine that she becomes *one of* the sisters in every sense of the term. She even looks back at her unfashionable and, by her own lights, "unfeminine" past self with a sense of befuddled embarrassment. When she goes back home for the summer her old friends are shocked by her transformation, dismayed that she has abandoned the sport she loved (shotput), and her endearing indifference to fashion. She appears, to them, to have been the victim of a body- (or brain-) snatching. I am inclined to side with Jamie's old friends in thinking something terrible has happened here. But are there any principled grounds for saying that, while Samantha has simply changed, Jamie has been alienated from her true and original self?

The defender of The Ideal of Authenticity as Psychological Independence faces a challenge: on what criteria should we decide which of Jamie's or Samantha's selves was her "true self?" It's not plausible to say that the external, social origin of Jamie's interest in fashion means that it cannot be part of who she really is. If we add to the story so that Jamie's overbearing father is responsible for her previous "tomboyish" ways, shall we then say that she was betraying her true self even before joining the sorority? If the social origin of some aspect of a person is sufficient for its not being part of her true self, what elements of our identities could be said to be authentic? The core of the problem lies in the fact that desires and interests and values always have (at least partly) "external" origins. "Who we are," in the deepest sense there is, is the result of numerous contributory factors: our physiologies (individual and species-specific), our interactions with other people, our interactions with various social and political institutions, etc. So an "external" origin can't easily explain why those suffering from psychological oppression (in Bartky's sense) are not their "true selves." In general, being influenced and even fundamentally changed by interacting with other people is a normal, unobjectionable, even desirable part of human life.

Comparing our intuitive responses to Jamie and Samantha suggests that the appeal to authenticity, in Jamie's case, even with its admirable feminist bent, is objectionably *ad hoc*. We are not inclined to see good or even morally neutral influences as oppressive; but when our deep values are threatened, we are inclined to see the source of those threats as subversive of authentic selfhood. But what makes the "good" social influences compatible with authentic selfhood but not the "bad" ones? There seems to be no *principled* metaphysical answer to this question, no answer that does not simply presuppose that the true self is, by definition, the moral self.[7] I suggest that our (in)authenticity judgments about Jamie and Samantha seem to be *un*principled, stemming from various other tacit value commitments. In overcoming various kinds of psychological dependence, a person *may* sometimes be better off in a number of ways. Negative feelings of alienation may subside. There is a meaningful moral sense in which we might say that a person who successfully resists or overcomes a certain kind of social pressure or oppression has been *liberated*. Making choices in accordance with one's deepest sense of what is right or healthy, rather than being browbeaten or coerced, is a real kind of freedom (the kind that compatibilists of free will and determinists of many stripes think is the only kind we have). But this is all perfectly compatible with denying that the "liberated" self is in any way more *true to itself*. If watching Oprah or reading the arguments of true-self feminists like Mary Daly brought Jamie to change her life "back," it seems both unnecessary and metaphysically silly to insist that this change is a return to her "original," "independent," "true," or "authentic" self. Better just to be happy and impressed, as we should be, that she's managed to reject a set of ubiquitous sexist values. Jamie's old friends should make their case to her by appealing to these moral considerations–and perhaps also to important considerations like friendship and mental and physical health. Authenticity talk, here, seems to miss and occlude these deeper issues.

REDIAGNOSING THE APPEAL OF AUTHENTICITY AS WHOLEHEARTEDNESS

Sergio, recall, was our paradigm case for thinking about authenticity as wholeheartedness. To motivate the thought that it would be better for Sergio to become wholehearted, we considered the ways in which his ambivalence might be psychically painful for him as well as irrational and morally harmful; the ambivalence might paralyze him or make him inconstant; it might preclude self-knowledge of a certain kind (e.g., knowledge of what he really wants); it might lead him to harm David, the object of his ambivalent affections. With these costs of ambivalence in mind, the advice to Sergio to settle how he feels (and thus settle who he is) is compelling. But what happens if we focus on something other than these costs?

Suppose that Sergio is content with his ambivalence (say, because he's a realist about love) and that he is honest with David about his feelings; suppose David is okay with it, too. Or imagine that Sergio's ambivalence about David protects him from the pitfalls of blind love and opens him up to other worthwhile experiences (for example, a rewarding relationship with Geoffrey). Imagine that Sergio is neither harming himself nor failing to live up to any basic moral expectations. Do we still think that Sergio is under an imperative to finally resolve his feelings one way or the other and become wholehearted? Those who think there is still something wrong with Sergio's ambivalence may be in the grip of an as yet unexamined commitment to the overriding value of wholehearted romantic love. Such people may draw the conclusion that anyone *not* so committed cannot live a fully good life. But this judgment seems quite different and significantly narrower than a general endorsement of The Ideal of Authenticity as Wholeheartedness.

To see this, consider cases of ambivalence where no deep value other than authenticity is implicated because the ambivalence is about something trivial (e.g., what kind of ice cream to order). Or consider cases where the wholehearted alternative to ambivalence seems morally or prudentially risky or objectionable. In such cases ambivalence no longer seems problematic, *qua* ambivalence. More generally, my proposal is that when we are disposed to see a particular failure of wholeheartedness as bad (recall here, Jordan, who does not commit to any one profession), we take this as an opportunity to reflect on our own possibly unexamined commitments. We may discover that we only think Sergio should be wholehearted because we value stable love; we may discover that we only think Jordan should be wholehearted in his professional path because we value stable employment. If Sergio's or Jordan's ambivalence did not conflict with these commitments of ours, would we persist in objecting to it? My own answer to this question is that a person can have both a meaningful and a good life with a pretty radical degree of ambivalence about many things (and I think this supports a fairly pluralistic view of the good romantic life).

I suggested in chapter 2 that, given the multiplicity of good things in the world and our disposition to be "strong evaluators" in Charles Taylor's sense (i.e., to weigh the significance of things),[8] both ambivalence and a persistent desire to overcome it may be partly constitutive of the human condition. Moreover, we are guaranteed to be ambivalent about all sorts of things simply because we don't know enough about them or have enough experience with them to render our attitudes and feelings determinate. And given our limited time and energy, we simply don't have the resources necessary to fully explore all these possibilities. If these points are right, then it is in fact a condition of living well that we *are* often ambivalent and conflicted in various ways: our ambivalence is evidence of our recognition of a variety of contingently and noncontingently conflicting goods; it is evidence that we take our choices seriously, that we are "deep" in Taylor's sense. There may sometimes be something to be admired or envied about the lives of unambivalent people; but such people may also sometimes seem to have a childlike naïveté about the complexities of things and the range of worthwhile activities. As I argued in chapter 2, wholehearted love, untainted as it must be by doubt and ambivalence, seems to be most characteristic of young love and young lovers, blind and intemperate.[9] In any event, taking authenticity as wholeheartedness as an *ideal* simply distracts us from these important discussions: some may think that a good life cannot be one that is significantly skeptical, stoical, or ambivalent; that a good life requires wholehearted love; that ideally, our basic commitments would never come into conflict; or even that the best lives involve stable devotion to a person, a cause, or an idea. These are deep and interesting possibilities worth discussing on their merits. Instead of advising Sergio to be wholehearted we might better ask him (and ourselves) about his (and our own) conception of the good romantic life or his conception of what makes someone worthy of love. We might ask Jordan what he's learned about life from all of his different jobs and ask whether he thinks he's missed anything by not picking a single, stable path. We might, simply, start conversations with the kind of ethical substance that talk of authenticity or of "finding oneself" so often obscures.

REDIAGNOSING THE APPEAL OF AUTHENTICITY AS SELF-KNOWLEDGE

I argued in chapter 1 that self-knowledge of many kinds is not good for us; in chapter 2, I argued that self-knowledge, as such, is not mandated by any rule of epistemic rationality nor is it reliably the best bet as far as facilitating practical rationality; and, in chapter 3, I argued that valuing self-knowledge too highly can be morally costly. So why is The Ideal of Authenticity as Self-Knowledge so appealing? I suggest that it is often invoked to promote a set of values that are in fact independent of the value of self-knowledge or authenticity. If this is right, this should provide yet more reason to be wary of The Ideal of Authenticity.

Recall *Jack, the Starving Artist,* who does not know the truth about his talents and for this reason is stuck pursuing dreams that he would be better off abandoning. Given his current unhappiness and the prospect of his future success as a lawyer rather than a painter, it seems like his friend's true-self advice is sound, purely from the perspective of Jack's well-being. But I think there is reason to be suspicious that this judgment is really (or primarily) about the value of self-knowledge for Jack. This is because many of us also endorse the following claim about the good life: that one's central life choices ought, when possible, make use of one's best talents.[10] Now, using one's talents does normally require a degree of self-knowledge—after all, to make use of one's talents one may need to know what they are. Likewise, it seems that matching one's choices to one's talents is a way of being true to oneself. So there is evidently some connection between the good-life claim about the value of using one's talents and The Ideal of Authenticity as Self-Knowledge. But, as we shall see, by way of a short analysis of the values embedded in the film *Good Will Hunting,* the connection is misleading.

In *Good Will Hunting,* the character of Will (played by Matt Damon) is effectively used to explore the complex relationship between The Ideal of Authenticity as Self-Knowledge and the idea that the good life requires one to make the most of one's talents. In a crucial scene near the end of the film, Will's therapist, Sean (played by Robin Williams), is probing Will's motives for resisting taking a job that will make use of his overwhelming mathematical abilities.

Sean's implication is that if Will can discover the subconscious feelings that are presumed to be the cause of his self-destructive behavior (Will gets into fights; he breaks up with his girlfriend for no apparent reason; he refuses to use his prodigious talents to improve his life), he will live a better life. As the conversation reaches its emotional peak, Sean asks Will what he wants to *do,* in the most existential of tones. We are clearly meant to understand that Will is being challenged to introspect and see that his official conscious answer (that he sees no reason to change his life) is not the real or true one. He's being asked to acknowledge the truth about who he *really* is and what he *really* wants, deep down. On the surface, the narrative seems to be reinforcing The Ideal of Authenticity as (psychotherapeutic) Self-Knowledge. Will's reply to Sean's question is telling, though, in what it suggests about *his* interpretation of Sean's implicit authenticity advice. Referring presumably to his mathematical talent, Will points out that he didn't choose to be so talented. The implication is that Will thinks Sean is telling him he's under some duty to *use* his natural talents, even if that's not what he (at least consciously) wants to do, even if he does not deeply identify with those talents, and even if developing them will not (Will thinks) make him happy. In other words, Will interprets Sean's invocation of The Ideal of Authenticity as Self-Knowledge as a *disguised* and manipulative way of recommending a different substantive view of the good life, namely the view that one should make the most of one's talents. At this stage of the narrative, Will is acknowledging one truth about himself (that he is talented) but is denying that this truth about himself has any special practical import.

Will protests that he not only sees nothing wrong with doing construction work (rather than math) but that he sees honor in manual labor, which provides people with basic things they want and need. Will thus shifts the conversation with Sean from the true-self-related question of what he "really" wants to the ethical question of what makes a job meaningful, honorable, or worthwhile. Sean quickly agrees that there is honor in manual labor and returns to the authenticity point, pressing Will to consider whether he is being honest with himself and whether his reasons for choosing manual labor are in fact not the products of a subconscious and self-deceived fear of success (presumably the product of his difficult childhood). Sean, of course, cannot bring himself to imagine the possibility that what is best for Will might be to stay with his friends and do manual labor. And this is because he cannot imagine that Will's therapeutic self-discoveries will not lead him to want to make use of his talents. But this is a conflation of different ideas and different values. The value of self-knowledge is orthogonal to the question of what job Will should pursue. And the film thoughtfully represents Will as recognizing the conceptual confusion involved in conflating the two ideas.

Two scenes later, a similar conversation occurs between Will and his best friend Chuckie (played by Ben Affleck), while they are working on a construction site. Initially, Chuckie's judgments appear similar to Sean's. Chuckie angrily admonishes Will to get out of construction and to escape their difficult life. Chuckie seems to be insisting, in the spirit of Sean's argument, that Will use his talents to improve his life and do something bigger and better. Again, Will takes the advice to involve an objectionably paternalistic claim about what kind of life is best for him, concealed by the rhetorical sheen of The Ideal of Authenticity. Will responds to Chuckie by rejecting the idea that he can only be true to himself if he pursues a fancy job in math. He denies that he would in any way be betraying himself by not devoting his professional life to an activity that he just happens to be good at. He thus explicitly rejects the idea that to live an authentic and good life, one's choices must match one's talents. Refreshingly and surprisingly (and unlike Sean, who does not deviate from his commitment to The Ideal of Authenticity as Self-knowledge), Chuckie clarifies that his advice has nothing to do with authenticity or Will's well-being. Chuckie disavows The Ideal of Authenticity by agreeing with Will that he shouldn't make all these choices because he owes it *to himself*. Chuckie's position is that Will ought to pursue a broader set of life experiences than is available to Chuckie and their group of friends. Whether Will identifies with his talents or is alienated from them, whether pursing them will make him happy, is simply not the point. Chuckie's point is that for Will to forego the winnings of the natural lottery (which in this case are intellectual and financial and experiential) would be wrong in itself. With this explanation of Chuckie's position in mind, the retort Will offers to Sean—that he didn't ask for his gifts—makes no sense. Neither his particular preferences nor his right to make his own choices are at issue. If Chuckie is right, the simple fact that Will has the opportunity to do something great is the reason to do it. In respecting Chuckie's position (his speech is a moving emotional climax), the movie appealingly refuses to romanticize working-class life; the lesson conveyed is that improving the material conditions of one's life (and by extension the lives of one's friends) is a good thing, independent of whether the work required to do so is the ultimate manifestation of a person's "true self." Unfortunately, and perhaps unsurprisingly, *Good Will Hunting* ends up siding with Sean and The Ideal Authenticity as Self-Knowledge. The result of Will's therapy is his coming to the "proper" self-understanding that his resistance to success is the result of low self-esteem induced by the childhood abuse he suffered. Will accepts this truth about himself, overcomes bad faith, and begins, naturally, to make the "good" choices that match this newfound knowledge. (He gets back together with his girlfriend and we are led to presume that he will get a job worthy of his talents.) In the end, the lesson of the film is that achieving authentic self-knowledge cannot fail to be best for us. And this is what is so striking about the film. After intelligently distinguishing between good-life claims that appeal to authenticity and those that do not, after acknowledging the coherence of Will's proposal that being true to his talents might not be best overall, the film regresses back to conflate these ideas, insisting after all, that being true to ourselves by gaining self-knowledge, using our talents, and being happy, all essentially amount to the same thing. *Good Will Hunting* thus demonstrates that The Ideal of Authenticity as Self-Knowledge is a basic *romantic* convention from which a Hollywood narrative cannot easily deviate.

The film effectively demonstrates the seductiveness of the claim that developing one's talents is a requirement of authenticity; but a careful reader of the film can also see that it enables us to problematize that claim. Suppose, for a moment, that someone had an unknown-to-them hidden talent for standing on one leg for a very long time. Would we think it important, on authenticity grounds, that the person discover this truth about himself and develop this capacity? I presume not. Perhaps if this talent turned out to be connected to some *other* activity that we thought had value, we might start thinking that it was a talent worth developing and that it ought to be thought of as somehow essentially connected with the person's true self. But what this example shows is that *which* talents we are disposed to identify as central to who we "really are" is, again, *ad hoc*. We want to say that Will Hunting's mathematical talent is (or ought to be) a core part of his lived identity. But this intuition now seems suspicious in light of the possibility that what we *really* think (pardon the expression) is that people should selectively identify with just those talents that we think have genuine value. So it looks like our authenticity judgments are, again, conveniently conforming to other value judgments that have nothing to do with authenticity. This is precisely the point that Will tries to make to Sean and Chuckie by arguing that he'd rather be a loyal friend and do honorable manual labor than develop his talents. The lesson I draw is that instead of invoking the value of authentic self-knowledge, better to follow Chuckie's lead and honestly say, simply, that we think people should, when they have the talent, use those talents to pursue opportunities that have distinctive value. We might add that identifying with those talents (rather than being alienated from them) will tend to improve well-being. But this is a far cry from saying that one's talents should be pursued simply because they are connected with the one's true self or because it is a requirement of The Ideal of Authenticity that a person recognize and identify with those talents. How transparent therapists should be with their patients about the purported instrumental value of self-knowledge is a question I do not address here. But that, too, is not simply an empirical question about the value, to health, of different therapeutic approaches. It is also an *ethical* question about the appropriateness of paternalism in clinical contexts, and *that* is a question that The Ideal of Authenticity as Self-Knowledge can also obscure.

As a subjectivist about well-being, my own view is that there would have been nothing wrong, per se, with Will's decision had he chosen to continue to work in construction with his friends. I also think there is no principled reason to think that this choice would be less authentic. The conviction that the choice to stay and work in construction would have been a betrayal of himself just shows how badly we want our conceptions of the good life to carry the authenticity stamp of approval. Moreover, even if Will, or *Jack the Starving Artist* for that matter, were to remain deluded about their talents, we cannot conclude that this might not be best for them. It may be hard not to be drawn to the idea that it is good to do what we are good at (though of course there are many exceptions, for example, when what we are good at is itself harmful or of no evident value). But if we are drawn to this idea, we should argue for it on its own terms and not insist that we should do what we are good at simply because it is the way to be authentic. To argue in this way is to confuse or ignore a substantive question about the value of self-knowledge, the value of developing one's talents, and, more generally, about the kinds of pursuits that make life worth living.

RE-DIAGNOSING THE APPEAL OF AUTHENTICITY AS MORAL CONSCIENTIOUSNESS

We established in chapter 1 that being morally conscientious is not reliably best for us (for example, because conscience often requires significant self-sacrifice), in chapter 2 that conscientiousness can be practically irrational (for example, because conscience might not cohere with rationally overriding elements of our motivational psychology), and in chapter 3 that it can also be morally wrong (because conscience can be misguided). Why, then, is the idea that it is best, all things considered, to be true to conscience so alluring? One possibility is that if being true to ourselves guaranteed that we'd be good, this would provide a very powerful solution to what I will call *the grounding problem*. The grounding problem, in a nutshell, is the problem of offering a satisfactory general answer to the question of why we should be moral *at all*. Given that morality plausibly consists in a set of (often demanding) constraints on how we should live, it seems eminently reasonable to ask *why* we should so constrain ourselves, especially when not doing so often appears advantageous in concrete and obvious ways. Now, if it were to turn out that being good simply amounted to being true to ourselves, this would significantly undermine the force of the why-be-moral question. This is because, as we noted in chapter 4, it is hard to see the question "Why should I be true to myself?" as a live question (especially if it reduces to "Why should I be me?" or the even more absurd sounding "Why should I do what I think is best?"). On The Well-being Account of The Ideal of Authenticity, the available solution to the grounding problem looks even more secure. After all, with the possible exception of some martyrs or perhaps some self-destructive masochists (depending on our understanding of masochism), we are all interested in our own well-being. The authenticity solution to the grounding problem would, on this approach, be backed by the further thought that being good is reliably best *for us*.

George Mavrodes says that it would be a "crazy world" if the fulfillment of moral duties could "result in the net loss of good to the one who fulfills them."[11] His reasoning about the grounding problem seems to go this way:

1. For it to make sense to be moral, being good must always be best for us, all things considered.
2. The observable evidence suggests that being good is often not best for us.
3. If being good is nevertheless best for us, it must be made so by compensation in some unobserved world.
4. It does make sense to be moral.

Conclusion: There must be compensation in some unobserved world.

The first premise (1) encapsulates the intuition that in order to solve the grounding problem, being good must ultimately redound to our benefit. The second (2) acknowledges the apparent evidence to the contrary.[12] The fourth (4) expresses a commitment to the belief that this is *not* a "crazy world," i.e., that this is not a world in which we are under moral requirements that are not good for us. To preserve the combination of these ideas, Mavrodes draws the supernatural conclusion demanded by (3). Now, notwithstanding what I take to be the morally objectionable selfishness of the idea that there would be no reason to be good if being good weren't reliably good for us, what this line of thought demonstrates, for our purposes, is what philosophical lengths we may go to in order to solve the grounding problem. The idea that doing good *must* be good for us is morally comforting. So is the idea, encapsulated by The Ideal of Authenticity as Moral Conscientiousness, that if we are just true to ourselves we will do what is morally right—that being true to ourselves is in fact *a matter* of doing what is right. By contrast, the thought that there might not be any general answer to the grounding problem can be a terrifying one—so terrifying that it compels many toward a belief in otherworldly compensation for the suffering of the virtuous. This belief would thus be an understandable (if, in my view, irrational), manifestation of the hope that none of us can escape the constraining authority of morality.

Philippa Foot, Michael Smith, and J. L. Mackie all offer accounts of the appeal of the Kantian Categorical Imperative that resonate with the psychological impulse for a solution to the grounding problem. In "Morality as a System of Hypothetical Imperatives," Foot offers this critical observation about the Kantian solution to the grounding problem: "[W]e are apt to panic," she says, "at the thought that we ourselves, or other people, might stop caring about the things we care about, and we feel that the Categorical Imperative gives us some control over the situation."[13] In other words, the idea that moral imperatives are categorical, in the sense of being binding on us simply in virtue of our rational natures, functions as a piece of metaethical fortification that quells the anxiety that comes from thinking that moral skeptics or, worse, immoralists who don't care about morality (or other people) at all might in fact be off the moral hook. The reason to worry that they *might* be off the hook comes from thinking about how non-categorical, *hypothetical* imperatives function. Recall from our last chapter that the normative force of hypothetical imperatives depends on the contingent interests or desires of those to whom they are directed. We withdraw such imperatives if it turns out that the person has no interest or desire that will be promoted by following them. So, if I tell you to practice your tennis backhand but it turns out that you have no interest in tennis, I take back my directive. By contrast, we are not inclined to withdraw moral imperatives even when we are pretty sure our interlocutors don't care about morality (or other people). But what reason could there be for any of us to do something in the absence of any interest or desire of ours that would be promoted by doing it? The answer, according to the Kantian form of moral rationalism, is that what we are morally required to do is solely determined by, and derivable from, formal rules of rationality. It thus has nothing to do with our desires or our idiosyncratic personal interests at all. In a similar, though less critical vein, Michael Smith observes that we do, and must, take moral requirements to be supported by *privileged* reasons, reasons that do not depend on pre-existing or contingent elements of a person's motivational psychology. Says Smith, we do not "rest content" at the thought that things could be otherwise.[14]

In *Ethics: Inventing Right and Wrong,* J. L. Mackie offers this account of the appeal of the Categorical Imperative:

> The moral Categorical Imperative . . . can be seen as resulting from the suppression of the conditional clause in a hypothetical imperative without its being replaced by any such reference to the speaker's wants. The action is still required in something like the way in which it would be if it were appropriately related to a want, but it is no longer admitted that there is any contingent want upon which its being required depends.[15]

Mackie's suggestion is that believing in the Categorical Imperative involves "suppression" or, we might better say, *repression,* of something patently obvious, namely that there is no such thing as "objective prescriptivity," that no norms are binding on us, independent of contingent facts about our particular aims and desires.[16]

Now, I agree with Smith that we do not normally "rest content" at the thought that there might not be any privileged defense of morality.[17] In the face of protracted moral disagreement, we are not content simply to say "To each her own," as if we were debating the merits of chocolate or vanilla ice cream. We persist in trying to adduce considerations that we think support our moral judgments—in the belief (or hope) that our interlocutors will somehow come to see things aright (i.e., as we do). But sometimes the experience of confronting apparently reasonable people with deep and intractably different moral orientations from our own, can and should shake us, and lead us to worry about the grounding problem; we might become less confident about our own moral judgments; we might even be drawn down the path of first-order moral relativism or moral skepticism—or simply to further ethical or metaethical inquiry.

The point here, though, in the spirit of Foot's and Mackie's critique of Kant, is that The Ideal of Authenticity as Moral Conscientiousness may be compelling to many largely because it seems to offer us a comforting solution to the grounding problem. If being good turned out to be a matter of being true to ourselves, the why-be-moral question would lose its *psychological* force. And if being true to ourselves were always good for us (as the Well-being Account proposes), this would just be the icing on the cake. But in light of the preceding discussion, I think we should be skeptical of both The Ideal of Authenticity as Moral Conscientiousness, as such, and the claim that this kind of authenticity is reliably best, all things considered. Rather than letting ourselves be seduced by the comforting nature of these ideas, I suggest, against Mavrodes, that we acknowledge that there can be good reasons to be good *that have nothing to do with authenticity or with our own well-being*. In other words, I suggest we look for ways of dealing with the grounding problem that do not rely on suspicious claims about the self or about the prudential value to ourselves (in this world or another) of being good.

Of course, this debunking diagnosis of the appeal of The Ideal of Authenticity as Moral Conscientiousness must be seen for what it is: an *ad hominem* and psychological account of why people might think that being authentic amounts to being good (and vice versa). The hope for a secure grounding for morality is surely a powerful force. But I acknowledge that our *motives* for being drawn to a certain metaethical view should not be taken, on their own, as any evidence that the view is mistaken. And I don't take myself to have refuted Aquinas' or Kant's proposed solutions to the grounding problem. But if the bit of armchair psychology I've proposed is compelling, it should prompt us, a least, to be yet further suspicious of the commitment to The Ideal of Authenticity as Moral Conscientiousness. Moreover, we needn't rely solely on *ad hominem* observations; there are solid metaethical grounds for suspicion of the idea of authenticity as moral conscientiousness as well. Against Kant, there is reason to doubt that we can derive substantive ethical duties from the formal rules of rationality. And if we are naturalists, we will be skeptical of the theistic commitments of the Thomistic version of natural law theory. Likewise, sociobiological understandings of human altruism should not incline us to think that only certain of our drives (say, the characteristically pro-social ones) are the ones that make us who we "really are." Indeed, the contingency of the evolutionary processes that produce biological change seems inconsistent with the essentialism of a moralized true-self metaphysics. Instead of hoping or insisting that being good must amount, somehow, to being true to ourselves, better to investigate the substantive moral merits of different moral principles and theories.

In the remainder of this book, I consider how three competing Moral Accounts of The Ideal of Authenticity function, problematically, in discussions of LGBTQ rights. I argue, in particular, against a popular but objectionably essentialistic authenticity defense of gay liberation; against Charles Taylor's "horizons"-based approach and, ultimately, against Leslie Green's authentic "inclinations" argument (though I am most sympathetic to his approach of the three). My hope is that by focusing on this concrete context of public discussion, I can demonstrate how The Ideal of Authenticity both permeates and distorts a vital discourse, directing us away from underlying and important ethical conversations.

AUTHENTICITY AND GAY RIGHTS

In his video for the "It Gets Better" Project, Barack Obama offers emotional support to young gay people with these moving words: "[W]hether it's your parents, teachers, folks that you know care about you just the way you are."[18] And he concludes, rousingly, with this: "As a nation, we're founded on the belief that all of us are equal and each of us deserves the freedom to pursue our own version of happiness; to make the most of our talents; to speak our minds; to *not* fit in; most of all, to be true to ourselves. That's the freedom that enriches all of us. That's what America is all about. And every day, it gets better."[19] Now, this is obviously not (nor, presumably was it intended to be) a well worked-out moral argument. The President's message is one of hope for those who are bullied and mistreated because of their sexual orientation. But the language is telling. Indeed, it plausibly alludes to all five of our conceptions of authenticity and powerfully resonates with the arguments and values of many LGBTQ activists.

What follows is a critique of three importantly different authenticity-based arguments for what I take to be an absolutely correct conclusion: that the lives of LGBTQ people are worthy of the same respect as anyone else's, in every respect. Homophobia and other phobias and biases against people with non-conforming sexual orientations or gender identities ought not to be tolerated, and we ought to be doing all we can to bring about the equal rights of and respect for all LGBTQ people. But because I am about to criticize a set of arguments that are both very meaningful for many people and that almost certainly have done (and may continue to do) a lot of good, I want to be clear that my purpose in criticizing these arguments is not to challenge their conclusions but to clear the ground for what I take to be *better* arguments for those conclusions.

Perhaps the most common version of an authenticity argument for gay rights and respect relies on a premise like one of these two, the first theistic, the second naturalistic:

- God determines everyone's sexual orientation and it is not changeable by us.
- Nature determines everyone's sexual orientation and it is not changeable by us.

In addition to one of these two premises, the fleshed-out argument relies on this further premise:

- It is perfectly morally appropriate to act in accordance with a sexual orientation that one has not voluntarily chosen and that is not changeable by us.

Now, I am not going to discuss the factual basis of either of the first two claims (I am skeptical of both). I am also going to assume, for present purposes, that defenders of both of these claims acknowledge the physical and psychological *possibility* of voluntarily sexual abstinence. Furthermore, I take "orientation" in all three claims to entail a stable pattern of sexual desire. The deductive conclusion (taking one of the first two premises, plus the third) is that it is perfectly morally appropriate for everyone to act in accordance with their respective sexual orientations. The third claim above is, of course, the normative one and it seems well-understood as asserting the idea that it is morally acceptable to act in accordance with one's essential or true sexual nature. The premise can thus be understood as entailing a logical connection between what we might call *sexual authenticity* and morality. Given the value assigned to sexual self-expression in our liberal society, it is unsurprising that the argument holds such appeal for so many. So, what is wrong with the third claim? Well, as stated, it morally legitimates anyone acting in accordance with any involuntarily determined sexual orientation. But consider the plausible hypothesis that some people have morally problematic orientations, say, orientations that dispose them to desire to harm others or that dispose them to desire sexual contact with those incapable of consent or, more generally, with those we simply think are inappropriate partners. If this is not an outlandish possibility, then the argument's conclusion is patently overbroad. Of course, the natural reaction to this observation is to deny that the premise is meant to apply to sexual orientations of all kinds. And herein lies the rub: in the absence of a clear account of why we should think that only certain orientations but not others are fixed by God or nature, or in the absence of a more detailed account of why only certain orientations are appropriately acted upon, the premise remains content-neutral. It proposes that we are all morally justified in living in accordance with our involuntarily determined sexual orientations. Now, if the premise is qualified to say that involuntarily determined orientations *that do not harm anyone* may be appropriately acted upon, it becomes quite plausible. But it should also be clear that now the talk of "involuntarily determined orientations" has lost its moral import. After all, why should it matter *morally* whether a non-harmful course of action is an expression of a voluntarily or involuntarily formed nature or disposition? Given the assumption that orientations are things we can choose to act upon or not, an appeal to "ought implies can" will not help here (see chapter 4). Moreover, the addition of the qualification evidently moves us away from a concern for authenticity to a concern about the harmfulness of different actions. This move seems wholly morally appropriate. It is the moral basis on which I think discussions of all behavior should proceed. But then why invoke the involuntary nature of the orientation at all? One *might* hold that, so long as there is no harm in doing so, there is special value in being true to our fixed but not our voluntarily formed orientations. But why think this? Again, on the assumption that it is possible to control the behavioral expression of our orientations, the ethical question we should be asking is this: what makes it reasonable or healthy or moral to choose certain modes of sexual expression rather others?

Another related concern about this kind of authenticity-based argument for sexual rights and respect is that it can make it look as if rights and respect are due to different orientations *because* they are not voluntarily determined. But what would or does this imply about the rights and respect due us if our behavior is *not* the product of any such determined nature? Would the implication be that if sexual (or other) orientations *were* in some way malleable (or more up to us than many people think) that this would somehow undermine the basis of and entitlement to equal rights and respect for those with unfavored orientations? The argument does not, strictly, imply that the answer is no, but the implication is there. And the implication is one that has historically been used to propagate *conservative* values, not progressive ones: the implication is that we all ought, morally, conform to our unchosen natures. But if nature can dispose us to bad, or if we are suspicious of our collective ability to judge what the parameters our essential natures are, we should resist linking arguments for rights and respect to claims about our essential natures. For this reason, I suggest we look to other arguments for equality and respect: arguments that do not hinge upon metaphysically suspect or biologically oversimplified assumptions about our natures; arguments that do not morally privilege "natural" behavior over "unnatural"; arguments that do not commit the naturalistic fallacy of drawing moral conclusions from what may (or may not) be facts about our fixed dispositions.

Charles Taylor's Dialogical Ethic of Authenticity

In *The Ethics of Authenticity*, Charles Taylor offers a critique of an importantly different authenticity argument for gay rights and respect. Taylor considers and rejects a view that proposes that "[a]ll options are equally worthy, because they are freely chosen, and it is choice that confers worth."[20] Unlike the essentialist defense of authentic sexuality above, here the argument for liberation hinges on the idea that chosen differences (interpreted here as behavior) are, as modes of "original" self-expression, valuable in themselves. One of Taylor's overarching concerns in *The Ethics of Authenticity* is to acknowledge something that he and I both take to be correct about the position of those he calls "the knockers" of "the contemporary culture of authenticity."[21] The knockers are correctly worried that idealizers of authenticity are overly individualistic in their account of the good and correspondingly prone to a problematic anything-goes moral relativism or subjectivism. Taylor thinks that we cannot make our lives "significant" on our own simply by glorifying them as the products of free individual choice. On the contrary, Taylor thinks that we must recognize the *external* "horizons against which things take on significance for us."[22] Indeed, according to Taylor, the very idea that our choosing something could confer value upon what we choose presupposes that "independent of my will there is something noble, courageous, and hence significant in giving shape to my own life."[23] In other words, Taylor thinks that in order to believe that authenticity as "self-determining freedom" really is valuable, we must not think of *ourselves* as the ultimate source of that value. Taylor thus thinks that horizons of significance are always the necessary backdrop for ascriptions of meaning or moral worth to our lives. In light of his critique of the idea that we can make our lives—including our sexual lives—significant simply *by choosing them*, Taylor proposes that to defend "the value of a homosexual orientation," one must "take into account the actual nature of homo- and heterosexual experience and life. It can't just be assumed a priori, on the grounds that anything we choose is all right."[24] One implication of this, which I agree with here, is that debates about the moral worth of different forms of life cannot normally be settled by the observation that a certain form of life—the merits of which are currently up for debate—has been freely chosen. Rather, such debates can only meaningfully proceed through discussion of the substance and quality of different lives and how those lives look relative to the evaluative standards that comprise our horizons of significance. Taylor thus *seems* to be offering a critique of an Ideal of Authenticity similar to a critique that I have been developing in this chapter: Taylor seems to be saying that arguments for gay rights and respect that focus on the value of authentic choice pull us away from necessary discussion of the substantive sources of worth, which have nothing to do with authenticity, per se, but are rather to be explored by looking outward, to the horizons of significance, which confer meaning to our lives.

Interestingly, though, this is not exactly Taylor's point. Taylor is criticizing what he calls the "contemporary culture of authenticity" which he thinks, with "the knockers," is objectionably relativistic, individualistic, hedonistic, and self-defeating. But his aim in doing so is not to reject the paradigm of authenticity at all but to defend his own distinctively *moral* conception of The Ideal of Authenticity. Taylor thus thinks that the way to think about the value of different sexual orientations *is* to think in terms of the value of authenticity. But to preclude the kinds of individualism and hedonism that "the culture of authenticity" succumbs to, his conception of authenticity integrates his central idea of "a horizon of significance" and highlights the "fundamentally dialogical" nature of the self.[25] According to Taylor, we define our identities "always in dialogue with, sometimes in struggle against, the identities our significant others want to recognize in us."[26] To be authentic, then, according to Taylor, is to construct a meaningful identity by thinking, *with others*, about what has moral worth. What are the implications of this conception of authenticity for gay rights and respect?

Leslie Green, whose authenticity argument I turn to next, points out a potentially conservative implication of Taylor's dialogical account of authenticity. Taylor's view, Green observes, has the implication that to be authentic, all of us, including those of us with nonconforming sexual orientations, must explore and defend the value of living in accordance with those orientations by assessing their merits *in dialogue* with others and in light of our collectively "given" horizons of significance. This, according to Taylor, is how we avoid the collapse into relativistic narcissism. But seeing as those horizons and the interlocutors with whom we may find ourselves in dialogue are the products of a very specific cultural history, the process of authentic inquiry, indeed *the ethic of authenticity itself*, morally demands that we respond defensively to what many of us would recognize as a culture of homophobia. Dialogical authenticity is thus constraining in a particularly troubling way if those who are historically marginalized must justify or explain themselves, in dialogue, with people who do not share the same horizons of meaning. Green's argument, in response to Taylor, is that in certain contexts, mere preference, qua authentic self-expression, *can* legitimate our choices and the lives that those choices embody. No further, "deep" justification is required. If called to defend gay life (something Green and I both think presupposes a basic moral mistake), Green thinks it wholly appropriate to respond this way: "I've chosen it because it accords with my inclinations, so it's no less worthy than yours which accords with your inclinations. It allows me to be myself, to pursue my own good in my own way, to be authentic."[27]

Green thus sounds here like he wants to endorse the position of the "boosters" that Taylor and I are concerned about. He seems to be endorsing the worth of acting in accordance with inclinations, *on the grounds that doing so is a form of authentic self-expression*. His language seems to resonate with the very liberal platitudes that both Taylor and I deem implausibly relativistic and individualistic (and that Obama's "It Gets Better" speech captures so nicely). The simple fact that one is pursuing one's own good in one's own way does not seem to have *moral* weight, as such, if morality is fundamentally about how we relate to others. To figure out whether a course of action is *morally* permissible or good, we need to know about the content of that action and its affects on the lives of other people. By invoking the value of authentic self-expression in defense of gay life, Green seems to be diverting us from this substantive moral point and returning us either to an unmoralized, Well-being Account of The Ideal of Authenticity, or to an implicit (if localized) moral relativism.

Now I actually think this is a somewhat uncharitable interpretation of Green's argument. A more charitable interpretation of Green's analysis would recognize his compelling claim that the objects of our sexual desire need *not* be morally significant at all so need not be *morally* justified, dialogically, against Taylor's horizon of significance. When deciding to whom we should direct our sexual energies, we needn't be "strong evaluators," making choices in light of our "deepest unstructured sense of what is important, which is as yet inchoate and which [one is] trying to bring to definition."[28] "Choosing" the sex or gender of a sexual partner really is, contra Taylor, morally equivalent to sexually preferring blond- or brown-haired people or preferring chocolate to vanilla ice cream—cases where "mere" inclination is taken to be sufficient on its face to justify a choice precisely because the choice has no particular moral significance (absent any pattern of oppression on the basis of these preferences). How others are *morally* affected by what we do with them lovingly and consensually is not normally related in any deep, stable or significant way to their hair color or their sex. So, on the reading of Green that I prefer, it makes sense to say that once we have established that the sex of those we desire is of *no special moral significance*, it is perfectly appropriate to choose sexual partners on the basis of mere inclination. I think this is Green's view. But he also says more.

Green seems to be saying that authenticity, as such, *can* and *should* do justificatory work in the argument for gay rights and respect. His view seems to be that authentic pursuit of our own well-being *is* a basic good, just one that needs to be constrained by relevant moral considerations. The presumption, then, is that *because* a choice is an authentic expression of one's desires, it has a degree of validity or worth. And here, I want to disagree. I think the simpler and better moral argument is that in the absence of any moral reason *not* to take a course of action, the fact that that course of action will promote the pleasure (or overall well-being) of the person taking it—and presumably also the pleasure of any others consensually involved—is sufficient justification to perform it. In other words, I am questioning what is being *added* by Green's observation that our sexual choices "allow us to be ourselves" and thus to be authentic. If this just meant that society and law ought to leave us free to make these decisions I would certainly agree. But by invoking authenticity Green seems to accept something that I do not and that I think we ought to reject: that part of the reason that it is "okay" to live a gay life is that it is a way of standing in some proper relation to *oneself*, a relation of authentic selfhood. The arguments of chapters 1 and 3 showed, among other things, that being true to ourselves is not our reliably best way of achieving our own well-being; that the value, even, of authentic well-being (if we could make out what this is) is no principled trump against other moral considerations; that being true to ourselves is no guarantee of a morally good or even morally permissible life because our "true selves" aren't intrinsically good. For these reasons I think that it is a mistake to invoke authenticity when trying to make our case (if we are forced to) for the worth of our sexual lives, especially if that case must be made to unsympathetic interlocutors who are often (I think correctly) suspicious of the individualism and relativism of the "culture of authenticity." I think that the legitimacy of sexual choices should be defended, if it is necessary that they be defended at all, on the grounds that those choices are part of the person's fulfilled and moral life, all things considered. What makes acting on inclination good, when it is good, is not that in doing so we are true to ourselves. It is that desire-satisfaction, as such, is among the most vital components of a good life.

I noted above that while Taylor sees merit in the concerns of the knockers of the culture of authenticity, the project of his book is to vindicate an Ideal of Authenticity that does not reduce to individualism, relativism, or hedonism. In my estimation, Taylor sees that an ideal of authenticity that really is, essentially, about how one relates to *oneself*, would not be sufficiently guided by external moral constraints (other people, objective moral standards), and would not capture the phenomenology of being a "deep" or "strong evaluator" which essentially involves looking *outward*, to horizons of significance, when trying to make important value decisions. What Taylor does, to preserve an ethic of authenticity, is thus to insist that being a strong evaluator, thinking *dialogically*, against *given* horizons of meaning, just *is* what it means to be authentic. The air of paradox should be evident here. It turns out that being true to oneself, far from being a matter of how one relates to oneself, is a *moral* ideal precisely because it is a matter of how we relate to *others*. Taylor goes so far in his reconstruction of the idea of authenticity as dialogical, that he proposes that our very identities, construed as "'who' we are, 'where we are coming from,'" are the products of internalizing the "tastes and desires and opinions and aspirations" of those we love (and presumably others as well).[29] Unsurprisingly, I find this compelling as an account of selfhood. My critical analysis of The Ideal of Authenticity as Psychological Independence suggested that there is little of a principled nature to say about where the self begins and ends. By comparing *Jamie the Sorority Sister* and *Samantha the Adaptive Friend*, each of whom internalize others' tastes and judgments and change, accordingly, over time, I argued that our intuitions about their relative degrees of authenticity are pretty *ad hoc*. I take Taylor's expansion of the idea of authenticity to accommodate dialogical thinking and given horizons and internalization of others' world views, to be a *reductio ad absurdum* of the idea of authenticity, rather than the insightful philosophical move that explains authenticity and vindicates it as an ideal. This is because I think that to be useful as a concept at all, authenticity must be understood, essentially, as a relation one bears to oneself.

So, given Taylor's evident sympathy for the knockers of the culture of authenticity (with its implicit relativism and hedonism), why does Taylor want so badly to preserve and defend authenticity as a moral ideal? Taylor asks himself this question. "Would it make sense to root it [the ideal] out?" he wonders.[30] He answers, in part, by pointing out that "we can practically *define* the culture of mainstream Western liberal society in terms of those who feel the draw of this [some form of The Ideal of Authenticity] and the other main forms of individualism."[31] What he evidently means by this is that it would not be *strategic* to oppose this cultural juggernaut; it should, rather, be co-opted. He concludes by asking, rhetorically, "Does the policy recommended here [in his book] make more sense in our situation, namely espousing the ideal at its best and trying to raise our practice up to this level?"[32] The implication is that Taylor thinks it makes more *practical* sense to try to leverage the pervasive commitment to The Ideal of Authenticity by reconceptualizing it and making it compatible with his own incredibly complex dialogical metaethical vision of what it is to be a "deep" person in an officially "disenchanted" materialistic world. I think there is something cynical about this approach. But, more importantly, I think it suffers most in virtue of its expansion of the notion of authenticity beyond its reasonable conceptual limits (and, I think, philosophical usefulness). Better, I think, to make the case that authenticity, if it exists at all, *is* about the self's relation to the self and argue that good, fulfilled moral lives are *not* lives focused on authenticity as the locus of our ethical and moral ideals.

Imagine that instead of framing our support for gay rights and respect in terms of the benefits or moral legitimacy of being true to ourselves, we framed it in terms of our collective responsibility not to stigmatize and oppress people for ideas, desires, and behaviors that are not only not directly harmful to others but that are, for so many, a vital part of our rich and flourishing lives. This claim itself can be and is debated. But that debate is a debate about two substantive things: what counts as harm and what makes our lives flourishing. These are difficult and profound questions but they are questions about how we treat *each other* and about the nature of human happiness, not questions about our formal relations to ourselves. They are questions that force us to think about where value resides *in the world* and about how to get along with each other, not questions about our own individual psychologies. Those questions (about our psychologies) are themselves difficult and profound. The thesis of this book is just that those questions—about who we "really are"—are not the questions that reveal to us any general answer to the overarching question that our ideals seem intended to answer: "How should we live?"

VALUES BEYOND IDEALS

I have argued in this chapter that in paradigm situations where authenticity is invoked as an action-guiding ideal, we can readily identify a variety of authenticity-*unrelated* values that are obscured by the talk of authenticity. Part of that argument hinged on the observation that we tend not to invoke the importance of others being true to *themselves*, when we reasonably judge that the practical outcome of their following our authenticity advice would be behavior that conflicts with *our own* value commitments. We don't normally tell people to be true to themselves when we suspect that their conscientious, strong-willed, self-knowing and wholehearted efforts to do so will result in harmful, morally wrong (by our lights) or self-destructive behavior. But if this is right, we ought to pay special attention to a set of cases where we *do* to stick with our be-true-to-yourself advice, even when we can guess that doing so means we are effectively advising people to do what we substantively disagree with. We can easily imagine Caitlin's doctor advising her to be true to herself even if she (the doctor) thinks abortion is wrong but suspects that Caitlin (or Caitlin's "true self") will think it is the best course. Or consider my own view (and that of many colleagues of mine) that I want my philosophy students to think for themselves, even if this means they will be led to disagree with me about things I care about deeply. Don't examples like this provide evidence of a commitment to an Ideal of Authenticity not reducible to or explicable in terms of other values (including well-being or rationality or morality)? In other words, is there any way to rediagnose examples like these in a way that shows it is not "really" authenticity, as such, that we care about? It seems, after all, that I myself care, *as such*, about authenticity as psychological independence (in the form of independent critical thinking).

There are two replies here that, together, I hope constitute a summing up of the central ideas of this book. The first reply is that endorsing the value of various conceptions of authenticity is not the same as endorsing any such conception *as an ideal*. I have had students who have reacted to the expectation that they engage in "independent thinking" with depression, nihilism and reckless drinking. To insist that a certain mode of critical or philosophical inquiry is the most reliable bet as far as these students' good lives is concerned would be absurd. I think there is *pro tanto intrinsic merit* to a certain kind of critical thinking, to authenticity construed in this narrow way. But I also think there are also plenty of contexts in which it is not reliably good to engage this mode of thinking.[33] I also think there are probably some kinds of people for whom, contingently, this kind of thinking is generally quite a *bad bet* as far as their living good lives is concerned. If I have overwhelming evidence that I am talking to a person for whom this kind of thinking would not be good, I do not nevertheless insist that a failure to think in this way is a failure to live rationally or morally or best. The second reply, building on the first, is that the arguments of this book have been meant to cast doubt on the plausibility that there is *any* unique value or good that might count as an ideal in the sense we have been employing. The central chapters of this book have been devoted to establishing that, though well-being, rationality, and morality are among the absolute strongest candidates for being ideals (this is why they seem so compelling as grounding accounts of authenticity), none of them qualifies as an ideal. This is because the range of things that matter to a good life is too broad and too complexly interwoven for the model of ideals to be useful. What can be useful, though, is occasionally being prompted to think about the values associated with different conceptions of authenticity and how they might be weighed against themselves and other values. In addition to thinking for oneself, it is in fact sometimes good to be strong-willed, to think conscientiously, to seek psychic integration and self-knowledge. All of these things have their place, but none of them is overriding; none of them has any "privileged rational justification" (as Michael Smith would say), or is a plausibly "comprehensive guide to conduct" (as Susan Wolf puts it). None of them is distinctly our reliably "best bet" for living the best lives we can. I doubt there is any one practical principle for living or even a set of consistent principles, that both have substantive guiding content (see chapter 4) and that would be reliably best for us to follow, as rule.

So, my critique of The Ideal of Authenticity is not a rejection of fundamental values like freedom, or rights, or choice, even liberally construed where each of these is preceded by the word "individual." There *are* ways of being ourselves (and being with others as free, responsible and interdependent creatures) that can and should be separated from the robust and problematic authenticity fetishism that saturates so much of our contemporary normative discourse.

NOTES

1. We are putting aside, for now, the question raised in chapter 5, whether we should construe this encouragement as advice at all.

2. Taylor (1991, p. 18).

3. When the subjectivist view is articulated this way, it should be clear that it is in fact an objectivist theory in another sense. The view is that what really is, objectively, best for us is what we reflectively judge to be best (perhaps in ideal deliberative conditions). So the subjectivist and the objectivist described above are really disagreeing about what is objectively good for everyone. For the subjectivist, a person's life goes well when she lives in accordance with her own best judgment about how to live. For the objectivist, a person's life goes well when she lives in accordance with certain perspective-independent facts about how it's best to live.

4. The case is adapted from Feldman and Hazlett (2008).

5. See Trilling (1972, p. 27). Apart from the incongruence between feeling and avowal we may also object to behavior of this kind on related but different authenticity grounds: people we think of as inauthentic manifest what we judge to be inappropriate concern to project a certain social image; people we characterize as "phonies" seem to be trying (and failing) to conform to some social expectation, rather than simply "being themselves."

6. Note the air of paradox here: if Samantha's colleagues evince an interest in baseball to get to know her better, they would seem to run afoul of the same authenticity concern.

7. See chapter 4 for a fuller discussion of the purported metaphysical connection between selfhood and the good.

8. Taylor (1976).

9. Moral saints, wholeheartedly devoted to their causes, can seem equally misguided in their single-minded pursuits. For a powerful account of the compelling if unappealing life of a person with wholehearted moral commitments, see Ian Parker's "The Gift" (2004).

10. Our judgments in Jack's case may also be affected by various cultural assumptions we make about authenticity and the arts. We often conceive of artists as specially engaged in the project of authentic self-expression in a way that others are not. For example, we don't presume that corporate lawyers or waiters are following their muses or their soul's call. We might say that the epistemic standards for self-knowledge are raised for those whose life projects are in some way thought to be specially justified on grounds of authenticity (consider how we give various "geniuses" special social leeway to pursue their projects). Given this, the failure of an artist to know the truth about his talents might seem especially pernicious.

11. Mavrodes (2007, p. 587).

12. Strikingly, this argument takes it as a given that in the world as we know it, being good is often not good for us. Inverting Mavrodes' logic, those not disposed to believe in another world (or a dimension of the soul/psyche which we do not experi-

ence but which determines what is really good for us) might reason in this naturalistic, though I think equally pernicious, way:

1. For it to make sense to be moral, being good must be good for us, all things considered.
2. The observable evidence suggests that being good is often not best for us.
3. If being good is nevertheless best for us, it must be made so by compensation in some unobserved world.
4. There is no compensation in an unobserved world.
5. Conclusion: It doesn't make sense to be moral.

As I explain below, my own preference is to reject (1).

13. Foot (1972, p. 315).
14. Smith (1994, p. 90).
15. Mackie (1977).
16. Ibid.
17. Smith.
18. Obama (2010).
19. Ibid.
20. Taylor (1991, p. 37).
21. Ibid., pp. 11, 31
22. Ibid., p. 37.
23. Ibid., p.39.
24. Ibid., p. 38.
25. Ibid., p. 33.
26. Ibid.
27. Green (1995, p. 389).
28. Taylor (1976, p. 299).
29. Taylor (1991, p. 34).
30. Ibid., p. 75.
31. Ibid.
32. Ibid.
33. Certain kinds of intimate interpersonal experiences or artistic or religious experiences may be incompatible with the kind of critical independent thinking in question here.

References

Allen, Ernest. (1997). "On the Reading of Riddles: Rethinking Du Boisian Double Consciousness" in *Existence in Black*, Lewis Gordon (ed.). London: Routledge.

Aquinas, Thomas. (1913). *Summa Theologica* London: R. T. Washbourne, Ltd.

———. (2008). "On Law, Morality, and Politics" in *Philosophy of Law 8th Edition*, Joel Feinberg and Jules Coleman (eds.). Belmont, CA: Thomson Wadsworth.

Arendt, Hannah. (2006). *Eichmann in Jerusalem: A Report on the Banality of Evil*. New York: Penguin Classics.

Arpaly, Nomy. (2003). *Unprincipled Virtue* New York: Oxford University Press.

Austin, J. L. (2008). In *Philosophy of Law 8th Edition*, Joel Feinberg and Jules Coleman (eds.). Belmont, CA: Thomson Wadsworth.

Baron, Marcia. (1988). "What is Wrong with Self-Deception?" in *Perspectives on Self-Deception*, B. P McLaughlin and A. O. Rorty (eds.). Berkeley: University of California Press.

Bartky, Sandra. (2005). "On Psychological Oppression" in *Feminist Theory: A Philosophical Anthology*, Ann Cudd and Robin Andreasen (eds.). Oxford: Blackwell Publishing.

Berkowits, Peter. (1995). *Nietzche: The Ethics of an Immoralist*. Cambridge, MA: Harvard University Press.

Brison, Susan. (2005). *"Outliving Oneself" in Feminist Theory: A Philosophical Anthology*, Ann Cudd and Robin Andreasen (eds.). Oxford: Blackwell Publishing.

Clifford, William. (2003). In *The Theory of Knowledge 3rd Edition*, Louis Pojman (ed.). Belmont, CA: Thomson Wadsworth.

Davidson, Donald. (1985). "Deception and Division," in *Actions and Events: Perspectives on the Philosophy of Donald Davidson*, E. Lepore (ed.). Oxford: Blackwell.

de Sousa, Ronald. (1976). "Rational Homunculi," in *The Identities of Persons*, Amelie Rorty, ed. Berkeley: University of California Press.

Doris, John. (2005). *Lack of Character*. Cambridge: Cambridge University Press.

Dreier, James. (2001). "Humean Doubts about Categorical Imperatives," in *Varieties of Practical Reasoning*, Elijah Millgram (ed.) Cambridge, MA: MIT Press.

Du Bois, W. E. B. (1994). *The Souls of Black Folks* Dover Publications, Inc.

Epictetus. (n.d.). *Enchiridion*. Elizabeth Carter (trans.). http://classics.mit.edu//Epictetus/epicench.html. The Internet Classics Archive.

Fanon, Franz. (1967). *Black Skin, White Masks* New York: Grove Press.

Feldman, Simon and Allan Hazlett. (2008). "What's Bad About Bad Faith?" *European Journal of Philosophy* (pp. 1-24).

Foot, Philippa. (1972). "Morality as a System of Hypothetical Imperatives." *Philosophical Review* (81) pp. 305-316.

Frankfurt, Harry. (2002). *Contours of Agency: Essays on Themes from Harry Frankfurt*. Cambridge, MA: MIT Press.

———. (2004). *The Reasons of Love*. Princeton, NJ: Princeton University Press.

Freedman, Carol. "'It's Your Illness Talking': The Uses and Abuses of 'Illness Talk,' in the Treatment of Eating Disorders" (unpublished).

Frye, Marilyn. (2005). "Oppression," in *Feminist Theory: A Philosophical Anthology*, Ann Cudd and Robin Andreasen (eds.). Oxford: Blackwell Publishing.

Gauthier, David. (2011). "Morality and Advantage," in *Ethical Theory Classical and Contemporary Readings 6th Edition*, Louis Pojman and James Feiser (eds.). Boston: Wadsworth, Cengage Learning.

Gilligan, Carol. (1993). *In a Different Voice: Psychological Theory and Women's Development*. Cambridge, MA: Harvard University Press.
Goldman, Alvin. (2002). *Pathways to Knowledge: Private and Public*. Oxford: Oxford University Press.
Green, Leslie. (1995). "Sexuality, Authenticity, and Modernity," *in Philosophy of Law, 4th edition*, Joel Feinberg and Jules Coleman (eds.). Belmont, CA: Wadsworth Publishing Company.
Grimshaw, Jean. (2005). "Autonomy and Identity in Feminist Thinking," in *Feminist Theory: A Philosophical Anthology*, Ann Cudd and Robin Andreasen (eds.). Oxford: Blackwell Publishing.
Guignon, Charles. (2004). *On Authenticity*. New York: Routledge.
Haney, Craig, Curtis Banks and Philip Zimbardo. (1973). "Interpersonal Dynamics in a Simulated Prison." *International Journal of Criminology and Penology* 1: pp. 69-97.
Harman, Gilbert. (2011). "Moral Relativism Defended" in *Ethical Theory* Luis Pojman (ed.) Boston: Wadsworth.
Hart, H. L. A. (2008). In *Philosophy of Law 8th Edition*, Joel Feinberg and Jules Coleman (eds.). Belmont, CA: Thomson Wadsworth.
Hazlett, Allan. (2013). *A Luxury of the Understanding*. New York: Oxford University Press.
Hoagland, Sarah. (1992). "Why Lesbian Ethics?" *Hypatia: A Journal of Feminist Philosophy* 7(4), pp. 195-206.
Hume, David. (1985). *A Treatise of Human Nature*. Oxford: Clarendon Press.
Hursthouse, Rosalind. (1999). *On Virtues*. Oxford: Oxford University Press.
James, William. (2003). "The Will to Believe," in *The Theory of Knowledge 3rd Edition* Louis Pojman (ed.). Belmont, CA: Thomson Wadsworth.
Jopling, David. (1992). "Sartre's Moral Psychology," in *The Cambridge Companion to Sartre*, C. Howells (ed.). Cambridge: Cambridge University Press.
Kant, Immanuel. (1933). *Critique of Pure Reason*. Norman Kemp Smith (trans.). London: Macmillan and Co.
———. (2002). *Groundwork for the Metaphysics of Morals*. Allen Wood (trans.). New Haven, CT: Yale University Press.
King, Martin Luther. (2008). "Letter from Birmingham Jail," in *Philosophy of Law 8th Edition*, Joel Feinberg and Jules Coleman (eds.). Belmont, CA: Thomson Wadsworth.
Kittay, Eva. (2005). "Vulnerability and the Moral Nature of Dependency Relations" in *Feminist Theory: A Philosophical Anthology*, Ann Cudd and Robin Andreasen (eds.). Oxford: Blackwell Publishing.
Kohlberg, Lawrence. (1984). *The Psychology of Moral Development*. San Fransisco, CA: Harper and Rowe Publishers.
Kuhn, Thomas. (1996). *The Structure of Scientific Revolutions*. Chicago: University of Chicago Press.
Lewis, David. (2003). "Elusive Knowledge," in *The Theory of Knowledge 3rd Edition*, Louis Pojman (ed.). Belmont, CA: Thomson Wadsworth.
Lofton, Kathryn. (2011). *Oprah: The Gospel of an Icon*. Berkeley: University of California Press.
Lynch, Michael. (2001). *The Nature of Truth*. Cambridge, MA: MIT Press.
Mackie, J. L. (1977). *Ethics: Inventing Right and Wrong*. New York: Penguin Books.
Mavrodes, George. (2007). "Religion and the Queerness of Morality," in *Ethical Theory Classical and Contemporary Readings, 5th Edition*, Louis Pojman (ed.). Belmont, CA: Thomson Wadsworth.
McGraw, Phil. (2003). *Self Matters*. New York: Free Press.
Mead, N. L., Baumeister, R. F., Gino, F. et al. (2009). "Too tired to tell the truth: Self-control resource depletion and dishonesty." *Journal of Experimental Social Psychology*, Vol. 45, pp. 594–597.
Mele, Alfred. (2004). *Irrationality: An Essay on Akrasia, Self-Deception and Self-Control*. Oxford: Oxford University Press.

Milgram, Stanley. (1963). "Behavioral Study of Obedience." *Journal of Abnormal and Social Psychology* 67 (4): pp. 371–378.

Millet, Kate. (1977). *Sexual Politics*. London: Virago.

Myers, B. R. (2011). "The Moral Crusade Against Foodies." *The Atlantic*, Available online at http://www.theatlantic.com/magazine/archive/2011/03/the-moral-crusade-against-foodies/8370/. Accessed January 30, 2012.

Nagel, Thomas. (1969). "Sexual Perversion." *Journal of Philosophy* 65 (January 16).

Nehamas, Alexander. (1985). *Nietzsche Life as Literature*. Cambridge, MA: Harvard University Press.

Nietzsche, Freidrich. (2011). "The Transvaluation of Values," in *Ethical Theory: Classical and Contemporary Readings 6th Edition*, Louis Pojman (ed.). Boston: Wadsworth, Cengage Learning.

———. (2000). *Mortal Questions*. Cambridge: Cambridge University Press.

Nozick, Robert. (1974). *Anarchy State and Utopia*. New York: Basic Books.

Nussbaum, Martha. (2012). *Not for Profit*. Princeton, NJ: Princeton University Press.

Obama, Barack. (2010). "Remarks of President Barack Obama for 'It Gets Better' Video" http://www.whitehouse.gov/it-gets-better-transcript.

Oshana, Marina. (2007). "Autonomy and the Question of Authenticity." *Social Theory and Practice* Vol. 33, No. 3.

Parfit, Derek. (1984). *Reasons and Persons*. Oxford: Oxford University Press.

———. (2011). "What Makes Someone's Life Go Best?" reprinted in *Ethical Theory Classical and Contemporary Readings 6th Edition*, Louis Pojman and James Feiser (eds.). Boston: Wadsworth, Cengage Learning.

Parker, Ian. (2004). "The Gift," in *The New Yorker*. Condé Nast Publications, Inc.

Piaget, Jean. (1965). *The Moral Judgment of the Child*. New York: The Free Press.

Plato. (1997). *Phaedrus, in Plato Complete Works*. Indianapolis, IN: Hackett Publishing Company.

———. (2005). *Apology*, in *Readings in Ancient Greek Philosophy, 3rd Edition*, S. Marc Cohen, Patricia Hurd, C. D. C. Reeve (eds.). Indianapolis, IN: Hackett Publishing Company, Inc.

Potter, Andrew. (2010). *The Authenticity Hoax*. New York: McCleland and Stewart.

Quinn, Philip. (2008). "The Meaning of Life According to Christianity," in *The Meaning of Life: A Reader*, E. D. Klemke and Steven Cahn (eds.). Oxford: Oxford University Press.

Rosenberg, Tina. (2011). *Join The Club*. New York: W. W. Norton and Company.

Sartre, Jean Paul. (1956). *Being and Nothingness*. New York: Washington Square Press.

———. (2007). *Existentialism is a Humanism*, C. Macomber (trans.). New Haven, CT: Yale University Press.

Scanlon T. M. (1998). *What We Owe Each Other*. Cambridge, MA: Harvard University Press.

Schneider, Nathan (2011) "What is Oprah?: An Interview with Kathryn Lofton" *The Immanent Frame*, http://blogs.ssrc.org/tif/2011/01/26/what-is-oprah-an-interview-with-kathryn-lofton/. Accessed October 27, 2014.

Shafer-Landau, Russ. (2003). *Moral Realism: A Defence*. Oxford: Clarendon Press.

Shapiro, Scott. (2004). "Authority," in *Philosophy of Law, 4th Edition*, Joel Feinberg and Jules Coleman (eds.). Belmont, CA: Thomson/Wadsworth.

Singer, Peter. (1972). "Famine, Affluence and Morality." *Philosophy and Public Affairs* Vol. 1 No. 3: pp. 229-243.

Smart, J. J. C. and Williams, Bernard. (1973). *Utilitarianism: For and Against*. Cambridge: Cambridge University Press.

Smith, Michael. (1994). *The Moral Problem*. Oxford: Blackwell.

Soberrecovery.com. (2002). http://www.soberrecovery.com/forums/best-soberrecovery/3985-thine-own-self-true.html last accessed January 15, 2012.

Stocker, Michael. (1976). "The Schizophrenia of Modern Ethical Theories." *The Journal of Philosophy* 73 (14).

Taylor, Charles. (1976). "Responsibility for Self," in *The Identities of Persons*, Amelie Oksenberg Rorty (ed.). Berkeley: University of California Press.

———. (1989). *Sources of the Self.* Cambridge, MA: Harvard University Press.

———. (1991). *The Ethics of Authenticity.* Cambridge, MA: Harvard University Press.

Trilling, Lionel. (1972). *Sincerity and Authenticity.* Cambridge, MA: Harvard University Press.

Varga, Somogy. (2011). *Authenticity as an Ethical Ideal.* New York: Routledge.

Velleman, J. David. (1992). "Against the Right to Die." *The Journal of Medicine and Philosophy* 17 (pp. 666-667).

Williams, Bernard. (1976). "Persons, Character and Morality," in *The Identities of Persons*, Amelie Oksenberg Rorty (ed.). Berkeley: University of California Press.

——— (1999). "Internal and External Reasons," in *Moral Luck.* Cambridge: Cambridge University Press.

Wolff, Robert Paul. (1998). *In Defense of Anarchism.* University of California Press.

Wolf, Susan. (2008). "Meaning in Life," in *The Meaning of Life: A Reader*, E. D. Klemke and Steven M. Kahn (eds.). Oxford: Oxford University Press.

——— (2011). "Moral Saints," in *Ethical Theory Classical and Contemporary Readings 6th Edition*, Louis Pojman and James Feiser (eds.). Boston: Wadsworth, Cengage Learning.

Young, Iris Marion. (2005). "Five Faces of Oppression," in *Feminist Theory: A Philosophical Anthology* Ann Cudd and Robin Andreasen (eds.). Oxford: Blackwell Publishing.

Zagzebski, L. (2003). "The Search for the Source of Epistemic Good," *Metaphilosophy* 34:1/2, pp. 12–28.

Index

About the Author

Simon Feldman is associate professor of philosophy at Connecticut College. He received his PhD in philosophy from Brown University and has been teaching undergraduates for seventeen years. Winner of his college's John S. King Faculty Award for Excellence in Teaching, Feldman teaches courses in ethics and metaethics, feminist philosophy, philosophy of law, and epistemology. His research explores the relationships between morality and rationality; partiality and impartiality; and selfhood and self-control. He has published on such topics as bad faith, self-knowledge, and the moral significance of not-in-my-backyard arguments in the context of environmental ethics. Feldman lives in Mystic, Connecticut.

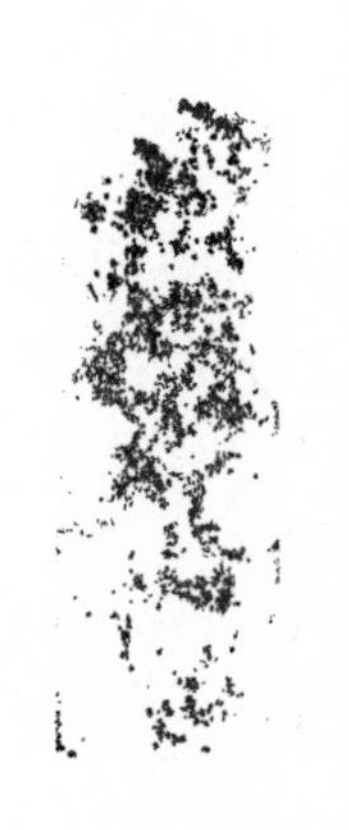